Hollywood

and the Catholic Church

Hollywood

and the
Catholic Church:

the image of roman catholicism
in american movies

by Les and Barbara Keyser

Loyola University Press • Chicago 60657

Photographs Courtesy of the Museum of Modern Art
Film Stills Archive.

Design by Carol Tornatore

LIBRARY OF CONGRESS CATALOGING IN PUBLICATION DATA

Keyser, Les J., 1943-
    Hollywood and the Catholic Church.

    Bibliography: p. 271
    Includes index.
    1. Catholic Church in motion pictures. 2. Catholics in motion pictures.
3. Moving-pictures—United States—History. L. Keyser, Barbara. II. Title.
PN1995.9.C35K48 1984   791.43'09'09382   84-12556
ISBN 0-8294-0468-6

CONTENTS

for Catherine

How but in custom and in ceremony
Are innocence and beauty born?

William Butler Yeats

A Prayer for My Daughter

preface

Irving Berlin's *There's No Business Like Show Business*, filmed in 1954 by Walter Lang, details the fortunes of the "Five Donahues," an Irish Catholic family song and dance act touring the vaudeville circuit, that one day faces an unusual crisis: son number one (Johnny Ray) has decided to become a priest, and Mom (Ethel Merman) and Dad (Dan Dailey) are flabbergasted. To ease their woes, the boy explains his vocation in show business jargon: "In a way, Dad, it's just a change of booking. You must admit that the Church has had a pretty long run." By the time of his departure for the seminary, the gregarious lad has developed a smooth patter about "going into rehearsal for four years," putting his "new act together," and presenting "new material" and "new costumes." Imploring his backstage compatriots to be sure to "find the time to come see me," the smiling apostle of a modernized ecumenical creed leads them in a rousing Tin Pan Alley rendition of "If You Believe."

The jump from chorus line to choir, from spotlights to candles, from palladium to cathedral, may have been easy for the young Donahue, but in American society at large there has been, more often than not, a tension between secular entertainment and spiritual enlightenment, between bijou and chapel. Critic Neil Hurley offers an important truth in his *Theology Through Film* when he suggests that American movies are for the masses "what theology is for an elite." Analyst Stuart Kaminsky details a similar argument in his important study of *American Film Genres:* ". . . genre film, television, and literature have to a great extent replaced more formal versions of mythic response to existence such as religion and folk tale." Anyone perusing the mass media section of a good bookstore today soon discovers that most analyses of American media develop this identification between the themes of contemporary popular art and the traditional concerns of established religions. Sometimes it seems as if media studies and religious studies are part of the same thing. Consider, for example, a very select group of recent titles: Tony Schwartz, *Media: the Second God;* Peter Biskind, *Seeing Is Believing;* Frank McConnell, *Storytelling and Mythmaking;* Thomas Martin, *Images and the Imageless;* James Baldwin, *The Devil Finds Work;* and Gregor Goethals, *The TV Ritual: Worship at the Video Altar.*

Church and cinema co-exist, commingle, and frequently compete in modern life. Each offers a vision of reality so complete that it threatens to preempt the other's existence. Yvette Biró maintains, for example, in her *Profane Mythology: The Savage Mind of the Cinema* that "In my view, today's film marches in one ambitious direction: it tries to take possession of human consciousness, to rule the total bustling life of our conscience." John Phelan, writing about *Disenchantment: Meaning and Morality in the Media,* also sees that we "virtually live within a 'media world' whose factitiously concocted morality is unconsciously shared, and abetted, by the great audience, which used to be known as the public." These critics suggest the context for this volume. Our analysis has as its initial premise the thesis Robert Sklar expounds in his *Movie Made America:* "Are we not all members or offspring of that first rising generation of movie-made children whose critical emotional and cognitive experience did in fact occur in movie theatres? American culture for us may be movie culture." Once this identification of American culture and media culture is made, it seems inevitable that any complete understanding of a significant segment of American life like the Roman Catholic Church must include a detailed sociological analysis of Hollywood's image of that group.

Our volume owes a great deal to other such sociological analyses of films, including feminist works like Molly Haskell's *From Reverence to Rape* and E. Ann Kaplan's *Women and Film;* black studies, such as Thomas Cripps's *Slow Fade to Black* and Donald Bogle's *Toms, Coons, Mulattoes, Mammies, and Bucks;* and religious overviews, such as Lester D. Friedman's *Hollywood's Image of the Jews.* Other texts which have influenced us include

Donald Spoto's *Camerado: Hollywood and the American Man* and Vito Russo's *The Celluloid Closet: Homosexuality in the Movies.* Our text shares the view of an ever broadening consensus that the shadows on the silver screen are important sociologically; that, to borrow Spoto's description, the larger-than-life images in films are "key reflectors of changing cultural images," that film characters are "mythic stencils, against whom the ideas of one's youth, adolescence, and maturity . . . are patterned," and that film narratives frequently show us "where we've just been or where we are."

Our focus is a new one, we believe, for Roman Catholicism on screen has received little critical attention, despite the fact that anti-Catholic prejudices are, nearly every sociologist and historian agrees, a most notable and lamentable feature of the nation's heritage. To trace Hollywood's changing image of Roman Catholicism, we have borrowed the useful critical method Lester Friedman employs in his important text on *Hollywood's Image of the Jew:* the "Catholic" films we discuss are films centering on Catholic issues or topics and not necessarily films made by Catholics; and the screen characters we discuss are persons identified as Catholics in the films, not roles essayed by Catholic actors.

We have not attempted to discuss every film about Catholics made in Hollywood; instead, our volume suggests various major themes and explores what we hope are important and interesting examples of these themes. Similarly, we have not attempted a definitive and exhaustive catalogue of Catholic characters. Instead, we analyze a number of key portrayals and examples of broad patterns and trends. Our focus throughout has been on the representative, the example that illuminates a motif or establishes the stereotype.

In *There's No Business Like Show Business,* young Father Donahue announces at his ordination that his calling card will read "Have black suit; will travel." We have tried to describe some of the many strange roads he and other Catholics have followed in American films. Taken all together, we believe, these Catholic pilgrimages on American screens constitute a catechism, the Hollywood catechism.

We use the metaphor "catechism" quite consciously. The famous *Baltimore Catechism,* or more properly, *A Catechism of Christian Doctrine Prepared and Enjoined by Order of the Third Plenary Council of Baltimore* (1885), detailed the intricacies of the Roman Catholic creed for American parochial school children by means of a mock Socratic dialogue, a complex, progressive, interlocking set of questions and formal answers; each year diligent pupils memorized more questions, mastered more elaborate answers, and pondered fuller explanations, as provided by Father Thomas L. Kinkead. Father Kinkead's announced intention was that the "questions on the same subject" which were repeated in the text would "bring out some new point" or at least "show their connection with the subject-matter there explained."

The films which are the subject of the Hollywood catechism are a less formal series of narratives enjoined by public curiosity about a minority religion and prepared by a long line of studio bosses, diligent censors, and committed artists. Each film with Catholic characters and themes raises new questions, offers further commentary and concerns, and provides still another image of the Church. Hollywood films offer no fixed canon for their public, but they do demand a Socratic dialogue. As Barbara Deming observed so astutely in her *Running Away From Myself* (1969), the movies do provide a haunting dream, a powerful if subliminal reflection of "the fears and confusions" that assail Americans. From *Intolerance* to *Flashdance,* from *The Sign of the Cross* to *The Exorcist,* they offer real clues about the psychic, economic, social, and theological problems that have marked Catholic life in America. Hollywood has provided us with a manual of often perplexing questions and frequently ambiguous answers concerning the dogma and ethics of this minority church, this immigrant church, this frequently misunderstood and often despised church.

acknowledgments

The original idea for this text belongs to Mr. Jerry Koren of the Loyola University Press. To him, and to Father Daniel Flaherty, the director of the press, as well as to our editor, Jeanette Ertel, at Loyola University Press, we are deeply grateful.

This book would never have been written had it not been for the kindnesses and example of Father Gene Phillips, S.J. Anyone who does serious research in film knows how well Gene Phillips writes, admires his acute analytical skills, and marvels at the breadth of his knowledge and the scope of his scholarship. We are also pleased to have Gene as a friend.

Our gratitude also goes to the dedicated staff at the Research Library for the Performing Arts at Lincoln Center; they work cheerful wonders every day. The Museum of Modern Art Film Study Center and their Film Still Archive were, as they always are, indispensable.

Special thanks must also go to Mr. Richard Hirsch and Mr. Michael Gallagher of the Division for Film and Broadcasting of the United States Catholic Conference, who graciously opened their files for us. Our many years previewing films with Richard and Mike have been considerably brightened by their wit, intelligence, and charm.

Barbara Keyser

Les Keyser

ONE

The Epic Film:
saints, sinners, and spectacles

I am reminded ... of another
memorable lunch in a suite at the
Dorchester when Mr. Sam Zim-
balist asked me if I would revise
the last part of a script which had
been prepared for a remake of
Ben-Hur. "You see," he said, "we
find a sort of anti-climax after the
Crucifixion."

Graham Greene
Graham Greene on Film

In the beginning, there was novelty. People crowded
movie theaters, as Professor D. J. Wenden demonstrates in his
The Birth of the Movies, just to see these lifelike pictures that
actually moved. And these early audiences were visibly shaken
by one-reel adventures: they ducked the waves in ocean scenes,
jumped out of the way of trains seen entering a station, and
cheered their favorite athletes on to victory in competitions long
since concluded. Faced with early cinematic tableaux of the
Bible and creation, some viewers marvelled that there had been

a camera in the Garden of Eden. Early films were clearly visceral experiences, not intellectual exercises.

Since space and time can be uniquely experienced in film, it was natural that film producers exploited the almost perfect subject for the camera, the chase. Accelerated, often comic explorations and voyages added a new kinetic rhythm to films, which producers hoped would tighten their hold on audiences. Even the chase, however, failed to sustain the original enthusiasm for movies, and small exhibitors began to worry about the demise of the whole business. Lecturing on "The Origin and Growth of the Movies" at Harvard, mogul Adolph Zukor, recalled his own troubles in these bleak days. By 1908, the chase was "wearing thin," Zukor observed, and he "could not carry on the business profitably." Producers wanted to keep making short, inexpensive films for quick sales; exhibitors were looking to Europe for more substantial and profitable attractions to build regular audiences. In 1908 Adolph Zukor discovered *The Passion Play*, filmed by Pathé in Paris, a hand-colored three-reel extravaganza he felt was "the first picture of any consequence," and he quickly booked it for his theaters.

When Zukor opened *The Passion Play*, he anxiously attended the screenings, trying to gauge audience response. Everything was going fine, he thought, until a Roman Catholic priest walked over to him and said he was going to have the local authorities close the theater since "showing a picture like that in a theater was sacrilegious." Thunderstruck, Zukor quickly tried to discover the priest's objections, only to learn that the cleric felt the whole film was fine. His complaint was that "the subject belonged to the Church and not the theater"; church and theater, he explained, had different missions. Frantically seeking to avoid this confrontation, Zukor appealed to the priest's charity by explaining what a personal calamity closing down would be for him financially. The priest thought for a while and finally agreed to let the show go on. For his part, Zukor's gamble on *The Passion Play* was rewarded; he showed the picture for months and "did a land-office business."

The key elements in Zukor's cautionary tale are a microcosm of the relationship between all of Hollywood and the One,

2

Holy, Roman, Catholic, Apostolic Church. Like Zukor and the priest, Hollywood and the Church both respected each other's powers; both tried to defend their respective domains; and both usually settled for an uneasy peace.

One other element concerning Zukor's story remains to be considered: it is a tale told by a Jewish businessman about a Catholic priest. As Lester D. Friedman demonstrates in his important sociological study, *Hollywood's Image of the Jew*, Jews held many important executive positions in Hollywood and controlled the image of their religion on film: "Unlike films about other American minorities, movies with Jews were often scrutinized by one segment of that minority group with the power to decide how the entire group would be presented to society as a whole." Catholics, on the other hand, like the priest in Zukor's vignette, often seemed the outsiders, the interlopers, when it came to Hollywood. Yet, like it or not, Catholics would also often be principal characters in film stories. And as films grew in influence, the American vision of Catholicism would come more and more to depend on the movies. For many Americans, the only priests or nuns they would ever see closeup would be on screen; for many others, the only Catholic liturgy or dogma they ever confronted was part of the Saturday matinee. Out in the real world, Hollywood and Rome could co-exist; in the darkened world of the theater, it was not the Baltimore catechism that expounded the creed, but the catechism according to Hollywood.

Zukor's account of a merciful priest and anxious exhibitor seems especially prescient when one considers the continuing tension in the first decade of the century between the patent companies' desire to keep film a one-reel commodity and film artists' desires to do more. The turning point may well have come on April 21, 1913, when an Italian religious epic, *Quo Vadis*, opened at the Astor Theatre in New York. Based on the novel by Henryk Sienkiewicz and directed by Enrico Guazzoni, *Quo Vadis* competed directly with live Broadway shows for the fashionable carriage trade; admission was an astounding one dollar. For this tariff, historian Louis Jacobs reports in his standard history, *The Rise of the American Film*, audiences enjoyed the "burning of Rome . . . the charge of Romans among Christian martyrs, the struggles of Roman gladiators, and bacchanalian orgies" presented with a "lavishness and splendor beyond anything the screen or stage had ever seen." This chronicle of the earliest Catholics and their sufferings paved the way for feature films in America and for more complex ideas in American narrative film. Realism and rhythm had not been lost; sensation and spectacle was still central, but there was a new seriousness and subtlety, a new scale of endeavor. The twelve-minute, one-reel short subject would be banished to a minor role; feature films would become the norm.

All these elements—length and grandeur, realism and sensationalism, Catholicism and spectacle—play a large role in what many consider to be the most important and influential film in the silent era and perhaps in the history of American film, David Wark Griffith's *Intolerance*, which was released in 1916, and which remains one of the most intriguing portraits of Catholics in cinema history.

Griffith's film is really four films in one, and Catholicism plays a key role in every narrative but one. Working without a script, Griffith limned, in the words of his subtitle, "Love's Struggles Throughout the Ages." As an early title card in *Intolerance* explained, "each story shows how hatred and intolerance, through all the ages, have battled against love and charity." The stilted diction and overblown emotions of these captions reveal the central paradox of *Intolerance:* Griffith's sensibilities hearken back to the conventions of the Victorian stage and to the ideals of the Old South, but his technique is as dazzlingly modern as his medium. In her seminal essay on *Intolerance*, "A Great Folly," Pauline Kael argues convincingly that Griffith was in his own way attempting "what Pound and Eliot, Proust and Virginia Woolf and Joyce were also attempting, and what he did in movies may have influenced literary form as much as they did."

Griffith's attempts to explain *Intolerance* to bewildered audiences sound very much like modern literary critics do when they define innovative narrative structures. Griffith looked for emotional links, not logical ones, proclaiming that in *Intolerance*

4

"events are not set forth in their historical sequence, or according to accepted forms of dramatic construction, but as they might flash across a mind seeking to parallel the life of the different ages." The metaphor Griffith constantly applied to his film was a river—natural, organic, and unified: *Intolerance*, he explained, had four stories the way a river might have four branches or currents. At first, Griffith noted, "the four currents will flow apart, slowly and quietly." But after a while, the currents merge most dramatically, as "they grow nearer and nearer together, and faster and faster, until in the end, in the last act, they mingle in one mighty river of expressed emotion."

To consider the components of *Intolerance* separately, then, belies the emotional and narrative unity Griffith sought. One must always remember that one episode, or one image of Catholicism, is to be considered in the light of the other stories and conceptions. There is a constant contrast and convergence, reinforcement and denial, affirmation and irony in Griffith's modernistic structure. The chronicle of the bloody Catholic persecution of Huguenots, for example, constantly reverberates with the images of Christ's miracles and his passion as presented in a second episode, the Judean story; and it is frequently counterbalanced by the persecution of Catholics by uplifters in the third segment, the modern story; or sometimes, it is offset by a parallel act of slaughter inspired by religion in another section, the Babylonian episode. The tapestry is as rich and subtle as the effect is grand and cumulative.

Griffith himself was mesmerized by the grand scale of *Intolerance*. His initial rough cut of the film, as David Cook notes in his *History of Narrative Film*, ran almost eight hours, and the director speculated on the possibility of screening *Intolerance* on two separate evenings. However, when *Intolerance* opened at the Liberty Theatre in New York, on September 15, 1916, it ran about three and one-half hours, or 13,700 feet. Because the film proved less successful at the box office than Griffith hoped, he began to trim sequences; then finally, in despair, he cut the original negative into separate features based on the longest episodes, *The Mother and the Law* and *The Fall of Babylon*.

Ironically, *Intolerance* had begun as a rather traditional

melodrama entitled *The Mother and the Law*, in which Griffith reworked a popular theme in contemporary fiction, the fall of rural innocence. In Griffith's variant, the innocents were Roman Catholic workers driven from their peaceful homes in the country by robber baron do-gooders and labor strife, only to be caught up in the crime and desperation of urban tenement life, abused by reformers, and railroaded by the legal establishment. The plot had the sensational twist that the Protestant progressives, the moral uplifters, the prohibitionists, and the Christian philanthropists were the heavies. A man later assailed for his sympathies with the Klan, D. W. Griffith, a Mason, was celebrating Catholic virtue and exposing Protestant pretense and hypocrisy.

In *Adventures with D. W. Griffith*, Karl Brown's readable and entertaining account of the man he considers the "Poor Icarus" of cinema, the author reminds his readers that Griffith's blistering indictment of many seemingly moral public figures, *The Mother and the Law*, was actually shot and completed, ready for the theaters, before the release of *Birth of a Nation*. Brown also notes how remarkable *The Mother and the Law* footage is. During the shooting of this feature, Brown and the crew all felt that Griffith "was ignoring or kicking aside all the principles of film-making as he himself had established them" by creating a film which was purposely "dull, drab, grim, and gray." Only later, Brown recalls, did everyone recognize the genius of the film because, as he puts it, the "constant and hammering insistence on the grim facts of life as it is lived, not as it is dreamed, carried the searing permanence of a Gorki or Dostoevsky, of Poe or Wilde."

With the release of Griffith's epic account of the Civil War and its aftermath, *The Birth of a Nation*, came a thunderstorm of criticism assailing his racism and glorification of the Ku Klux Klan. *Birth of a Nation* became, according to the leading authorities on censorship and the law, Edward DeGrazio and Roger Newman, in their book, *Banned Films*, the most widely attacked and frequently censored film in history. It seemed that everyone wanted to stop it from being screened, and, as Lillian Gish reports in her autobiography, *The Movies, Mr. Griffith, and*

6

Me, Griffith was willing to go anywhere and confront anyone who challenged the right of *Birth of a Nation* to be exhibited. Many film historians try to paint a picture of a repentant Griffith, stung by criticism, offering *Intolerance* as an apology for his earlier work. Nothing could be further from the truth. *Intolerance* is Griffith's apologia for freedom of expression in cinema; Griffith took the anti-reformer, anti-censor tale of *The Mother and the Law* and developed it into an impassioned fugue on intolerance and hypocrisy, a spectacular testament to intellectual freedom and cinematic daring. William Everson is absolutely correct in his landmark survey, *American Silent Film*, when he describes *Intolerance* as an "angry (if not always logically presented) cry of protest against the meddlers and would-be censors who would limit Griffith's freedom of expression on the screen."

The Mother and the Law footage which appears as the modern story in *Intolerance* is shocking, both sociologically and thematically. It's no wonder Lenin assumed Griffith was a communist and invited him to manage the Soviet film industry or that *Intolerance* became a basic text for Russian filmmakers interested in montage and revolution. The modern story centers on class warfare, with morally corrupt bosses devouring pure, unselfish workers; there is no equivocation whatsoever. The ugly capitalist bloodsuckers are modern day Protestant Pharisees and the victims are working-class martyrs with hearts as pure as gold.

No footage in the modern episode lacks a clear thematic import, and the titles hammer the point home. When we meet Miss Jenkins (Vera Lewis), "the unmarried sister of the autocratic, industrial overlord," the issues are joined; she is no longer young, so she smiles bitterly in envy of youth. Her rejection at a ball launches this angry old maid into a war against dancing, drinking, courtship, and fun. Joining some "ambitious ladies in the Midwest," Miss Jenkins heartily agrees that "we must have laws to make people good." Significantly, the specific focus of these reforms is on areas where Catholics were frequently seen as morally insensitive by Protestant Americans, dancing and drinking.

The "Vestal Virgins of Uplift" are most distressed that there is "drinking" and "dancing in cafes." Their arguments are, however, immediately undercut by Griffith's images of orderly, peaceful family fun, and by a quick cut to an episode at the Jaffa gate in the Christ story, which mocks the Pharisees for disrupting the vitality of Jewish life with empty ceremony and mindless legalism. Later titles confirm the impression of profitless meddling as Miss Jenkins is cited for "aligning herself with modern Pharisees" and the workers at a dance are sanctioned in their festivities by a quote from Ecclesiastes, "To everything there is a season . . . a time to mourn and a time to dance. . . . He hath made everything beautiful in his time." In all these juxtapositions, Griffith obviously wants the differences in interpretations of a moral life to be a critical focus. He is debunking the very foundations of a reform movement as he lauds a more natural joy in living and inner grace. The more he punctures the balloon of pious platitudes and perversely inspired puritanism, the more he highlights the value of his protagonists' simple virtues. The modesty and piety of Griffith's heroine, a young Catholic girl (Mae Marsh), are all the more luminous when contrasted with Miss Jenkins's vanity and egoism. Similarly, the young man (Robert Harron) who embraces Catholicism when he marries the young girl, becomes all the more pathetic and pitiable a victim when, having been drawn into crime by abject need, he repents only to be unjustly condemned for a murder he didn't commit. The priest on Death Row in *Intolerance* actually staggers at the enormity of the injustice as the innocent boy walks to the gallows.

Griffith's savage debunking of the hypocrisy of evangelical puritanism is coupled with the sharpest possible social criticism. Mr. Jenkins (Sam de Grasse), for example, finds moral vigor attractive only when he considers the practical impact on his business; his conscience and his pocketbook are closely joined. He firmly supports his vigilant sister's indignation for the most capitalist of reasons; when he watches the workers dance, he laments to a friend, "Ten o'clock! They should be in bed so they can work tomorrow." Griffith explores this link between puritanism and capitalism to its almost laughably

8

illogical conclusion. As Miss Jenkins needs more and more money to reform the workers, her brother decides that profits must be higher, so wages must be cut. One of the union organizers in *Intolerance* puts it all most succinctly: "They squeeze the money out of us and use it to advertise themselves by reforming us."

The inevitable result of Jenkins's order is a strike, so brutally presented that David Platt, in a neglected article on *"Intolerance"* in *Jewish Currents* (December 1976), assumes Griffith must have been influenced by, and commenting on, the Ludlow, Colorado, 1914 massacre, when Rockefeller mine guards burned down workers' tents, killing eleven children and two women. In *Intolerance,* it is the boy's father who dies in a very moving sequence. Film critic James Agee, in a 1948 *Nation* review, suggested how remarkable this whole sequence was, noting that "the realism of these short scenes has never been surpassed, nor their shock and restiveness as an image of near revolution."

After the strike is broken, the union members and their families, whom *Intolerance* labels the "many victims of the Jenkinses' aspirations," are forced to emigrate to the "great city nearby," and Griffith offers a concise lesson in urban sociology, echoing in large part the themes he had explored in his landmark 1912 social problem film, *The Musketeers of Pig Alley.* Each of his protagonists is forced to make a moral choice. The boy quickly succumbs to the temptations of the marketplace; unable to find food, he stumbles over a drunk in the street and takes his watch and wallet. One might note the irony here; Griffith is not blind to the evils of alcohol and gives a clear representation of them in *Intolerance.* These images, however, like most others in the film, are constantly being balanced and modified by others. The result is a kaleidoscope of shifting and interrelated patterns.

The Catholic girl, "The Dear One," who is a symbol of all the Catholic immigrants confronting the new morality of America's great cities, tries to emulate the walk of a girl of the streets and meets the boy, who tells her, in his newly acquired argot, "Say kid, you're going to be my chicken." Her father (Fred

Turner), however, chases her upstairs, and forces her to kneel before a statue of Madonna and Child, demanding that she "Pray to be forgiven." Overwrought as these scenes may seem today, they are interesting as prototypes for the many Hollywood images of Catholics and romance which follow. Griffith establishes many of the key conventions: Catholics are immigrants; they live in crime-ridden ghettoes; they are desperately trying to be assimilated; their parents cling to traditional values; their women are conscience-stricken virgins with repressed sexual desires; and their religion demands ritual, statues, penance, and unnatural postures. Most interestingly of all, Griffith also supports the idea that the older generation can never be assimilated; the "inability to meet new conditions" brings death to the Dear One's father. The immigrant church, as Catholicism was frequently labelled, had to change dramatically, the message seems to be, if it was to survive in the American metropolis. This one theme of assimilation haunts three decades of ethnic films. Hollywood tried to define the place of Catholic, Jew, and Protestant, Irish, Italian, and Wasp in the "melting pot"; this art so popular with immigrants became the arbiter of the new Americanism, preparing the way for Harvey Cox's "secular city."

Intolerance also hammered at the sexual theme rather daringly. Catholic girls in American film are both virginal and sensual. When the boy and girl return from a Coney Island Day, he assumes more romance is to follow: "Nothing doing with that good night stuff. I always go inside to see my girls." The Dear One slams the door, imploring her saints to "Help me to be a strong-jawed Jane." She then links her virtue with her faith and heritage: "I told you before—I promised Our Lady and I promised father that no man would ever come in this room." This trinity of faith, family, and fidelity is the cornerstone of virtually every melodrama involving a Catholic girl ever to come from Hollywood; the road from *Intolerance* to *Looking for Mister Goodbar* and *Flashdance* is straight and narrow.

At first, the boy reacts angrily, declaring, "Just for that, I'll never see you again." As she hears him go, she wavers and calls for Bobby. Her capitulation results in his own surrender.

10

She will not have to deny her moral principles after all; he returns and proposes marriage as a revealingly straightforward contract: "I was thinking—suppose we get married, then I can come in." Once again, Griffith establishes a Hollywood archetype. Catholic girls are not lovers; they are wives. Matrimony is the *sine qua non*. Fittingly, Griffith links the matrimonial theme to the question of drinking and dancing by highlighting the miracle of Christ changing water into wine at the feast at Cana in his abbreviated treatment of Jesus's life, and he links marriage to political power and religious unity in both the Babylonian and French episodes. In the modern story, however, marriage is seen principally as a redemptive act. After their wedding, the girl teaches the boy Catholic prayers; and as a title indicates, "strongly braced in the Dear One's sweet human faith, [he] sets his steps with hers on the straight road," vowing that he is through with his old life.

The boy's moral salvation is counterpointed in the modern story by the degradation of "the Friendless One" (Miriam Cooper); she listens to a "musketeer of the slums" because she is desperately hungry. Within a short time, she is wearing fancy gowns and drinking champagne, but her inner life has been destroyed. Griffith captures this quite effectively in a closeup of her vacant stare in the midst of frivolity, an insert shot of her toying with a withered flower, and a quick cut to a closeup of a nude statue, a whiskey bottle, and a book shelf dominated by a copy of *The Loves of Lucille*. She and the boy both work for the same gangster; the boy is blamed for the murder she commits; and his rescue from the gallows is made possible by her confession. Her prostitution is obviously a serious social problem and moral concern for Griffith, but again he sees both sides of the issue, and mocks the reformers for their self-righteous raid on a brothel. In a mostly comic scene of a police roundup, matronly dowagers are scandalized by girls in low-cut gowns, and the title cards scathingly observe that "When women cease to attract men, they often turn to reform as a second choice." Griffith, as he so often does in *Intolerance*, chides the sanctimonious even as he deplores the conditions they pretend to correct. The brothel of the modern story is echoed in both the slave markets of Babylon and in the temples of the goddess Ishtar. Griffith constantly demands that we balance one impression with another, that we avoid blind prejudice and intolerance.

Griffith had, it might be remembered, used a quote from Longfellow as a headnote for the official programs for *Intolerance*:

> "Why touch upon such themes?" perhaps some friend
> May ask, incredulous; "and to what good end?
> Why drag into the light of day
> The errors of an age long passed away?"
> I answer: "For the lesson that they teach;
> The tolerance of opinion and of speech."

Many contemporary viewers and even later critics have accused Griffith of equivocating, of posing ambiguous and contradictory images, and of garbling his message. The complexity and contradictions are actually central to the articulation of his key theme; like Walt Whitman, Griffith was singing a song which contained "multitudes."

This diversity and richness is central to an understanding of the presentation of Catholicism in *Intolerance*. The same faith which reforms Bobby and makes the Dear One a radiant madonna figure serves as a guise for political persecution in the French episode. The creed which condemns Christ to agony on Calvary in the gospel episode is the only succor available to the boy on death row. The religious warfare of the Babylonian episode is a spectacular prelude to the Christian utopianism of the epilogue where images of an everlasting armistice are suffused in a "white cross of light," which becomes brighter and brighter.

At every turn, Griffith invites his audience to see in new ways. When the boy is framed and carted off to prison, Griffith reminds his viewer that jail is "the sometimes House of Intolerance." In the courtroom, Griffith offers a disarming portrait of the boy's inarticulate and inexperienced attorney unbalancing the scales of justice with his most damaging plaint, "I mean—can we hang—I mean, it's only circumstantial evi-

12

dence." The unjust verdict of guilty is underscored by Griffith's impassioned anti-capital punishment title "an eye for an eye; a tooth for a tooth; *a murder for a murder*" and by his quick cut to the trial of Jesus and the order "Let him be crucified."

As Griffith brings the modern story to its breathtaking conclusion, he focuses on the Dear One's maternal instincts and the blindness of both reformers and public, who heap praise on Miss Jenkins. The wholesale acclaim for reform stands in marked contradistinction to the private virtues of motherhood, love, and prayer. On death row, Bobby receives the last sacraments, and Griffith dramatizes the role of the priest. In 1910, Griffith had done an interesting short, *The Way of the World*, about a young priest who emulated Christ by taking religious preaching to the marketplace; and in *Intolerance* he is both reverent and punctilious in his portrait of Catholic ritual. Griffith even employed a real clergyman to act in these prison scenes so they would be exactly right.

The priest as death-row counsellor will become a convention in later crime movies, largely because his presence provides a convenient *deus ex machina* to assuage demands that "crime does not pay" on film. Pat O'Brien's Father Jerry in *Angels With Dirty Faces* and William Gargan's Father Dolan in *You Only Live Once* are the progeny of Reverend A. W. McClure's Father Farley in *Intolerance*. And like Father Farley, most Hollywood priests will be a little overwhelmed by harsh realities and the cruelties of the world. Isolating priests as social workers or confessors made them seem a little unfit for the real world; their holiness seems commendable yet a trifle unworldly and unrealistic. In his key scene in *Intolerance*, Father Farley seems on the verge of fainting; at the gallows, the priest falters, drops his Bible, and needs a guard to steady him. For all his assurances that it was nothing, this stumble establishes the Hollywood myth that sanctity is a trifle weak-kneed. Father Farley's humanism, though founded on the rock of the Church, seems crushed by the injustices of contemporary life.

Griffith's attention to Catholic liturgy in these scenes may have been unrecognized and unappreciated by non-Catholics. The highly praised shot-by-shot analysis of *Intolerance* done by noted film enthusiast Theodore Huff for the Museum of Modern Art demonstrates that the meticulous Huff may have missed some of the film's nuances even after rigorous study. For example, in the scene Griffith introduces with the title "The last sacrament," when the priest prepares for the sacrament of Penance by putting on his stole, Huff offers the rather unintelligible gloss that "the priest removes his hat—kisses scarf—puts it around his neck—Boy leans toward him—crosses self—repeats words after the priest." The concept of confession and forgiveness is obscured in Huff's account, and this oversight may reflect a lack of perception any non-Catholic viewer would be prone to. Similarly, when the priest gives the boy Holy Communion, Huff glosses the scene in detail, but with little recognition of the sacrament: "the priest makes sign of the cross, gives tablet to Boy—he swallows it—looks upward—smiles forward into the arms of the priest." Huff's tablet for a Catholic viewer is a consecrated host, the veritable transubstantiated body of Christ. Any time Catholic forms, sacramentals, and liturgy are featured on screen, this problem of misinterpretation is present.

So, too, when Griffith turns to the history of Catholicism in his Judean and French episodes, he raises the whole question of history and its treatment in film. Griffith was well aware, as he wrote in the *Boston Journal* in April of 1915, that "one man's orthodoxy is another man's heterodoxy" and that "one man's judgment is another man's prejudice." For all his evocations of the past, Griffith plumbed the depths of libraries and frequently even footnoted sources in title cards. Yet the selection of details and their interpretation were always his; for all the authenticity of decor, there was still the necessity of a point of view in the narrative. A good example of this comes in his presentation of Catherine de Medici and the Saint Bartholomew's Day Massacre in *Intolerance*.

In her autobiography, Lillian Gish details the far-reaching research that went into *Intolerance*. Although her role was brief, she was very involved in the film and frequently discussed characters with Griffith. She felt "too young and unworldly" to understand Catherine de Medici, so she asked the director about the best interpretation. Griffith told Gish: "Don't judge. . . . Always remember this, Miss Lillian, circumstances make people what they are. Everyone is capable of the lowest and the highest. The same potentialities are in us all—only circumstances make the difference." Yet in *Intolerance* Griffith has Josephine Crowell play Catherine as such a grotesque monster that most critics fault her performance. William Everson is quite correct when he asserts that "the fault is Griffith's as much as hers." The power-mad Catholic Catherine obviously was meant to balance the insanely jealous Miss Jenkins. Each uses morality as a cloak for her real motivations.

This personal and political dynamic in the French section serves, as Paul O'Dell observes in his *Griffith and the Rise of Hollywood,* to mute the anti-Catholicism of the entire Parisian episode. When Catherine is introduced, the title informs all viewers that the queen mother "covers her political intolerance of the Huguenots beneath the cloak of the great Catholic religion." Anti-Catholicism is further mitigated by the mirror image we are given of Catholics and Huguenots. Confronting the opposition, Catherine whispers to her son, "What a wonderful man, the Admiral Coligny, if he only thought as *we do.*" Simultaneously, Admiral Coligny tells his friends, "What a wonderful king, if he only thought as *we do.*" In his avoidance of allusions to specific religious and doctrinal issues and in his focus on personality and prejudice, Griffith set the precedent for most religious epics to follow. Religious intolerance is usually presented in a different guise in Hollywood films; cinematic exposition rarely treats doctrine *per se* or religion *qua* religion. Differences are more often than not translated into some other metaphor. Instead of pagans versus Christians, for example, it's the Roman Empire against apostles of democracy and human equality. Aside from the title identifying Huguenots as the Protestants of the day, *Intolerance* does not define the theological and moral issues at all. The entire focus is on politics, intrigue, and revenge.

In *Intolerance,* the bloody massacre of Saint Bartholomew's Day is justified, to some degree, by the passions Catherine inflames with her account of the Protestant slaughter of Catholics at Nîmes. Catherine convinces the king that it is a question of "destroy or be destroyed." Even on the day of the actual massacre, religious battlelines are somewhat obscured. In the face of the soldiers' ghastly actions, a priest hides a little Huguenot girl under his cloak, lies to the pursuers, and saves her life. Griffith's priest on death row and his merciful priest in Paris are clearly meant to be positive poles, even if Catherine and her Catholicism can cause great bloodshed.

This avoidance of the direct presentation of purely religious controversy is notable even when the clash is between two pagan cults, as it is in the Babylonian sequence. As Robert Sklar astutely observes in his *Movie Made America: A Cultural History of American Movies,* it takes several viewings of the Babylonian episodes to "understand that a vengeful Spartan God is competing with a goddess of Pleasure." In Babylon and in France, much more attention is paid to the plight of lovers and the fate of newlyweds. Personal tragedies overshadow any historical considerations, and this becomes the hallmark of American historical film. Sweeping conflicts and cataclysmic changes are usually in the background. The narrative energy depends on the relationship· between two or three principal characters whose fate it is to endure the impact of the changes in the culture. If Griffith's modern story is an essay on capitalism and unionism, immigration and assimilation, Protestantism and Catholicism, criminal justice and morality, it is, first and foremost, a picture of Bobby, the Dear One, and their baby. One might never understand the Huguenot controversy from *Intolerance,* but one is hard put to forget the image of Prosper (Eugene Pallette) dying beside his betrothed, Brown Eyes (Margery Wilson).

The Christ story in *Intolerance* is the least developed episode, and its importance largely rests in its indirect commentary on other sections. Griffith's preoccupation with marriage in *Intolerance,* for example, is mirrored in the two episodes he chooses to treat in Christ's public life, the marriage feast at Cana and the trial of the woman taken in adultery. Griffith had essayed a biblical epic earlier in his *Judith of Bethulia,* his last film for Biograph, and was, at this time, also trying to secure

16

the rights to film *Ben-Hur*. Griffith used Howard Gaye regularly to play Christ and kept him on contract for the role. But as Karl Brown reports in his first-hand account of the filming of *Intolerance*, Griffith was never really satisfied with the total effect of his performance (Brown 1973). The director constantly chided his assistants that he wanted his Christ to be "mysterious, mysterious." It's too bad that Griffith didn't know that the other cinematic genius of his age, Charles Chaplin, wanted desperately to play Jesus Christ. Chaplin often told friends, "I'm the logical choice. I look the part. I'm a Jew . . . And I'm an atheist, so I'll be able to look at the character objectively."

Like so many later Hollywood directors, Griffith also worried about the slightest taint of blasphemy or sacrilege, so he had rabbis and ministers on set to check details. As Brown describes it, the Judean sequence had "three directors"; "in addition to Griffith, Rabbi Myers was there to direct the Jewish details of this Christian drama, while Father Dodd [an Episcopalian] was there to keep this event in Jewish history in line with Christian beliefs." The rather short scenes of the Passion and Crucifixion in *Intolerance* offer scant hints as to how Griffith himself might have handled this material in a larger work. The scathing portrait of the Pharisees as "meddlers" decrying "the revelry and pleasure-seeking among the people" augment Griffith's attack on reformers, but they might also suggest the general approach he would take to the New Testament, presenting it as a repudiation of legalism and an affirmation of charity.

The final segment of *Intolerance*, the Babylonian episode, is, as Thorold Dickinson suggests in his *A Discovery of Cinema*, Griffith's *folie de grandeur*. Volumes have been written about Griffith's extravagant sets, lavish costumes, and gargantuan expenditures on this pagan spectacle. The siege of Babylon in Griffith's presentation, Charles Higham gleefully reminds readers in his *The Art of the American Film*, is "fictitious, since that city in fact fell to the invader without a struggle at the time." Griffith created his own battlefield saga, with huge moving towers covered with oxhide, awesome weapons, rock-throwers, catapaults, battering rams, crossbows, and cauldrons full of burning oil. Contemporary reviewers like George Souele of

The New Republic, in fact, attacked *Intolerance* because it spent so much energy on the "surprising, the enormous, the daring, the sumptuous" that it gorged the senses. The love scenes were just as overwhelming as the battles; Belshazzar's court was overpopulated by dancing girls in diaphanous gowns, and the heroic prince spends much of his time assuring his princess that "the fragrant mystery of your body is greater than the mystery of life." Griffith's Babylon became, as filmmaker Kenneth Anger suggests in his insider's view of *Hollywood Babylon,* "something of a reproach and something of a challenge to the burgeoning movie town—something to surpass, something to live down." Critics like Paul O'Dell see *Intolerance* and its epic grandeur "at the root of the rise of Hollywood" since only grand studios could ever create such sweeping visions of the past. Others like Charles Higham maintain that *Intolerance* turned the greatest intellects against cinema for fifteen years, convincing them that Hollywood would "never be anything but a side show or circus for the enjoyment of the masses." Griffith had explored quite serious themes in *Intolerance,* but the power of his imagery, his ability to recreate history on a spectacular scale, was what most impressed his contemporaries. *Intolerance* provided the impetus for a huge number of religious spectacles, more inspiring in physical terms than moral or intellectual ones. Many of these films would, perforce, treat Catholic characters and themes, but most of the time any interpretation, indeed any idea at all, would be buried under layers of costumes, hidden behind huge fortresses, and trodden under by innumerable horses.

The master of this Hollywood genre was Cecil B. DeMille, who frequently tried to link his productions with Griffith's masterpieces. In his *Autobiography,* DeMille takes great pains to assure his readers that he recognized Griffith's preeminence: "Many years ago, some people used to flatter me by saying that Griffith and I were rivals. Griffith has no rivals. He was the teacher of us all." Such modesty is atypical of DeMille. More to the point is Gabe Essoe's description in *DeMille: The Man and His Pictures:* "With open-throat shirt, puttees, Louis XV hat, a drooping pipe and silver bugle, Cecil B. DeMille strode across the earlier twenties Hollywood landscape like a colossus, establishing an extravagant prototype of the film director." Half the anecdotes about Hollywood in the twenties and thirties involve C. B. DeMille, his personality, and his mega-films.

DeMille's canon is so large it is easiest to talk about the types of religious epics he made. One genre he immortalized is the biography of saint and statesman. Perhaps the best example of DeMille's hagiography, *Joan the Woman* (1916), starring Geraldine Farrar, was a rather unsubtle manipulation of history which DeMille himself described as a "call to a modern crusade," the First World War. Film historian Jack Spears cites Ms. Farrar in his *Hollywood: The Golden Era* as accepting the role because she knew that in the hands of DeMille Joan's story would be "the greatest pro-Ally propaganda," and DeMille himself often lauded the film as the beginning of his love affair with the spectacular. Most critics are less impressed, and see the film, as John Howard Lawson does in his *Film: The Creative Process*, as "a burlesque of the emotional effects that are so richly achieved in *Intolerance*."

Propaganda or burlesque, *Joan the Woman* raises some of the issues that haunt any analysis of Catholicism in film. The major problem contemporary Catholics found with *Joan the Woman* was the villainy of the clergy. If Jewish groups were loud in their protests against films that pictured them as Christ killers, Catholics were equally fervent in denouncing movies that emphasized the dark days of the Inquisition, the terror of the cloister, the mystery of the Process, and the omnipresence of the rack and the screw. Bishop Cauchon and his shadowy cohorts in *Joan the Woman* were the very sort of ornately robed Inquisitors who riled Catholic sensibilities. The pictorial treatment of these clerics makes them seem as implacable as they are inhumane. Their posturings make the cassock and cowl the very image of cruelty, vanity, self-indulgence, and inscrutability. As Charles Higham indicates in his uncharacteristically circumspect biography *Cecil B. DeMille*, the controversy over *Joan the Woman* was furious, and DeMille suggested "rather desperately" to his distributors that two versions be circulated: "In the strong Catholic communities, those scenes relating to the

Catholic church might best be spared; while in Protestant portions of the country, it might be desirable to retain such scenes." DeMille and Hollywood were more than willing to tailor their cloth to suit contemporary fashion, and the historical epic became more a sociological curiosity than a mirror of the past. Professor Morris Dickstein, writing about these "Time Bandits" in *American Film* (December 1982), sees this adaptation as an inevitable process: "History, *wie es eigentlich gewesen*—as it really was—is a will-o'-the-wisp, an impossible dream, or a convenient cover for the concerns of the moment."

Still another problem for the contemporary audiences of *Joan the Woman* was the treatment of sex. While the film had none of the bathtubs and couches that would characterize DeMille's later opuses, there was a love interest added, and Joan's rejection of this dalliance leads to her betrayal. D. W. Griffith was, Lillian Gish reports, quite shocked that—even before Joan of Arc was canonized—DeMille could add love scenes to her story. Explaining his ire, Griffith told Gish: "I'll never use the Bible as a chance to undress a woman!" DeMille's creed, which became Hollywood's gospel, was almost the opposite; history and the Bible could justify almost any debauchery and licentiousness. Moral purpose overwhelmed, DeMille and Hollywood thought, any need for restraint, since the end always justified the means. Thus, as Murray Schumach proves in his perspicacious chronicle of censorship in American film, *The Face on the Cutting Room Floor*, "Sunday school stories become perfect pastures for men who want a maximum of lust with a minimum of interference from the code and civic and religious organizations." DeMille discovered the perfect way for Hollywood to have its cake and eat it too; religious epics allowed one to be pious without being prudish, to cling to the City of God and to foray widely in the City of Man, to appease moralists and to sate the demand for sensationalism.

Joan the Woman, by focusing on her asceticism and her visions, also established a disturbing equation between Catholicism, spiritualism, and suppressed sexuality, which haunts all later treatments of the Maid of Orleans and many interpretations of other saints. Catholic author and intellectual Gilbert

20

Keith Chesterton is quoted in Harry Geduld's anthology *Authors on Film* as fearing "a real danger of historical falsehood being popularized through the film, because there is not the normal chance of one film being corrected by another film." An even more real danger is that one film reinforces the other, and every exercise in the epic genre becomes a variant on earlier themes. If John Ford the artist can expand the horizons of the Western to incorporate more sweeping concerns, it is also true that DeMille, the progenitor of historical epics, can so define the vistas that little real complexity is possible. Coincidence or not, the treatments of Joan of Arc which follow DeMille's, notably Victor Fleming's 1948 *Joan of Arc* with Ingrid Bergman, and Otto Preminger's 1957 *Saint Joan* with Jean Seberg, all seem trapped in DeMille's one-dimensional universe, and they never rise to the poetry of Maxwell Anderson nor to the irony of George Bernard Shaw. Some explanation of this lack of subtlety and complexity may be found in a most felicitous criticism by Anthony Burgess, cited in John Baxter's *Hollywood in the Thirties*. Burgess postulates that the danger with portraying absolute good poised against evil incarnate is that our natural propensity is to rest in a hackneyed response to simplified situations. Art, Burgess suggests, frequently lies in "the tension between the subject matter and what is made of it." Always to choose "enlightening topics," as DeMille and Hollywood epics do, is to risk sententiousness and superficiality. As Burgess warns, "A moral stock response comes more easily to most people than a genuine aesthetic transport." Historical epics from Hollywood do not aspire to a rarefied bliss; DeMille's reputed instructions to his crews, "Hit sex hard," were much more down to earth. In her brilliant article for the January 1976 *Film Comment*, "For God, Country, and Whoopee: DeMille and the Floss," by far the best critique of his films in English, Ruth Perlmutter offers a structuralist summary of the faults in DeMille's epic which might also be used as a summary of the limitations he introduces to the historical genre. DeMille offers, she observes, "no moral equivocations" and "no subtle psychological nuances." In aesthetic terms, she notes, the result is deadly dull: "The lack of unresolved tensions, the absence of irony, the encasement in a plot-heavy narrative typical of melodrama are iso-morphic with the cultural tendency to 'pragmatic acquiesence' and cognitive anesthesia."

DeMille deadens senses and sensibilities in many of the other genres he pioneered and perfected. His *King of Kings,* for example, a silent rendition of Christ's life, became, in the words of Wilford Beaton in *The Film Spectator* (11 June 1927), "the picture which will tend to standardize the world's conception of the New Testament." Christ, as played by H. B. Warner, is static, other-worldly, dignified, and a trifle effete; he is a Hall-mark-card Jesus, pious and untroubling. John Steinbeck's epi-grammatic reaction was most revealing: "Saw the movie; loved the book."

DeMille realized he was on touchy ground when he treated the Messiah, so he gave Hollywood an epic lesson in how to defuse controversy. Rather than alienating any denomination, he used would-be religious critics as consultants and he invited them to his set for interminable Bible readings and prayers. The result was less an ecumenical council and prayer meeting than a well-publicized clerical junket. DeMille was especially fearful of the Catholic reaction, so he employed Father Daniel Lord, co-author of the Motion Picture Production Code, as tech-nical adviser for the film. As DeMille somewhat smugly recalls in his autobiography, one of his "brightest memories" was of Father Lord on the set of *King of Kings* offering sunrise Mass every morning; it was, DeMille declares, "like a continued ben-ediction on our work." It was also—and this lesson would not be lost on Hollywood producers for years to come—a good insurance policy against future attacks on the film. Hiring Cath-olic technical advisers became roughly analagous to obtaining an *imprimatur*. It did not assure there would be no controversy, but it did smooth the way to the theater.

Seeking a consensus on Christ's life which would offend no religious group often resulted, of course, in a rather bland definition of Christianity and sanctity. Dialogue, parables, and pronouncements give way to lush inspirational music, heroic postures, mysterious back-lighting, and unearthly halos. Christ's life translated into striking tableaux; indeed, every once in a while, everything seems to freeze so the audience will have time to recognize the painting. In his anecdotal history of early motion pictures, *A Million and One Nights,* Terry Ramsaye describes the filming of *The Passion Play* for Lumière in 1898. The director evidently thought he was making lantern slides and screamed "Hold it!" whenever he attained the desired effect. DeMille and others who have filmed the life of Christ in Hollywood have likewise directed with the same panache. Ruth Perlmutter is again describing the whole genre when she attacks DeMille's style because "every shot is self-contained and self-explanatory." As she notes, his world and the life of Christ as seen in Hollywood is "a tight little world" where "a homogenous constancy, of *mise-en-scène,* costumes, and historical period exists within a three dimensional space, the so-called window on the world of Renaissance illusionism."

Paradoxically, the further Hollywood drifted from historical accuracy, the greater the emphasis on illusion and physical details became. Even DeMille admitted that his vision of *The Crusades* (1935) "telescoped" history, arguing in his *Autobiography* that audiences came to be "entertained not educated," so he could not subject them to "a day to day chronological presentation of actual fact." *Scientific American,* on the other hand, found the exacting reconstruction of "armor, swords, shields," and the Siege of Acre worth exploring in the pages of its August 1935 issue. The most interesting questions about *The Crusades,* however, were raised by Graham Greene in his review for *The Spectator.* Greene, a Catholic, noted that this stirring pageant of Catholic kings off to conquer infidels had "nothing Romish" about it; it appeared, he suggested, as if it had "been written by the Oxford Group." Rome, papal authority, and the Holy Empire were studiously ignored; Richard Coeur-de-lion, Greene perceptively observed, was presented "through the pious and Protestant" eyes of DeMille. Hollywood historical films merged all faiths under one banner; Hollywood was clearly happiest when it arrayed true believers against clearly villainous heathens, huns, and pagans, in a manner uncomplicated by any church doctrine.

Greene's acute analysis also pinpoints the sexual metaphor

which holds *The Crusades* together as a narrative. Saladin (Ian Keith) may be a crafty, suave, potent opponent for Richard (Henry Wilcoxon), but he remains exotic and erotic enough to make his proposed liaison with, and dominance of, Berengaria (Loretta Young) seem faintly miscegenetic and perverse. Richard, for his part, as Greene writes, closely resembles "those honest, simple, young rowing-men who feel that there's something wrong about sex." Hollywood spectaculars transform and transmute serious topics into more easily assimilated romantic triangles. Instead of the struggle between Catholicism and Islam for the Holy City, *The Crusades* offers Richard the misogamist fighting Saladin the polygamist for the favors of a winsome maiden. In Hollywood, any jolt of amazing grace was quite likely to be accompanied by an irresistible arrow from Cupid's bow. The line between eros and agape is seldom hard and fast. Usually conversion to Catholicism is as easy as falling in love; to be smitten is to be halfway to heaven.

The high priest of camp, Cecil B. DeMille, a more complex personality than his debunkers realize, used historical genres as an outlet for his excesses; he patented the immoral morality play to exercise and exorcise his personal demons. DeMille offered America "sword and sandal," "bathrobe and beard," Christian and lion epics which struggle hard to seem to chant Catholic glories but delight quite contentedly in pagan rhapsodies. Nero's fiddle sounds most vibrantly in all of DeMille's orchestrations. When he adapts *The Admirable Crichton* for the screen as *Male and Female*, a fleeting allusion in Barrie's play inspires a lush excursion into psychologically revealing master-slave domination games, as the ornately coiffed and stylishly attired Catholic maid (Gloria Swanson) dies swooning in an arena of lions. *Male and Female* is but a modest prelude, however, to *The Sign of the Cross*, DeMille's ode to "delicious debauchery."

DeMille always protested that *The Sign of the Cross* was on the side of the angels and that the Catholics were the heroes, but their sanctity is just too banal to hold a candle to Charles Laughton's Nero. All the juxtapositions in *The Sign of the Cross* suggest DeMille's adoration of the pagan aristocrats and his very grudging reverence for the deadly dull catechumens. DeMille's epic follows the text of Wilson Barrett's old play rather closely, but it is visually a lot different from earlier adaptations like the 1909 Vitagraph one reeler, *The Way of the Cross,* the 1910 Selig one reeler, *The Christian Martyrs,* and Adolph Zukor's 1914 *The Sign of the Cross,* starring Dustin Farvum as Marcus Superbus.

Zukor's advertising emphasized the "extravagance of scenes and spectacular effects," the "faithfulness to the original settings," and the "most sumptuous and lavish production," claiming that the whole project "glows with Titianesque luxuriance of coloring," but in fact, Zukor's "gallery of startling scenes" involves in large part a parade of pious posturings, redolent of Victorian prayer cards. In Zukor's primitive hagiography, the Catholic martyrs may be boring "helpless ones," but the Romans clearly are the villians who defile virtue.

Compared to Zukor's version, DeMille's avant-garde Romans debauch more freely and make sin look rather more appealing than the agonizing death of a Catholic true believer. As the weekly *Variety* noted in 1932, *The Sign of the Cross* has "sight stuff that hasn't been duplicated since the silent picture days." Karl Struss, the cinematographer, shot the whole picture through bright red gauze, a technique often used in silents, to help capture a nostalgic mood, and Cecil B. DeMille pointed his camera to emphasize every voyeuristic delight.

A measure of how important sub-text is in *The Sign of the Cross* may be found early in the film, after the two aged Christians meet. As they draw a cross on the ground, the film cuts from that crucifix to another cruciform, a wooden beam carried by a scantily clad girl bearing buckets of water. A subliminal pattern is established by DeMille's loving focus on this pagan's ample cleavage; the cross of these old philosophers will always be the abnegation of her sensuality and eroticism. All the pagan women obviously revel in their flesh and display their bodies flamboyantly; the Catholic women are modestly, indeed prudishly, garbed until they are stripped naked, humiliated, and chained at the phallic stake. Thus the most famous scene in the film features Poppea (Claudette Colbert) luxuriating in a bath of milk, as she implores Dacia to "Take off your clothes, get in here and tell me all about it." DeMille's coy focus on glistening bare backs, smooth legs, and almost exposed breasts is clearly designed to titillate audiences. Later this ardent pagan empress strives mightily to have Marcus Superbus (Fredric March) doff his clothes, share her dreams, and make her his slave. She even attempts to warm Mercia the Christian virgin (Elissa Landi) "into life" when she discovers her rival for Marcus's love is "frozen with virtue." Far from providing a paean to Christian modesty, these visual dalliances celebrate the carnality of the Roman Empire most unabashedly. Studiously crafted sequences of Colbert and her lovely handmaidens and dramatically lighted visions of Laughton on his pillows wallowing in rapturous delight dominate DeMille's glowing tribute to pagan excess.

Similarly, DeMille's feverish attention to the sufferings of early converts finally becomes an end in itself. All the emotional climaxes in this film revolve around scenes of torture and suffering. DeMille's obsession with cruelties inflicted on adolescent boys, prepubescent orphan girls, and nude young women lead Fred Lawrence Guiles to a striking aside in his history of Hollywood's stormy relationship with famous writers, *Hanging on in Paradise*. As Guiles views Hollywood, the focus is always on "sanitized illusion," assuming one can accept "the sadism of Cecil B. DeMille's Biblical dramas as pure in intent." In his disturbing parenthesis, Guiles opines that making such a leap to faith in DeMille was "a very difficult thing to do, but . . . was managed neatly by every Christian Church in this country and abroad."

When the vehement Catholic attacks on DeMille's 1932 Christmas present, *The Sign of the Cross*, came, religious critics mainly ignored the sadism and focused on the dance of "The Naked Moon" as performed by Ancaria (Jazzelle Joyner); the nudity and implied lesbianism in this attempt to loosen Marcia's inhibitions shocked Catholic audiences. The whole film industry felt the Catholic pressure, and the famed guardian of Movie Morals, Will Hays, had one of his many highly publicized "secret meetings" with a determined DeMille. When Will Hays asked, "What are you going to do about the dance?" DeMille's celebrated reply was succinct: "Not a damned thing." As a result of this impasse, DeMille's purported homage to the earliest Catholic saints became, according to the noted Catholic intellectual, Moira Walsh, writing in *America*, "one of the contributing factors in the formation of the Legion of Decency."

In *The Sign of the Cross*, DeMille does allow a few minutes for preaching, but even then he undercuts the true believers with his visuals. As Catholics pontificate about a Christ who "proved there is no death," DeMille cuts to Romans killing the saintly sentinels guarding the grove. And when the sermon concludes with a call to "carry a new life to your brothers" and "a freedom as vast as heavens," archers shoot down the preacher and Roman legions round up all the worshippers. This disjunction between the assertions of the Catholic faithful and the realities of the physical continues in the arena scenes. Mercia and her colleagues reassure themselves that "There is no death, only a crossing over," but their songs cannot disguise the enormity of the prison doors, the agony of the long climb up the stairs to the arena, nor the reality of the lions. Even the noble Superbus cannot accept the religion of these zealots; as he tells Mercia, "I believe in you . . . not this Christ." Although he is full of "happiness and strange hope," he embraces salvation because he dreams of an eternity in her arms. His conversion hardly seems the Catholic journey from eros to agape; he seems merely to have rejected pagan promiscuity in favor of the sacrament of matrimony when he declares, "I can't sing the hymn or look up. I'll be believing in you my wife." Just like Bobby in *Intolerance*, and later Hollywood converts in epics such as *The Robe*, Marcus Superbus finds his God through a Catholic maiden. This identification of Catholicism with romantic love, of faith with sexual fidelity, cuts across every Hollywood genre. Cool gangsters melt, hardened soldiers disarm, and hellish demons depart when true love flourishes. Constantine's message, "in this sign you shall conquer," is translated by Hollywood into the cliché "Love conquers all." In the Hollywood catechism, to be loved by a Catholic is a benediction, but to love a Catholic is a plenary indulgence. Affection for a

Catholic provides actual grace; marriage with the right Catholic assures sanctifying grace.

It was DeMille's treatment of the Middle Ages that reinforced Hollywood's tendency to view bows and arrows, swords and shields, peasant uprisings and religious wars, as a domain for overgrown, over-age boys. Allan Dwan's 1923 *Robin Hood* with its derring-do and buffoonery pushed the Crusades far to the background and used its one notable Catholic, Friar Tuck, as a focus for slapstick humor. Similarly, *Cardinal Richelieu* (1935), a George Arliss vehicle, had its Catholic hero switch hats rather cavalierly. As the chameleon courtier tells his queen in her boudoir, "Tonight I am his Majesty's minister, tomorrow a cardinal." The same sort of frenetic masquerade and constant disguise characterized the saga of the three musketeers in its various incarnations. Hollywood seemed intent in its costume dramas on adventure without controversy, period touches without historical accuracy. The dominant tone for these stagey epics is exemplified by Michael Curtiz's hugely successful *The Adventures of Robin Hood* (1938), an Errol Flynn swashbuckler shot in ravishing color, which reduces any moral questions about the ethics of civil disobedience or of "stealing from the rich to give to the poor" to juvenile banter. When Robin (Errol Flynn) recruits Friar Tuck (Eugene Pallette) to provide his men "spiritual guidance," their stylized encounter is larded by ironic barbs, slapstick pratfall, and enough comic asides to dismiss any serious considerations out of hand. Friar Tuck, for example, declares he has "vowed poverty," but one glance at this corpulent hedonist engenders Robin's riposte, "If this is poverty, I'll gladly share it." Hollywood's Sherwood Forest is so obviously green tinsel and harmless whimsy that the monastic life can be mocked with impunity. Nobody worries about Friar Tuck's soul, as this cardboard caricature huffs and puffs his way through the trees, frolicking at banquets and vowing to convert his companions from their "thieving ways." This outlaw friar's only recourse to religion comes when he tests Maid Marian's sincerity. In solemn tones, he inquires if she is "a good daughter of the Church" and "true to Robin," a seeming corollary of Catholicism. Catholic cathedrals and ceremonies fare no better in medieval costume dramas. Michael Curtiz carefully re-creates a religious coronation ceremony at the end of *Robin Hood* only to have it disrupted; the stately procession of the Black Canons dissolves into a farrago of spirited swordplay.

The Adventures of Robin Hood was, as Rudy Behlmer indicates in his "behind-the-scenes" look at *America's Favorite Movies*, "physically the biggest film undertaking since D. W. Griffith's *Intolerance*." Much of the planning for the film centered on the treatment of Catholicism. All the research for the film led screenwriter Roland Leigh, who developed the original concept for this project, to see the villains in extant Robin Hood sagas as "bishops, abbots, and friars who bled the poor in order to enrich themselves." According to Behlmer, Leigh's earliest notes define the quandry most pointedly: "Undoubtedly in medieval times the church took unwarranted liberties with its power and influence. Equally undoubtedly we have no desire to offend either the Catholic or Protestant church of today . . . a tactful compromise will have to be arrived at." In the final editing of the film, any serious Catholic problem has disappeared; the religious issue is reduced to the frivolity of Friar Tuck and the exoticism of the Black Canons. Whenever Hollywood found substantial problems in portraying medieval Catholic personages, it usually sidestepped the serious issues or framed the problems in such obscure terms that viewers could be offended, if they were offended at all, only by the process of evasion and trivialization. Studying Catholicism in American films frequently involves a recognition of such omissions and obscurantism. A similar technique of avoidance and reductionism haunts director Curtiz's 1960 *Francis of Assisi*, in which the aura of spirituality is rendered by pregnant pauses, empty stares, unspeakable lines, crucifixes, cosmic voice-overs, and stigmata. To define Francis's sanctity, various characters mumble that he "seems not of this world" or complain most uncomprehendingly that dancing with him is "like dancing with a ghost." When Francis (Bradford Dillman) rails against "the emptiness, the hypocrisy, and the shallowness" around him, he is also summarizing the major flaws critics isolate in his film biography.

Critics were even less kind to Franco Zeferelli's *Brother Sun, Sister Moon* (1973), which refurbished the friar as a flower child in a mod world animated by the vapid music of Donovan. The nadir for these medieval saints' lives comes, however, in Edward Dmytryk's Italian-American production of *Cronache di un Convento, The Reluctant Saint* (1959), featuring Maximillian Schell as Joseph of Copertino. As the reviewer for *Esquire* observed at the time of its first American release, Schell's duck-like walk, imbecilic grin, exaggerated clumsiness, and outspread hands failed to convey any sense of sanctity, humility, or rapture; these broad gestures were rib-ticklingly funny. And the arch visions of his levitations, the reviewer for *Saturday Review* concluded, pushed the film very close to being "the first anti-church comedy." The final scene of the saint being held down so he won't drift away from a religious procession, is, in the words of *Saturday Review*, "as hilarious as any scene from a Laurel and Hardy two reeler." Many Hollywood treatments of historical Catholicism finally crack under the strains of lofty reverence and degenerate into high camp.

Hollywood rarely had time for complex theology and windy sermons, though John Ford does manage in *Mary of Scotland* (1936) to capture the fury of an irate John Knox damning Papists. His vitriol is more than balanced, however, by the radiant beauty of Katharine Hepburn as the doomed Catholic. Normally, however, cathedrals, pulpits, and gargoyles serve as mere backdrops to more athletic accomplishments. Warner Brothers' stirring adaptation of *The Hunchback of Notre Dame* (1936) and other historical extravaganzas featured more of Quasimodo and Esmeraldo, more beauty and the beast, more swords and horses, and fewer images of cross and crozier. Hollywood history for the next two decades demanded mammoth sets, stock characters, elaborate chases, fiendish intrigues, sterling heroes, predictable melodrama, and superheated romances. Stars, sentiment, sex, and sets became Hollywood's formula for success; larger than life epics showcasing celebrities in lavish though anachronistic costumes filled neighborhood theaters where patrons clamored for grand emotions and free dishes. Historical spectaculars became, as Michael Wood re-

30

marks in his insightful analysis of *America in the Movies*, "demonstrations of what a studio could do; they were the last grand flings of those factories of illusion."

Faced with possible extinction in the 1950s, Hollywood looked to ever bigger screens and ever greater spectacles to conquer television. DeMille, tinseltown's most celebrated prophet, could hardly have foreseen the proliferation of titles based on biblical material. Beginning again with *Quo Vadis* (1951) and *The Robe* (1953), Hollywood churned out an endless list of extravaganzas, including such clinkers as *The Sign of the Pagan* (1954), *The Silver Chalice* (1954), and *The Big Fisherman* (1959). Paul Newman spent a good deal of money for ads asking his fans not to watch *The Silver Chalice*, his first film, labelling it "the worst film to be made in the entirety of the fifties." Most other entries in Hollywood's toga sweepstakes could easily vie for the title; it would be quite a chariot race. As Lester Friedman points out in his chronicle of Jews in these films, "these biblical epics prove a vast Sinai of tedium and mediocrity relieved only occasionally by some small cinematic interest."

Dull as they may be aesthetically, these excursions during the fifties into the earliest ages of faith do provide a fascinating chapter in the Gospel according to Hollywood. The more Hollywood tried to avoid doctrinal issues while focusing on primitive Catholicism, the more it needed to explore the sociology of what historian M. L. W. Laistner in his *Christianity and Pagan Culture in the Later Roman Empire* terms "perhaps the most far-reaching revolution that the world has seen." Necessity became the mother of invention, and a glorious irony of this period is that by avoiding so-called religious questions, Hollywood offered perspicacious insights into the evolution of early Catholicism.

The best of the biblical films, *The Robe* (1953), director Henry Koster's big screen spectacular, photographed in Cinemascope by Leon Shamroy, and planned by Twentieth Century Fox as the answer to the challenge of television's small screen, provides a brilliant exegesis of the underlying causes for Rome's persecution of Catholics. The film expands dramatically on Lloyd Douglas's popular novel and seems to cull many of its best insights from Herbert B. Workman's turn-of-the-century classic analysis of *Persecution in the Early Church*. Workman's scientific analysis of a religious phenomenon is the very approach Hollywood, consciously or unconsciously, adopted. Workman demonstrated convincingly that Roman persecutions were "not theological, or the outcome of esoteric doctrine of worship, or the result of certain ethical postulates. Nor were they the result of animosity."

Instead, Workman postulated five main "internal" causes for the persecution of Catholics, and *The Robe* skillfully embodies them all. The first and foremost reason for the vicious attacks on the Christian sect was, Workman shows, the power it had as "a disintegrating factor upon the Roman *familia*." Early churchmen discouraged marriage and forbade intermarriage; traditional family bonds and marital arrangements were renounced in favor of ecclesiastical ones. Established customs like the Roman *patria potestas* obviously contradicted the new faith. If, as so many epics suggested, marriage with a Catholic led to faith, conventional marriages with pagans were dangerous for catechumens. At the conclusion of *The Robe*, this convention surfaces most powerfully. The Christian maiden, Diana (Jean Simmons), refuses a pre-ordained union with Caligula (Jay Robinson) and walks off with her newly chosen and converted husband Marcellus (Richard Burton) into "his new kingdom." Caligula jests about their voyage "to meet their king," but the loud chorus of alleluias, their radiant smiles, and the clouds forming in the heavens all suggest Hollywood's traditional happy ending.

Workman's second argument, that the Christian rejection of slavery threatened the empire, becomes the dominant theme in *The Robe*. Rome, the opening narration intones, contains "more slaves than citizens," and Leon Shamroy's camera glides leeringly from one trader's stall to another, as they expose their wares. This visual panorama of the "traffic in human souls" spares no energy to suggest that naked women are being auctioned, though the camera is always discreetly placed to avoid frontal nudity. When Marcellus buys Demetrius (Victor Mature), a rebellious and educated slave, his servants try to assure the newcomer that "to be a slave in this household is an honor." Demetrius sneers back that "to be a slave anywhere is to be a dog." Even when Marcellus tries to befriend Demetrius, the embittered slave obviously savors his insulting retort: "Friends cannot be bought, not even for three thousand pieces of gold." Demetrius becomes a Christian and eventually converts his master in an evocative realization of Workman's thesis that early Christianity's immediate willingness to accept slaves into the faith and ordain them as priests was "a revolution, silent, unheralded, the full effect of which it is difficult to exaggerate."

Workman's third explanation of the persecution of the early church involved the new conception of property that faith entailed. Early Catholics felt that the end of the world was near; a view, Peter Nichols argues in his fine account of *The Pope's Legions*, which "probably distorted a number of decisions in the first years of the Church." As a result of this preoccupation with a new world, early churchmen scrupulously avoided the blandishments of this life. When Marcellus hunts "the big fisherman," he baits impoverished Catholics by offering them any price they want for their cloth cloaks. Then their spiritual leader appears and reminds them, "We pray to be free of greed." When he further challenges them with the query "Shall we turn dishonest because life is hard?" the faithful flock sheepishly return Marcellus's coins. Such disregard for material wealth made this band of outsiders threatening to an empire built on trade and plunder and sustained by ambition.

Workman also theorizes that "the secret rites and ceremonies" of the primitive church generated intense fear and hatred. In the Roman world of superstitions, new sects frequently took on the aspect of dangerous magicians and black arts. Christianity, with its mysterious sacraments, especially Communion, reeked of debauchery and cannibalism. Caligula in *The Robe* frequently refers to Christ as "this dead magician," and even doctors friendly to individual Christians rail against the new "sorcery." The totemism of the sect and its isolation from mainstream culture are always evident in *The Robe*; the Christian quarter seems a quite different world from the palace. Historian Louis DeWohn in his sweeping history of the Catholic

Church, *Founded on a Rock*, posits such isolation, the *Disciplina Arcani*, as the most notable feature of early Church life: "Christians had a way of holding themselves aloof." Non-Christians, DeWohn declares, were not allowed at Christian services, and even those receiving instruction in the faith "were allowed to stay only during the first part of the Mass, up to the Offertory." Hollywood audiences had the same partial view of Catholic ritual; in the most hackneyed of the epics, a few minutes of ceremony would quickly be interrupted by slaughter. In *The Robe*, Christians are transformed into a loveable group of martyrs mesmerized by doleful folk songs, and their piety inspires a routine production number.

Workman's last thesis isolates the "individualistic spirit" of the early converts as a major cause for their persecution. Rome had to eradicate citizens who avowed their loyalty to a throne outside the empire. In *The Robe* and other epic fantasies of the fifties, this theme allows Hollywood to confuse faith and patriotism; the Christian's losing battle with Rome and their sufferings become a metaphor for the birth of democracy. Biblical epics in the age of Truman and Eisenhower celebrate the birth of Americanism and manifest destiny, not the origins of faith and Catholicism. The Catholics in the epics of the fifties are good guys, not because they worship the true God but because they love their mates more than life itself, cherish their freedom, and die bravely for their Bill of Rights. In *The Robe*, one almost hears "The Star Spangled Banner" and "Battle Hymn of the Republic" in the background when an aging but savant emperor predicts the inevitable fall of his totalitarian regime: "When it comes, this is how it will start. This is the greatest madness of all . . . man's desire to be free. Some obscure martyr in some obscure province, then madness, infecting the legions, rotting the empire." Having just crushed a thousand year Reich in Europe and deflated an empire of the Rising Sun in the Far East, self-satisfied Americans could relish the Christians' defiance of Rome. Martyrdom was made palatable by historical distance; all these images of gladiators and beasts disemboweling true believers were acceptable because Americans knew that democracy would eventually destroy all the emperors. Michael Wood addresses this issue perceptively in *America in the Movies* as he exposes Hollywood's attempts to gloss over hard questions. Biblical epics, he suggests, "invite our sympathies for the oppressed, of course—all the more so because we know that by generously backing these losers we shall find we have backed winners in the end."

Depending entirely on one's preconceptions, these "winners" could be the first illustrious evangelists for the Catholic faith, the heroic avatars of American democracy, or the beguiling apostles of romantic love. Audiences varied widely in their reactions, and Hollywood relished the ambiguity. Movies were "better than ever" and epics were engineered to lure everyone to the same box office for a red carpet, road show attraction, demanding an increased admission charge. For a young Catholic school girl like Gina Cascone, this multiplicity of possible reactions generated some hilarious misunderstandings. She gleefully reminisces in *Pagan Babies and Other Catholic Memories* about her burgeoning awareness that the nuns who taught her were seeing one film while she enjoyed quite another. For her cloistered tutors, *Quo Vadis* (1951) was a "Catholic training film" canonizing Christian martyrs and preparing the faithful to endure similar torments in defense of the Baltimore catechism. The young starstruck Gina was more entranced by Hollywood's image of Deborah Kerr giving her all for the love of Robert Taylor. For Gina, *Quo Vadis* was the film in which "After a really steamy romance, their love conquers the Roman Empire, and they ride off into the sunset together." As Gina notes, "According to the nuns, I missed the main thrust."

Critic and social commentator Julian Smith details another provocative example of the varying reactions religious epics fostered in his unjustly neglected study of Hollywood film and Viet Nam, *Looking Away*. Smith recalls an impending scandal in his hometown, Covington, Louisiana, when the local theater manager booked an "Eyetalian sex epic." Somehow, he reports, the controversy did not come to the attention of the "good sisters," and they marched their charges, the students of St. Peter's and St. Scholastia's to a special matinee at Mr. Sale's theater "to see the very same spectacle our parents forbade us."

Julian Smith humorously dates his "latent sadomasochism" to a scene in which "a Roman centurion raked the naked breast of a crucified virgin with what looked for all the world like the kind of gardening prongs my grandfather stocked in his hardware store." Where the nuns saw the stalwart faith of "virgins who refused to join the terrible orgies and were thrown half-naked to the lions," others, like Smith, were more interested in the half-naked bodies.

Some measure of how hard Hollywood worked to eliminate the doctrinaire from religious epics, replacing creed with more generalized and earthly emotions, can be found in the evolution of *Ben-Hur* from the fevered polemics of General Lew Wallace's purple prose to the studied non-sectarianism of William Wyler's 1959 *Ben-Hur*. Wallace's tale of the Christ unabashedly heralded its author's dramatic conversion to Christianity. No subtlety conceals Wallace's fervent plea for all men of good faith to be born again in their Redeemer's embrace. The message of salvation so illumines *Ben-Hur* that this popular fiction was endorsed by the Holy Sea and blessed by Pope Leo XIII.

During his life, Wallace zealously assured that only believers adapted his work for stage and screen. If it had not been for the Christian half of the Klaw-Erlanger partnership, *Ben-Hur* would not have opened at the Broadway Theater in 1899, where half a million theater-goers saw it the first season. Sidney Olcott filmed *Ben-Hur* in 1907, racing chariots drawn by firehouse horses around Paine's Fireworks Show in Manhattan Beach, but the Kalem Company later lost an important Supreme Court copyright case because they had not cleared the rights to the novel with Wallace. This 1907 production, Kevin Brownlow points out in his indispensable collection of interviews with early filmmakers, *The Parade's Gone By*, was only a "little film" of a race despite the vaunted claims to be "sixteen magnificent scenes with illustrated titles, positively the most superb motion-picture spectacle ever made."

In 1926 Fred Niblo filmed *Ben-Hur* again; this time, the film was not little; it was, if anything, too big. Kenneth MacGowan's delightful survey *Behind the Screen: The History and Techniques of*

36

the Motion Picture labels the project "probably the most extraordinary example of an overshot budget." Notable largely because it marks matinee idol Francis X. Bushman's attempted comeback, this *Ben-Hur*, Robert Sherwood accurately charges in his review for *Life*, consists largely of an "orgy of huge sets, seething mobs, and camera effects," which contain "little of the spirit of the original story." This 1926 silent version, however, does preserve that one critical idea, Wallace's overworked major theme: the Jewish hero, Judah Ben-Hur, does find Christ and embrace a New Testament faith founded in charity. Reunited with his family, Judah Ben-Hur proclaims his newfound joy in Christ via a title card: "O day of gladness! Thrice blessed—that giveth me mother, sister, and thee." In 1926, Christianity provided the apotheosis.

In 1959, the muscular and handsome Judah Ben-Hur, as portrayed by filmdom's demi-god, Charlton Heston, makes no such avowal of faith. As Bosley Crowthers astutely notes in his panoramic discussion of *Vintage Films*, "no conversion of the hero to Christianity was implied." In the place of overt religious conversion, Crowther continues, Hollywood offers "a sense of spiritual movement toward the idea of the brotherhood of man." Jew and Gentile, Catholic and Baptist, Hindu and Moslem could be equally satisfied with the ecumenical humanism of this *Ben-Hur*; Hollywood's catechism assured that there was none of General Lew Wallace's partisan evangelizing to fret over. When well-defined creeds offend audiences, Hollywood will gladly pluck them out. In place of the old gods, Hollywood provides its own deities. The startling thing about the 1959 *Ben-Hur*, Donald Spoto correctly intuits in his provocative overview of *Camerado: Hollywood and the American Man* was the transcendental power of the new superstar. As Ben-Hur, Charlton Heston need not cling to Christianity; the miracles of Hollywood technology have elevated his imposing figure "to the ranks of a religious savior." Spoto perceptively isolates a cosmic shift. In this 1959 *Ben-Hur*, Heston need not go to Christ because Heston himself has become Hollywood's new Messiah, a savior created by the twentieth century's marvelous dream machine. Charlton Heston has been transfigured, in Spoto's words, into "our *deus ex machina*, all made up and smiling, come to save us with outstretched arm and dazzling, but somewhat spiritless, glance."

As Heston ascended to his heavenly throne, Hollywood pictured Jesus descending to earth, incarnated as a man of no special distinction. In a fascinating espousal of a "God is dead" theology, Hollywood movies de-mythologized Christ, his disciples, and all the generations of believers who followed. Divinity was out; humanity was in. The screen abounded with parables from a relevant revisionist Gospel. Holy Scriptures gave way to cinematic caricatures. Christ became a fledgling superstar and his Catholic co-religionists a gaggle of groupies. *Godspell* (1973) and *Jesus Christ Superstar* (1973) were merely the loudest entries in a cacophonous litany. Johnny Cash prepared a Nashville vision of an itinerant hobo in *Gospel Road* (1973), and Nicholas Ray saw his own teenage Jesus with neatly shaved armpits in *King of Kings* (1961). Director George Stevens turned *The Greatest Story Ever Told* (1965) into a prolonged game of *Hollywood Squares;* as Shana Alexander complained in her aptly titled critique, "Christ Never Tried to Please Everybody," "The total effect of Stevens' avowed reverence was one of 'sets by Hallmark' and 'panorama by Grand Canyon Postcards'." God's grandeur was inadvertently reduced to tedious schmaltz; his gospel became little more than another logo or merchandizing gimmick. Independent filmmaker Robert Downey's scathing satire of these new, all-too-human Hollywood messiahs, *Greaser's Palace* (1972) presents a zoot-suited Jesus who botches his cure of a cripple ("I can crawl, I can crawl!") and meanders aimlessly on his way to Jerusalem "to be actor-singer-dancer" in fulfillment of the prophecy, "It is written that agent Morris awaits me."

Show business and salvation always seem to be bumping into each other, whether it is God as performer or performer as God. The priest who challenged Adolph Zukor's right to screen *The Passion Play* because the cathedral and the theater were two markedly different domains had intuited an ineffable problem neither he nor Zukor could resolve. The same Americans who crowded the neighborhood bijou for Saturday matinees were filling the pews Sunday morning at the local church. Yet the pictures they saw on Saturdays and the sermons they heard on Sundays almost always seemed to come from different catechisms.

TWO

Crime Movie:
immigration, gangsters, and guns

Some people think the Crucifixion only took place on Calvary. They better wise up. Taking Joey Doyle's life to stop him from testifying is a crucifixion—Dropping a sling on Kayo Nolan because he was ready to spill his guts tomorrow—that's a crucifixion. Every time the mob puts the crusher on a good man—tries to stop him from doing his duty as a citizen—it's a crucifixion. And anybody who sits around and lets it happen, keeps silent about something he knows has happened—shares the guilt of it as much as the Roman soldier who pierced the flesh of Our Lord to see if He was dead.

Father Barry in *On the Waterfront*

On November 6, 1928, Alfred Emanuel Smith met Franklin Delano Roosevelt at the 69th Regiment Armory in New

41

York City; it turned out to be one of the most important nights in American history. These two Empire State politicians, renowned champions of immigrants and other urban poor, had come to the clubhouse of New York's famed fighting Irish, a notable bastion of Catholicism, urban pride, and ethnicity, of machine politics, wet sentiments, and ferocious ethnocentricity, to celebrate the crowning victory for the "Happy Warrior," an end to Prohibition, and the beginning of a new cosmopolitan era; but before they left that night, the raucous strains of "The Sidewalks of New York" had been muffled, their Jazz Age values had been rebuffed, and the victory belonged to the descendants of the "Order of the Star Spangled Banner," to the apostles of the "Dry Messiah," Bishop James Cannon, and to the small-town fundamentalists who found their silver tongue in William Jennings Bryan and their clubhouses in the American Protective Associations and the Ku Klux Klan. It was as though D. W. Griffith's *Intolerance* had come to life and the Jenkinses were ruling the land.

Al Smith's loss was a staggering experience for American Catholics, coming as it did in the decade that fostered the enactment of harshly restrictive immigration laws and a resounding victory for the Eighteenth Amendment to the Constitution. Prohibition was, as Garth Jowett cannily observes in his essay "Bullets, Beers, and the Hays Office," a markedly anti-papist piece of legislation: "In reality this [Amendment] meant the assertion of power by the Protestant, rural, native American, and was directly aimed at the emerging power of the Catholic and Jewish immigrants and the urban middle class." The nightmare for Catholics culminated when Al Smith received only 87 electoral votes to Herbert Hoover's 444.

Al Smith's defeat was so crushing largely because the whole campaign had been remarkably bitter. In a stirring speech in Oklahoma City, Smith had reaffirmed the "constitutional guarantee that there should be no religious test for public office" as "the most vital principle that was ever given any people," but his candidacy did become a *de facto* trial for Catholic rights and acceptance in America. Propaganda painted Smith, who never operated a motor vehicle, as a drunken driver

42

menacing law-abiding temperates, and pictured his abstemious wife as an alcoholic floozie. Widely circulated pamphlets spoke of Papal Wings at the White House, Cardinals patrolling the halls of Congress, and of obsequious public officials, including the Commander in Chief, genuflecting to kiss the rings of Catholic clergymen. New York was pictured as "Satan's Seat," a modern day Sodom and Gomorrah of foreign accents, swarthy men, dark women, saloons, brothels, and worse. All the old prejudices were stirred up: Catholics were sinister foreigners with secret allegiances to an Inquisitorial Empire, or they were genetically inferior peasants breeding huge cadres of sub-human juvenile delinquents, alcoholics, nymphomaniacs, and drug addicts who would infect American values, corrupt native institutions, and pollute the genetic pool. Catholic sacraments and ceremonies were presented as orgiastic and licentious; the Catholic immigrant's lifestyle was denounced as perverse and scandalous. No wonder, then, that according to Thomas M. Coffey in his history of Prohibition, *The Long Thirst*, Al Smith, once the smiling Golden Boy of Tamanny and the Irish crown prince of urban America, but now a defeated, crestfallen, and embittered Democratic presidential candidate, left the armory that November night a broken man, lamenting to his dazed supporters that "the time hasn't yet come when a man can say his [Rosary] beads in the White House."

If they weren't welcome in the Capitol building during Prohibition, the paraments of Catholicism filled movie screens during this era of bootleggers, flappers, and gunsels. The outlaws of the twenties and thirties were iconoclasts and immigrants—predominantly Irish and Italian Catholics—while the heroes were native-born champions of Americanism, Protestantism, Yankee traditions, and assimilation. Cathedrals and crucifixes, Roman collars and confessionals, shrines and scapulas, all became important icons in a vibrant new film genre full of booze, broads, machine guns, and speakeasies. The three most famous gangster films of all time, Mervyn LeRoy's *Little Caesar* (Warner Brothers, 1930), William Wellman's *Public Enemy* (Warner Brothers, 1931), and Howard Hughes's *Scarface* (Hughes Production—United Artists, 1932) are essentially

Prohibition parables delineating the war betweena puritanical Protestant native establishment and free-spirited Catholic immigrants intent on making it to the top of the world, any waythey can. The superficial tension between the law and the mob, between drys and wets, between treasury men and rum runners, is overshadowed by rich psychic, religious, sexual, and cultural clashes.

Little Caesar, for example, was intended by Jack Warner, according to Gerald Peary in his fine introduction to the Warner Brothers Screenplay Series edition of the complete script, as a "thinly disguised portrait of Al Capone." There can be no doubt that the crowds who stormed the Strand Theater in New York on opening day in a riot that brought out the mounted police had come to see headlines transferred to the screen. Several key incidents had clear analogues in reality, but the film did much more than give an objective account of garish funerals, ritualistic executions, and bloody machinations. Caesar Enrico Bandello was novelist W. R. Burnett's vision of an immigrant MacBeth, destroyed by his vaunting ambition, a Horatio Alger figure gone berserk; in *Little Caesar,* Burnett tried, as he told Ken Mate and Pat McGilligan for a January 1983 *Film Comment* interview, to present a world "seen completely through the eyes of a gangster." Earlier fictions, Burnett noted, always showed the gangster as "some son of a bitch who'd killed somebody," and society would then send representatives to go get them. In *Little Caesar,* Burnett boasted, "I treated 'em as human beings."

Edward G. Robinson's landmark performance as Rico makes this stunted megalomaniac almost tragic; as incarnated by Robinson, this small-time hood is as contradictory a presence as his oxymoronic nickname. Rico's meteoric rise, his dazzling energy, and his glittering affluence almost prove him worthy of the classic title Caesar. He has the speed, drive, and pep the Charleston era adored. This power-mad tyrant's demoniac energy ignites the screen like a Roman candle. Yet an undertone of pathos and confusion haunts this biography. Rico is a tiny man in a land of gigantic heroes, a twerp in the age of Lindbergh; his bootlegging racket is penny-ante shenanigans in a universe of robber barons and trusts. Even his hyperbolic rhetoric finally deflates in a maudlin, desperate aspiration: "Mother of Mercy, is this the end of Rico?" (a Hollywood bowdlerization of Burnett's more ironic and blasphemous "Mother of God, is this the end of Rico?") As Eric Rhode observes in his *History of the Cinema*, Rico was almost too enigmatic a personage to serve as a protagonist in a mass audience film. As Rhode indicates in his complex and rewarding analysis, director Mervyn LeRoy and scriptwriter Francis Faragoh are "clearly baffled" by Little Caesar, so "while they recognize his statistical significance— many immigrants, wishing to be accepted, suffered his kind of rejection—they seem unable to dramatize his fate within any of the accepted modes of fiction."

To appreciate Rico fully, one must recognize his grotesque perversion of the golden rule, his distortion of capitalist ideas of competition, and his repudiation of American mores. In the place of Christ's lovingly turned cheek, Rico offers a sadistic dogma of toughness. As he condemns Sam Vettori at the Club Palermo in Little Italy, he tells Sam: "You've got so you can dish it out, but you can't take it no more. You're through." Rico has just as little sympathy with capitalism's open marketplace, laissez-faire economics, and endless diversity. His inversion of the social structure involves exclusive territories, absolute control, and amoral domination. In the place of the success ethic and the American Dream, Rico preaches to Otero about man's inevitable failure, as he declares "the bigger they come, the harder they fall. . . ," a nightmarish lesson he eventually reinforces by his own precipitous decline. Even more noticeable, however, is Rico's lack of American roots and his alienation from traditional kinship structures. Rico finds a morbific surrogate mother in Ma Magdalena (Lucille La Verne), the most scrofulous wicked witch of the decade. He is at his nadir when he is ensconced in her dark, womb-like hideout. Unmarried and a seeming misogynist, Rico has a homosexual affinity for a male dancer whom he fears he likes "too much."

Another clear opposition in Rico's life involves the Catholic Church. Here Rico sets the pattern for many classic gangsters. Raised in an immigrant Catholic culture, Rico has fallen from grace, and he views the Church as something he has put behind him, an old world weakness, irrelevant in the present century and especially alien to his new milieu. Yet Rico does not embrace the Protestantism of his new country; instead he becomes the "Catholic who has turned his back on the Church," a type described by Carl Jung in his landmark discussion of *Psychology and Religion*. Lapsed Catholics, Jung observed, usually develop "a secret or manifest inclination toward atheism" whereas backsliding Protestants usually follow "a sectarian movement." The explanation Jung provides complements the idea of negation so evident elsewhere in *Little Caesar;* "the absolutism of Catholicism," Jung argues, "seems to demand an equally absolute negation, while Protestant relativism permits variations."

The absolute split between Catholicism and the atheistic gangster can best be seen in the brutal assassination of Rico's henchman Tony Passa (William Collier, Jr.), who is shot on the steps of a Catholic church because he heeds the admonitions of his loving Italian mother and tries to recapture the sanctity and innocence of his youthful days in the church choir with the beloved Father McNeil. Tony becomes the perfect foil for Rico; his mother is the Madonna balancing Rico's Magdalena; his fits of conscience are the antithesis of Rico's cocky amorality; his silent death and salvation the repudiation of Rico's grotesque final ejaculation and sure damnation. Tony's mother, interestingly, doesn't use traditional apologetics to win her son back; her immigrant Church isn't a haven for philosophizing, casuistry, and contrition. It is instead a sensuous warm place, cozy, familial, and nurturing. The grace Tony Passa needs comes from rich memories, as his mother rhapsodizes about deeply felt, quite tangible pleasures: "You remember when you sing in choir with Father McNeil . . . You in white, remember? The church was beautiful . . . you little boys with long hair . . . the big candles . . . flowers. . . Remember, Antonio?" Tony's mother's loving, ironic reverie is the antithesis of the many post-modernist explorations of the psychic links between guilt-wracked Catholics and organized crime, like Martin Scorsese's exquisite *Mean Streets* (1973).

In each analysis, however, sacraments and sacramentals

provide a tangible counterpoint to the immutable codes and rituals of *la famiglia*. Body and soul, freedom and guilt, Catholicism and individualism war in gangster films, whether one sees the Church as the home of choir boys or as the dark citadel of foreboding commandments and dreadful punishments. Rico's last prayer is so baleful because he has lost the rest of the litany; in the place of hyperdulia he has only an hysterical void. He can no longer recognize or appreciate his damnation or his lost salvation. There will be no big candles, no hymns, and no asperges; his epitaph is a billboard for *Tipsy Topsy Turvy* at the Grand Theater.

When irate guardians of public virtue railed against *Little Caesar* for glorifying criminals and for suggesting that violent crime does pay off in wine, women, and song, Edward G. Robinson constantly pointed to Rico's catastrophic fate, arguing in his oft delivered speech, "The Movie, the Actor, and Public Morals," that Rico died "like a rat" and that the whole movie pointed to the traditional Christian lesson that "he who lives by the sword shall die by it, or, the wages of sin is death." Most critics of the film were not mollified, however; they knew there was more to these superheated biographies. Fifty years later, sociologist-film critic Jack Shadoian would come very close to defining that "something else" in his exciting study of *Dreams and Dead Ends: The American Gangster/Crime Film*. As Shadoian so vividly demonstrates, "The gangster's fizzy spirits, classy lifestyle, and amoral daring were something like an Alka-Seltzer for the headaches of the depression." In the theater, Shadoian shows, a curious dialectic was set in motion by the gangster: "a dialectic of the audience's fantasies and dreams and a rote Christian morality." Gangster films were hammering home the inadequacies of both Catholicism and Protestantism, yet they were haunted by the ghost of religion past, a sensual religion of ritual, liturgy, and certainty, of priests, altar boys, celebrations, and incense, and the ghost of religion future, a puritan creed of personal rebirth, divine election, and amazing grace. No synthesis was readily apparent between the aspirations of materialistic Americans and the strictures of spirituality, between Old World Catholicism and New World pluralism, so gangster films were made of these irreconcilable tensions, with protagonists positioned on the cutting edge between cultures, countries, and creeds.

In *The Public Enemy*, the polarities are embodied by Ma Powers's two sons, Tom (James Cagney), described in the film's ads as "the cold-blooded hot-head whose guns roared across the decade of death," and Mike (Donald Cook), a war hero whose exploits in France tossing hand grenades have made him the pride of the neighborhood. Hollywood always linked the Irish to drunkenness and pugnacity, so there's little wonder that this immigrant family's get-togethers enshrine the beer keg or that the clan ends up in a brawl. Hollywood's Irish are all shantytown papists, full of blarney and bluster. Hard as it may be to believe now, both film companies and critics overlooked then the ethnic stereotypes which seem so blatant today. In fact, to defuse any charge that they were glorifying these bootlegging sons of the sod, the producers added a title card to *The Public Enemy* disavowing any such seditious intent: "It is the intention of the authors of *The Public Enemy* to honestly depict an environment that exists today in a certain strata of American life, rather than glorify the hoodlum or criminal." Actually, the feverish tone of their advertising copy better captures their real intentions and defines the film's box office appeal: "It is real, real, devastatingly real. A grim depiction of the modern menace! Come prepared to see the worst of women and the cruelest of men—as they really are!" All this may seem ludicrous to audiences generations removed from Prohibition and the Irish Potato Famine, but to even the most sophisticated contemporary viewers, *The Public Enemy* was both engaging and alarming. The worldly reviewer for the *New Yorker* actually equated this sensational melodrama with stellar journalism; "It [*The Public Enemy*] was the kind of work that Joseph Pulitzer would have done had he been born half a century later and been a movie magnate instead of a newspaper publisher."

It's doubtful any journalist would have created the symmetrical psychological paradigm the film does. *The Public Enemy* culminates with a harrowing confrontation, as the two brothers meet for the last time, one trussed up like a mummy, the victim

48

of his own lawless urges, a bloodied relic of gang warfare, the other submerged in his matriarchal family, psychologically shattered by his own moral principles, a disillusioned and shell-shocked veteran of an absurd World War. In the background, a Victrola mocks each of their dreams with its eviscerating refrain "I'm forever blowing bubbles."

The Public Enemy never confronts the boys' faith directly, yet their nationality, ethnicity, and cultural Catholicism inform every scene. Ex-priest James Kavanaugh constantly reiterates in his agonized spiritual autobiography, *A Modern Priest Looks at His Outdated Church*, the inexorable link between life-style, ghetto, tradition, and Catholicism: "To be Irish or Polish or Italian was to be Catholic. . . . To commemorate the customs and folkways of Europe was as religious as to observe the rubrics of the Mass." Parish dinners, elaborate weddings, christenings, and wakes were, Kavanaugh postulates, "more the mark of a Catholic community" than Sunday Mass. In *The Public Enemy* one cannot remain oblivious very long to the Black and Tan Cafe, the cheerful matriarchy, the long suffering Molly (Rita Flynn), or the shadowy, inarticulate policeman father (Purnell Pratt) so addicted to the sound of the strap on bare bottoms. Putty Nose and the pool hall, the Irish wake for Larry Dalton, Paddy Ryan's backroom, and the Powers's kitchen are almost mythic settings. Even Ma Powers's (Beryl Mercer) language has an unmistakable lilt born of a religious piety so deeply engrained that it has substituted intimacy for reverence and linked the Divine Presence quite naturally to quotidian existence. When Tom snarls at his slow-witted brother, Ma Powers's automatic response is larded with imagery once religious but now notable only for its ethnic flavor: "Don't, Tommy boy! He ain't himself. Don't get him excited! This trip was too much for the poor soul. Lord have pity on him . . . he's been through too much."

The Public Enemy has as its focus the trials and tribulations of these two sons and their mother's futile efforts to contain them under one roof. The American experience is tearing her family apart, and with the family go all the old religious values, all the old civilities, all the old rituals. Ma Powers does everything she can to keep her boys from fighting because "fighting ain't right for two brothers," but Tom will just never be able to abide Mike's "preaching." These two siblings are the Janus-faced twins of conformity and rebellion, ethnicity and assimilation, law and disorder, obedience and defiance, optimistic faith and pessimistic determinism. Mike Powers is the good boy, the brave Marine, the faithful street-car conductor, the dutiful son, a stiff man weighted down by respectability, manners, and taboos. The flux of American life and the disillusionment attendant on the war shatter his wits and leave him a hollow zombie immobilized in his ghetto prison. Tom Powers, the mischievous son, cannot be repressed; he is a cocky street-fighter, mercurial in his emotions, and buoyant in his material successes. Cagney keeps his character Tom constantly dancing across the screen with Dionysian energy as he devours every second of his brief life. Nothing seems more natural for Tom than shoving a grapefruit in his girlfriend Kitty's face.

As Paul Rotha notes in his *The Film Till Now: A Survey of World Cinema*, that one phallic thrust and the allied joke about Kitty as "a wishin' well" might well have undermined the good intentions of Kubec Glasmon and John Bright, two druggists from Chicago who based their original story for *The Public Enemy*, entitled "Beer and Blood," on the exploits of some regular gangland customers including bootleggers Frankie Lake and Terry Druggan. These amateur storytellers, Glasmon and Bright, Rotha opines, had intentions which were "undoubtedly sociological," but the audience reactions to Cagney in the film were "frequently romantic"; in this era, Rotha reports, "Young girls longed to have grapefruit pushed in *their* faces, and the tough, not to say sadistic heroes in the persons of Cagney and Clark Gable became the beau ideal of men and women alike."

Tom Powers is so kinetic a presence that even his bullet-ridden body must be strait-jacketed to keep him still. The scholarly Lincoln Kirstein echoed Rotha's recognition of Tom Powers as a new kind of pop idol in his essay "James Cagney and the American Hero," written for *The Hound and the Horn* in April 1932: "Cagney may be a dirty little low-life rat . . . but when his riddled body is propped up against his mother's door, mummied in bandages and flecked with blood, we catch our throats and realize this is a hero's death." In the film, Jean Harlow as Gwen Allen also suggests how Cagney as Tom Powers has once again inverted all the traditional values, making evil good, cruelty kind, and self-absorption captivating: "You're so strong. You don't give—you take. Oh, Tom, I could love you to death." In the original shooting script by Harvey Thew, even the good brother Mike finally succumbs to Tom's animal magnetism. Instead of the final shot in the release print of *The Public Enemy* of a phonograph grinding away at the end of a record, the shooting script published as part of the Warner Brothers screen-play series describes an additional sequence, in which Mike walks to the closet, stuffs hand grenades in his coat pockets, and marches out of the family home to avenge his brother. This shooting script underlines the theme of a beseiged Irish im-migrant family by noting that "his brother's fate has turned him [Mike] into a killer" and then the script turns the screw one more time by ending with a shot of Mrs. Powers in her bedroom, oblivious to Tom's death and Mike's decision, as she lays out a dressing gown and slippers for her Prodigal Son and sings her "Irish song" quite happily.

The forces that had attacked *Little Caesar* were just as dis-gruntled with the truncated version of *The Public Enemy*. The middle-of-the-road Americans who had supported Prohibition had dreamed of a new millenium when America went dry. As Herbert Asbury reports in his "informal history" of the period *The Great Illusion*, rabid true believers had expected Prohibition to be heralded by "a covey of angels bearing gifts of peace, happiness, prosperity, and salvation"; instead, they were in-undated by "a horde of bootleggers, moonshiners, rumrunners, hijackers, gangsters, racketeers, trigger men, venal judges, cor-rupt police, crooked politicians, and speakeasy operators." And if all this reality was unsettling and discouraging, the glorifi-cation of these foreign urban demons on the silver screen was the last straw, the crowning indignity.

The most disturbing of all the early movie gangsters was Ben Hecht's Antonio Camonte, the hero of Howard Hawks's *Scarface*, a protagonist who shared much more with the man

51

Al Capone than matching initials and a similar physiognomy. *Scarface* was, as David Thomson boldly labels it in *Overexposures*, "a masterpiece of sardonic contempt," a striking demonstration of his thesis that the crisis in American filmmaking involved in part a split between the mass audience and the creators of this popular art: as Thomson views it, "The people of America have struggled for fifty years not to notice the scorn that their most treasured medium holds for them." Like the producers of *The Public Enemy*, the creators of *Scarface* tried to circumvent negative reactions with a prefatory title card; this time, they piously labelled their film an "indictment of gang rule in America and of the callous indifference of the government to this constantly increasing menace to our safety and liberty." The punch line to this disclaimer was a series of rhetorical questions meant to shift the burden of any guilt to all true patriots: ". . . the purpose of this picture is to demand of the government: 'What are you going to do about it?' The government is your government. What are *you* going to do about it?"

Once the pious formalities are dispensed with, the screen explodes with visual and aural fireworks that rank as director Howard Hawks's very finest work. *Scarface* is, in the words of the under-appreciated film savant Manny Farber, a "photographic miracle," with chiaroscuro images of Italian gangsters "as varied and shapely as those who parade through Piero's religious paintings." In Hawks's impassioned apostrophe to the Thompson sub-machine gun, an expressionistic city pulsates to the rat-a-tat of the new technology and glitters with the seductive flicker of neon lights. And for the first time, as Roger Dooley reveals in his *From Scarface to Scarlett*, an affectionate appreciation of the films of the thirties, the talkies found their real voice in "the gritty realities of contemporary urban America." Only the sound film, Dooley observes, could surround audiences with "the sob of nightclub saxophones, the bark of an automatic, the chatter of a tommy gun, the roaring motors and squealing tires of a getaway car rounding a corner, [and] the wail of police sirens. . . ." The silence of the American lone prairie was shattered by this new cacophony imported from the teeming metropolis.

Hawks self-consciously embellished his narrative of Tony's life with disarming and highly evocative visual and aural allusions. His Italian immigrant hero wears his ethnicity, his nationalism, like a badge of defiance inherited from the Old Country. Tony Camonte (Paul Muni) whistles the same melody from *Lucia di Lammermoor* before each of his murders; the melody poses the operatic question, "What restrains me in such a moment?" The allusion is deeply ironic since clearly this hulk of a man knows no restraint. American civilization has little sway for this gigantic immigrant. Tony defiantly lights his matches on the badges of overfed, clumsy Waspish detectives. His characteristic gesture is a defiant Italian salute which jauntily gives American law the back of his hand. For an American woman, however, the same gesture becomes a stylish challenge and invitation. Like so many immigrants, Tony speaks a body language which threatens a puritanical universe. Tony's verbal assault on the Protestant ethic is another interesting recasting of the Golden Rule: "Do it first, do it yourself, and keep on doing it."

Director Hawks places all of Tony's bloody machinations in a religious context by employing a noticeable, almost obtrusive visual symbol, the cross. As Robin Wood demonstrates in great detail in his masterful assessment of *Howard Hawks*, "the image of the cross pervades the whole film." It is one of the first and last things the audience sees; Tony's scar is cruciform; and every killing is accompanied by its formal presence. This "pervasive image," Robin Wood concludes, carries with it "associative emotional overtones" which give Tony's killings "a particular flavor of profanity."

Tony's Catholic mother (Inez Palange) lumbers around the kitchen, glowering under a shawl that makes her look like a Tyrolean gypsy who wandered onto the set, having lost her way to a vampire film on the backlot. This matriarch has not lost her distinctive Old World morality, but there is little reference to organized Catholicism, beyond some holy pictures, crucifixes, and statues. This is, however, not surprising—Italian Catholicism in America was less institutional and public and more familial and private. In America, Italian laity despised the Irish clergy who had laid seige to the cathedrals a generation before the *contadini* reached America's shores. Cinematic Italians like Tony's mother did, however, imbue their households with the sober dichotomy between Christ and the Devil, between good and evil; the aura of evil spirits, the evil eye, and patron saints is as omnipresent as the food and wine she so diligently prepares for her son. Tony's mother is so totally intemperate in her hatred for her wayward son that her words take on the air of an exorcism; her own son has become her private Lucifer, her personal anti-Christ. Tony's father is absent, so it falls to her to keep their daughter Cesca (Ann Dvorak) from accepting the booty of their corrupt son. In a key scene with Cesca, the mother erupts in almost evangelical fury, demanding that her daughter give back "the *bad* money." Tony, she warns, is all "smiles on the top, but whatta he think . . . he's gotta a lotta trick . . . he donna give nothin to nobody for nothin." When Cesca protests that she can take care of herself, the mother admonishes her confused child that "alla the times, Tony he say like that to me. . . . Afterwards he no belonga to me. He is no good, and now you start to be justa like him."

The sexual dynamic in *Scarface* is of a dark cast, for the linkage between this brother and sister is assertively psychosexual. W. R. Burnett in his interview with Ken Mate and Pat McGilligan revealed that he had been the first writer asked to do a script for *Scarface* based on the original story by Armitage Trail. Producer Howard Hughes, Burnett recalls, was intent on including incest as a major theme, so when director Hawks rejected Burnett's script, Hughes gave the redoubtable Ben Hecht ten days to create a fiction with more of the flavor of the Borgia family reincarnated in contemporary Chicago. Hecht obviously enjoyed mingling Machiavellian evil with gangster posturing, so he churned out a potboiler whose tone was more redolent of Renaissance court intrigues than the venal world of Chicago's corrupt mayor, William Hale Thompson.

Hecht boldly creates two siblings just made for each other. Cesca tears furiously at the bars of her ethnic cage; the ghetto cannot contain this would-be flapper. Manny Farber saw a perverse choreography in her gestures when he described her "striking out blindly with the thinnest, sharpest elbows, shoving aside anyone who tries to keep her from the sex and excitement of a dance hall." Tony's movements are more clearly a mating dance. He can't keep his mind or his hands off Cesca. Early in the film, she shrieks in terror that he doesn't act like a normal brother, and her mother reinforces this fear when she warns Cesca that to Tony "you justa another girl. He mixa you up in his bizaness. He maka you bad justa like him." By mid-film, Tony has lost all control; totems and taboos have been swept aside. He tears his sister's dress off when he finds Cesca "dressing up like that so fellas can see you." When the mother bursts in on this scene and sees the half-naked Cesca cowering before her brother, she again warns, "I tell you lotsa time. He hurt you. He hurt you. He hurt everybody." Largely prompted by sexual jealousy, Tony shoots Cesca's new husband. Yet when Cesca comes to Tony's lair to kill him, she cannot shoot her alter ego, her psychic twin, and she collapses in his arms, declaring, "You're me, I'm you, it's always been that way." As the two siblings approach incestuous fulfillment, the native forces of law and order bombard the steel shutters these two soulmates have put between themselves and the restraints of civilization.

Some measure of the inferiority of Brian DePalma's 1983 remake of *Scarface* to the original can be found by comparing Hawks's soul-searching conclusion and the tame, anti-climactic striptease Mary Mastrantonio does for Al Pacino. In the original version, Cesca bares her soul; in the remake, Tony Montana's sister undrapes her breast and little else, and when that fails to move Tony, she shoots him a few times to equally small effect. DePalma's narrative offers an updated vision of criminality for the eighties; bootlegging has been replaced by drug dealing, Chicago transformed to the Sunbelt's Miami, and Hawks's Dagoes reincarnated as *Marielitoes* who are "gonna get us every fucking thing there is." Eventually, however, the Southern hemisphere accents wear thin, the moral level is obscured in some totally unbelievable drivel about post-Watergate corruption and Wasp disingenuousness; and all that remains is a mountain of cocaine, which has an unfortunate tendency to stick to Tony Montana's nose like the pale greasepaint of a maudlin clown. As Pauline Kael aptly remarked in her December 26, 1983 review for *The New Yorker*, the whole feeling of DePalma's overlong epic is "limp," and it "may be the only action picture that turns into an allegory of impotence."

The contrast between DePalma's allegory of impotence and Howard Hawks's ode to phallicism is dazzling. In the original *Scarface*, Tony's *rispetto* is clearly linked to his sexual powers. At lunch with a woman, Tony cannot keep his mind on the food or his virility under wraps. The shards of dialogue leave little to the imagination, though the camera placement keeps the visuals comparatively tame. The girl, for example, implores Tony, "Please, my stockings—hands off—no, feet off." Tony assures her he knows "lots of girls," and his toying with food becomes a fitting metaphor for sexual foreplay. Tony's final encounter with Cesca in Hawks's epic would have been even more libidinal, if not for the fateful intrusion of civilization and its restraints. At the very instant Cesca and Tony recognize their kinship and begin to acknowledge each other as facets of the same whole, a policeman's bullet careens off the steel shutters, mortally wounding Cesca. Her dying wish is that Tony put his arms around her "for just a minute."

Tony is unmanned by the death of his only love and too frightened to live alone in his New Land; he begs the police for mercy, then runs through the door, and dies in the street. Just as a detective prophesied earlier in the film, Tony falls "right where the horses had been standing." Hawks's plan to use manure in this last shot was never realized in the release print. Instead, extant versions conclude with still another of the ironic visual commentaries so popular in crime movies, a closeup of an ad for Cooke Tours promising native Americans and restless immigrants that "The World is Yours."

Manure or not, Italian Catholics felt besmirched by *Scarface* just as pressure groups elsewhere felt threatened by these gangster idylls. Influential voices were growing ever louder in a chorus of demands that something be done to make films more responsible. Robin Wood maintains that the fear of censorship was so great at this time that "an embarrassingly hammy scene with a newspaper editor," prepared by a director other than Hawks, was edited into *Scarface* to placate moralists. In this sequence, the fictional Mr. Garston, publisher of the *Evening Record*, serves as a stern mouthpiece for all the so-called Progressives who believed that salvation was merely a matter of the correct legislation. In his harangue, Mr. Garston bellows demands for new gun laws that put weapons in the same class as "drugs and white slavery" and for a "deportation act" with teeth in it. The answer to crime, he argues, is to make more laws and to see that they're obeyed, "even if we have to have martial law to do it." This fascistic patriot steamrolls any concern for civil liberties with a xenophobic reminder that half the gangsters "don't belong in this country" and aren't even citizens. This jingoistic sentiment is echoed by an obsequious foreigner with a heavy accent who laments that "Thatsa true. They bringa nothin but disgrace-a to my people."

Tacked on sequences weren't enough, however, and Hollywood was a town under siege. Back in 1930, movie producers had tried to dissipate public anxieties about the Fatty Arbuckle case and some other dreadful personal scandals by adopting a production code, drafted by two leading Catholics, Father Daniel Lord and publisher Martin Quigley, and enforced by a leading Protestant deacon, Will Hays, a Republican of unassailable probity. The next few years saw much waffling and major revisions in the Code, however, with much smoke and little fire in the Hays office. Only the formation of a Roman Catholic pressure group, the Legion of Decency, in 1934 gave the Production Code its teeth. Thereafter, for three decades, American filmmakers had several monitors to appease: the most liberal was the Motion Picture Production Code Office, then there were local licensing boards in some key markets, and finally there was the Legion of Decency in New York, whose avowed purpose was to see that movies were moral, inoffensive to Catholics, and punctiliously loyal to the industry's own Production Code.

Historians and scholars have widely diverse opinions on how all these pressures shaped Hollywood films, but because of its sectarianism, the Legion of Decency is the most bitterly debated phenomenon. No one denies its influence, however. Richard Corliss, a Catholic by education, did his master's thesis at New York University on the Legion, and *Film Comment* reprinted his essay in its entirety as the bulk of its Summer 1968 issue. Corliss makes the point that the Legion was very effective as a pressure group because its threatened economic boycott was well aimed, well timed, and well organized by the hierarchy of the Church. The Catholic threat to withhold patronage from immoral films and theaters which habitually displayed them was awesome; immigrants were not only the subject of many films, but they were also the most frequent patrons. Urban Catholics were the mainstay of first run theaters; without their dollars, the industry could not go on.

The harshest critics of the censors lambast their pettiness, stupidity, and moral smugness. Philip French, for example, dismisses the Production Code in his chronicle of *The Movie Moguls* as a partisan Catholic document, reeking of Thomistic philosophy in its references to natural law, larded with specific provisions on Catholic concerns like suicide, and haunted by a generally supererogatory and Jesuitical morality. French suggests that "the offensiveness of the Code lies in its tone, the comedy in its explicitness." Another harsh critic of the Code and the Legion, Alexander Walker, has a chapter on "One Man's Poison" in his *Sex in the Movies: the Celluloid Sacrifice*, in which he maintains that the self-imposed industry guidelines as reinforced by the Legion were "one of the most restrictive, unrealistic, and hypocritically observed codes of conduct ever clamped on creative people . . . a series of anachronistic thou-shalt-nots." Walker develops his analysis by showing that no narrative could have lived up to the Code's provisions if it had not been for the "compensatory values" approach Joseph Ignatius Breen, a distinguished Catholic layman, introduced when he took over the chairmanship of the Production Code Administration Board in 1934. Breen, Walker indicates, "secularized his Church's technique of expiating sin" by allowing producers to show individuals violating Code standards so long as the malefactors were suitably punished. The Breen office became, Walker's analysis intimates, a sort of Confessor General making sure that individual filmmakers provided proper penance and retribution for each moral transgression. The absurdity in all this, Walker argues, is that the compensation principle which makes the Code "workable" also makes it "worthless," inasmuch as he feels it "has fostered a view of morality that is frequently false and hypocritical—in which sin and punishment are nicely adjusted to each other, yet the link between cause and effect is seldom made convincing." Critic Michael Leach in *I Know It When I See It: Pornography, Violence, and Public Sensitivity* is both harsher and more forgiving than Walker. The Legion, he writes, has "scrambled more brains and smeared more works of art than all the Cracows from the beginning of time"; but the time has come, he feels, to look back on those days "with humor and forgiveness" and with the "hope that they don't return in different clothes to haunt someone else."

Among the critics who are more supportive of the Legion of Decency and the Production Code, Jack Vizzard, an ex-seminarian who was technical adviser on a number of films treating Catholic topics (for example, *The Nun's Story* and *Heaven Knows, Mr. Allison*) also emphasizes the need to place things in historical perspective. *See No Evil*, his insider's account of life in the Production Code Office, where he was the Catholic voice for years, lays bare an anti-semitism rarely discussed in the context of censorship. It was more than a case of Catholics upset at inadequate moral safeguards in Protestant films, or Protestants inflamed by the glorification of Catholic criminals, or even of both groups of Christians incensed at the glorification of criminal elements. Under it all, Vizzard insists, was an abiding distrust of Jews. Catholics and Christians, the Knights of Columbus and the Daughters of the American Revolution, all imagined that a Zionist demon was creating a new enticing "this worldly" Jerusalem in the backlots of Hollywood—so enticing that both priests and ministers feared a modern celluloid hedonism would overwhelm all spirituality. Vizzard depicts these fears quite poetically when he declares that the Jews in Hollywood seemed like the tempters on Mount Tibi Dabo; these semites in the foothills of Mount Lee, he observes, presented a "glittering and seductive picture of the cities of the earth, as though they were not ephemeral, as though they would not melt away like a mirage once one reached out to touch them." His voyage from seminary to Production Office thus resembled a new Crusade: "I was rushing down out of the theological hills to save the world from those goddamn Jews." In his memoirs, Vizzard admits that all this anti-semitism seems preposterous now, but one long generation ago, he asserts, "this state of miasma" was very real.

The Code and the Legion, their defenders claim, did little more than articulate and reinforce a national consensus of proper American values. Film reviewer Charles Champlin, writing about "What Will H. Hays Begot" in *American Film* (October 1980), opines that the Code of the 1930s "fairly embodies the aspirations of most of the audience toward the good life," where virtue triumphs and sacrifice and heroism are rewarded. The Code merely reinforced, he assumes, Hollywood's "tendency to an optimistic, idealized, and escapist world." Scandinavian sociologists Leif Furhammar and Isaksson Folke, writing about *Politics and Films,* speak of a censorship in the United States no less stringent than that in the Soviet Union, with a Production Code that "in practice became a declaration of faith in a particular social system." The Code, as they perceive it, was "shaped by the collective value judgments of the public" and was highly political inasmuch as "it reflects and preserves the imagined aims and favourite myths of society by presenting them in attractive forms." John B. Phelan reiterates many of these same arguments in his more theologically oriented study *Disenchantment: Meaning and Morality in the Media.* The Legion did not impose Catholic morality on America, Phelan observes; it imposed instead "the bland formulas of middle American bourgeois values for as long as they represented the mainstream." Phelan is most dramatic in his disavowal of a sectarian moral role for the Legion; as he sees it, "Anyone who asserts that the Legion was some sinister force for 'Catholic Dogma' simply has not taken the trouble to look at what the record shows."

Any chronicle must also show that the Legion and the Code were effective. No major Hollywood film was released without the distinctive logo indicating Board approval; and, as James Hennessey reports in *American Catholics: A History of the Roman Catholic Community in the United States,* by 1938, 93 percent of all new films were "classed in one of the two highest categories" of Legion ratings. Daring gangster films had, inadvertently or not, speeded the repeal of Prohibition and the onset of an ongoing censorship. Edward G. Robinson would never be Little Caesar again. In 1933, his Little Caesar had already become a bit of an anachronism, and now as Bugs Ahearn, "The Beer Baron," cast adrift in a new wet era in Roy del Ruth's *Little Giant,* he wants nothing more than to "mingle with the upper classes" and "be a gentleman" in California. *Little Giant* is comedy, not drama, though, so improbabilities abound, and, as Bugs Ahearn ruefully observes, "the toughest mug in Chicago comes out here and gets trimmed by a lot of fats with handkerchiefs up their sleeves" in a film that ends not with corpses on church steps but instead with Runyonesque gangsters playing a hilarious game of polo. By 1940, Robinson was *Brother Orchid,* a criminal who discovers that real peace, contentment, and courage reside in the monastery. This Lloyd Bacon comedy, as John Baxter remarks in his comprehensive *Hollywood in the Thirties,* was "undoubtedly not to be relied on as a picture of monastic life," but it was a clear indication of how total a victory the forces of conventional values had won: they had made clowns of the gunmen. And while not every bootlegger would accept the tonsure, there were other employment opportunities around on the side of the Golden Rule. James Cagney, for example, went from being the *Public Enemy* to perennial outings as one of the *G-Men* (1935). Hollywood could keep all the gunplay and violence so long as it was compensated for with hymns to the burgeoning forces of federal law and the scientific sleuths in the Department of Justice and the Federal Bureau of Investigation. In Carlos Clarens's detailed survey *Crime Movies,* the best book on this subject, Clarens shrewdly links this switch to the other side of the law not only to the forces of censorship but also to the new political and social realities of the Roosevelt years. Gangsters, like the rest of America, were getting a New Deal.

Part of this new reality, however, did involve some Hollywood kowtowing to the Legion of Decency and to the Roman Catholic Church. Priests were to become major heroic figures in crime films; shoulder to shoulder with FBI men, revenue agents, and other agents of morality, they became part of a phalanx for truth, justice, and the American way. Super-padre would be born around the time Superman came crashing down from Krypton, and for years a few Latin mumblings and a breviary could quiet the most savage beast and transform the most hardened heart. Every priest became an amalgam of Father Flanagan and Father Coughlin, of Bing Crosby and Pat O'Brien; the new armament was moral, the new weapons rosary beads, chapels, and poor boxes.

The progenitor of this piety as power was all America's favorite Irishman, Pat O'Brien, whose performance as Father Jerry Connolly in Michael Curtiz's *Angels With Dirty Faces* (1938) would make Jesus himself proud to share his initials. The film, a mammoth popular success, propelled all of Hollywood to a new Christology in its portraits of Roman Catholic prelates. Andrew Bergman in his *We're in the Money: the Depression and Its Films* suggests that producers had been looking for a new hero, a workable *deus ex machina* to trumpet suitable moral sentiments, only to find in the priest even more than they needed. The priest was, after all, "classless" but "within the system," authoritarian and detached yet "sympathetic to the boys," and above all, he was "dramatically feasible" since parish churches were a major part of the urban scene. Breen's compensatory value system could be appeased, movies could be realistic, their sentiments could harken to New Deal mottoes, and the Legion of Decency could have its heroes; it was almost too good to be true.

Angels With Dirty Faces (1938) is, as Leslie Halliwell labels it in his *Film Guide*, "a seminal film for all kinds of reasons." As Halliwell suggests, this Warner Brothers offering "combined gangster action with fashionable social conscience," "confirmed the Dead End kids as stars," and "provided archetypal roles for its three leading players." Of equal importance is the fact that this modest project became the prototype for so many other images of urban Catholics and their life-styles. *Angels With Dirty Faces* raises in its short duration virtually every important question about Catholicism and crime in America. Its main theme, to borrow a journalistic description from one of the fictional news stories featured so prominently in its frequent montages, concerns "the battling, two-fisted clergyman of the lower East Side [who] offered a feisty challenge yesterday to underworld vice." On this level, the film offers an oblique commentary on Father Charles E. Coughlin, the Radio League of the Little Flower, and all the Catholic social activism modelled on the liberal doctrines of *Rerum Novarum*. On another level, *Angels With Dirty Faces* explores the question of the social causes of crime, the environmental influences, and the moral choices. To understand Rocky Sullivan (James Cagney) and Jerry Connolly is to be immersed once again in Irish culture, to visit the deterministic universe of *Dead End* (1937), but also to consider the world of free will and autonomous choice implicit in *Manhattan Melodrama* (1934). *Angels With Dirty Faces* also confronts the whole issue of juvenile delinquency. Pat O'Brien is an erstwhile Father Flanagan, but his labors are more troubled and his victories less certain.

On still other levels, *Angels With Dirty Faces* brings noteworthy attention to the importance of mass media in character formation and moral education, develops the image of the priest as death row counsellor into a full-blown movie convention, and redefines the Church's role as one of several social institutions aiding immigrants in their quest for the American Dream. O'Brien's ambitious athletic program, a personal CYO, foreshadows the half-way house programs of *The Hoodlum Priest* (1961) and the controversial "worker priest" of *On the Waterfront* (1954).

While *Angels With Dirty Faces* did have Father J. J. Devlin as technical adviser, he was not a regular on the set, and James Cagney in his autobiography, *Cagney by Cagney*, reports how he and Pat O'Brien, two Irishmen raised in the Church, made yeomanly efforts to keep the film true to the rigors of their Church. As Cagney recalled the project, he and his co-star "knew the ceremonial forms and very well did we know them"; the producer, writer, and director were all Jews, so they could not be expected to know much about the Catholic ethos. One example Cagney offers of the changes he and O'Brien made involved the staging of their first meeting as adults when the notorious gangster comes to see his old friend, now a parish priest. Originally, the script had called for Cagney to confront O'Brien in the confessional. Cagney and O'Brien refused to play the scene, however, arguing that the sacrament of Penance called for clearly established ritualistic language and to do anything else would be inauthentic. Instead of meeting in the confessional, then, Cagney and O'Brien meet in the aisle of the church and move quickly to the sacristy.

From this moment on, *Angels With Dirty Faces* poses a moral tug of war between two very attractive characters; the dazzling energy of the street-wise Rocky is pitted against the relentless rectitude of Father Jerry. The narrative energy of the film depends quite heavily on the audience's divided loyalties. Rocky sweeps audiences off their feet immediately; Jerry's appeal is more plodding but nonetheless powerful. The ads for *Angels With Dirty Faces* were quite stylish and symbolic; an inkblot divides itself into faces, a dark snarling Cagney with Medusa-like hair and a bright, smiling, well-groomed O'Brien with angelically clear eyes. The copy echoes the priest's vow to protect his boys from the pernicious influence of Rocky Sullivan, yet it confirms the close link between an all encompassing evil and transcendental virtue. In the ad, Father Connolly admits quite boldly that "there stands a killer—judged, condemned, ready to meet his maker" and that "There, but for the grace of God, stand I, Jerry Connolly, priest." The film well confirms his judgment. For all the oppositions between priest and gunmen, the audience recognizes their personal affinities. Jerry and Rocky are archetypal male buddies, one of the many incarnations of the team of James Cagney and Pat O'Brien, and their linked humanity overpowers any thematic focus on law and order, damnation and salvation. The contemporary film critic

64

Otis Ferguson was right on target when he declared that this movie team did "more than any other combination to search out and show in theater terms the obscure tie that exists between men who share the same dangers, privations, and sack of Bull Durham." The resolution of *Angels With Dirty Faces* has little to do with public executions, private prayers, policemen, or confessionals. Two marvelous performances submerge these ideas in a picture of male bonding that becomes standard in war movies, crime films, Westerns, and horror films. The more sharply the line is drawn between protagonist and antagonist, the more the underlying identification of the two becomes clear. Psychological doubling plays a key role in much narrative art— Sherlock Holmes is really Moriarity and vice versa—but in Hollywood crime films, the mirror imagery is startlingly important. The idea of a hoodlum priest really isn't paradoxical at all. The gangster and the priest are both perpetual outsiders, one engaged in a quest for Heaven and surrounded by nuns, indulgences, and vows, the other ensnared in a seamy underground of gun molls, blackmail, and double crosses.

James Cagney delineates every nuance of the hoodlum counterculture perfectly. Cagney based his characterization, he admitted, on a gangster he knew when he was a child, a pimp who greeted all his johns with "Whadda ya hear? Whadda ya say?" In *Angels With Dirty Faces* Cagney made his street-wise public enemy a cynical prophet of the Depression; anyone can see, he constantly avers, that the moral life ends for most people in quiet despair and economic desperation. Father Connolly doesn't ever really deny Rocky's assertion; in fact, his abiding lament pillories the inequities of the American system: "What earthly good is it for me to teach that honesty is the best policy when all around they see that dishonesty is a better policy . . . that the hoodlum and gangster is looked up to with the same respect as the successful businessman or popular hero?" Rocky and Jerry agree about social justice; it's just their responses to the system which differ.

Several other clear links are established between Jerry and Rocky. Born in the Irish ghetto, they both start out on a boisterous life of crime, but one day in a botched heist, Jerry eludes the cops because he can run faster, and Rocky is railroaded to reform school and inevitable perdition. The boys agree it's "the breaks" that condemned one and liberated the other. Interestingly, this plot twist also establishes an immutable genre convention. Every priest has Superman's athletic prowess hidden under his Roman collar. Pat O'Brien not only runs faster as a child; he also becomes the football hero who dashes ninety yards against New York University for Fordham. If it had not been for local color in this episode, no doubt Jerry would have been one of the four horsemen of Notre Dame. A major tenet of Hollywood's catechism is the inevitable link between Irishmen and Notre Dame football. The alleged prowess of Catholic athletes is a more timeworn tradition than later stereotypes of Negro jocks. Hollywood never let audiences forget the halo around *The Babe Ruth Story*, the fact that "somebody upstairs" loved Rocky Graziano, or that Knute Rockne was an all American. Notre Dame, in fact, became so cognizant of its media image that it started—and lost—a very famous film censorship case in an attempt to block the release of *John Goldfarb, Please Come Home* (1965), scripted by Catholic author William Peter Blatty. The authorities in South Bend were aghast at the film's images of the fighting Irish frolicking in harems, surrounded by concubines with pulsating and bejeweled navels and entertained by Shirley MacLaine's gyrating, well-exposed buttocks.

Pat O'Brien's knockout punch is another axiom of the Hollywood catechism. On screen, priests had to rival Jack Dempsey with the ferocity and efficacy of their punches. In *Angels With Dirty Faces*, a pool-room taunt from a kibbitzer, "What's the matter, can't you get them to go to heaven with you?" is met with a one punch rejoinder that settles any questions about O'Brien's physical powers. Given O'Brien's football heroics, this knockout is a lot more believable than Father Barry's (Karl Malden) one punch knockdown of the slightly drunk ex-professional boxer, Terry Mallow (Marlon Brando) in *On the Waterfront*. And it is surely more dramatically acceptable than the elaborate machinations in *San Francisco* that were meant to assure the audience that Father Tim (Spencer Tracy) could easily have defeated Blackie (Clark Gable) in a fistfight over a woman's virtue but chose not to. In her book, *Kiss Hollywood Goodbye*, Anita Loos recalls that Joe Breen objected to the original draft of the scene, fearing audiences would identify with Gable and rejoice in his humiliation of the Church. So an elaborate sequence in a gymnasium was added to show that Father Tim "could easily outbox, outslug, and outsmart Blackie." In this context, Father Tim lets Blackie knock him out, presenting, in Loos's words, "the other cheek" of Christianity and emerging as "the hero of the encounter."

Most modern critics of *Angels With Dirty Faces* ponder the concept of Christian heroism in that film, agonizing over the dynamic appeal of Cagney and the rigidity of O'Brien. Some, like Stanley Solomon in *Beyond Formula: American Film Genres*, find that "the overt moral conclusion is reversed" as Michael Curtiz "no doubt intended" since "Cagney emerges as a hero. . . ." The problem with this view is that Pat O'Brien also emerges as a hero. Curtiz clearly presents the priest as a powerful agent for profound social change and gives him many of the most insightful speeches. Father Connolly is no simplistic do-gooder with a limited perspective on reality. He agitates for sweeping reforms, not cosmetic touches. When Rocky offers him money, he refuses to compromise. Like Rocky, he's a big timer and small potatoes don't interest him. Once he thought he could solve problems from the "bottom up," but now he knows that he's "gotta start from the top down." Father Connolly wants more than a little oasis of morality in a corrupt world; he demands epic changes.

A measure of the importance of this scale of endeavor in *Angels With Dirty Faces* can be found in a comparison to its sequel, *Angels Wash Their Faces* (1939). In the latter, the priest has disappeared, and his replacement is a bumbling assistant district attorney (Ronald Reagan), intent on wooing his sweetheart and winning a playground for the local toughs. None of his clumsy ventures work on either project, however, until "Boys' Day" puts the Angels in charge of City Hall. The kids eventually pillory some hoodlums and garner the recreation area they sought. Father Connolly would have been livid at such co-optation. A key theme in *Angels With Dirty Faces* is his constant harangue that "selling out" is the worst evil of all. In his radio crusade, Father Connolly reveals that he was offered a large allocation for a sports center to "shut my eyes, stop my ears, and hold my tongue." Michael Curtiz intercuts Connolly's message with a comic shot of the three criminal conspirators (James Cagney, Humphrey Bogart, and George Bancroft), who look for all the world like the three monkeys who hear no evil, see no evil, and speak no evil. Father Connolly refuses the substantial bribe because it would treat only symptoms and ignore the real disease. His call for action is both stirring and sweeping: ". . . an isolated playground is not rooting out the crime itself. We must rid ourselves of criminal parasites. . . .We must wipe out those we have ignorantly elected and those who control this diseased officialdom behind locked doors." Father Connolly's activism clearly mirrors the emergence of widespread Catholic political and social activism, the landmark work of the National Catholic Welfare Conference, and the heroic dedication of Monsignor John A. Ryan.

Contemporary audiences would also recognize the fictional Father Connolly's affinities to one of the age's most dynamic media heroes, Father Flanagan, whose film biography was released the same year. In *Boys Town*, Spencer Tracy won his second straight Academy Award as best actor, portraying a personal friend; according to his biographer, Romana Tozzi, Tracy gave the Oscar to Flanagan with the inscription "To Father Edward J. Flanagan, whose great human qualities, kindly simplicity and inspiring courage were strong enough to shine through my humble efforts." Eventually all America would hear of Father Flanagan, his famous attack on California's Whittier Reform School, and his contretemps with Washington's Governor Roland H. Hartley; it was hard to ignore a man who lived by the gospel that "There is no such thing as a bad boy." With Mickey Rooney as the boy and Spencer Tracy as the priest, *Boys Town* packed them in at Saturday matinees and made this orphanage an American institution. A well-oiled media campaign, centered on the heart-rending motif "He ain't heavy, he's my brother," eventually solved all of Father Flanagan's financial woes; some critics, in fact, later charged that

Boys Town was raising funds out of proportion to its needs. The surprise box office success of *Boys Town* and the mass appeal of Mickey Rooney as the mayor of the orphanage generated a quick and less successful sequel, *Men of Boys Town* (1941), in which Father Flanagan (Spencer Tracy) called for "250 Boys Towns, and I don't mean Catholic Boys Towns or Jewish Boys Towns or Protestant Boys Towns . . . just places run by men of good will." These ecumenical sentiments don't convince his Jewish business associate, however, who argues, "You show me 250 Father Flanagans and I'll show you 250 Boys Towns."

Flanagan's modest declarations probably didn't affect audience perceptions very much either, for who but an Irish priest like him could face down evil wardens and sadistic guards? When a particularly obnoxious guardian of public morals warns Flanagan, "If you had that collar turned around, I'd convince you pretty quick," Flanagan takes his collar off and thrashes the startled official. Irish priests were, after all, fighting priests. In 1948 when Pat O'Brien played the life of a Saint Louis priest who cared for homeless newsboys, the studio wanted everyone to know that this was *Fighting Father Dunne* (1948), an urban equivalent of Father Duffy (also played by Pat O'Brien) of *The Fighting 69th* (1940). "Fighting" was an important word in the Hollywood catechism, invariably linked to Irish clergy and laity. The original release of the war epic, *The Sullivans* (1944), the true story of five Catholic brothers who die on the same ship, was unsuccessful; the film did a land office business, however, under the improved title, *The Fighting Sullivans*.

These spunky pictures of Catholics flooding the screen in the first decade after the foundation of the Legion of Decency led many commentators to suspect that producers were courting special favors. Even Margaret Thorp, a contemporary commentator who bent over backward to avoid contravening the Legion, acknowledged in her historically interesting *America at the Movies* (1939) that "certainly when he makes a picture like the one about Father Flanagan in *Boys Town* the producer hopes for such support as that got by pastoral letter and radio address from the Bishop of Omaha and many other priests." Father

Connolly in *Angels With Dirty Faces* may well have been another covert appeal for special consideration. His overweening virtue compensates for a great deal of Cagney's steely-eyed cynicism. Cagney dismisses cops as pathetically stupid, runs roughshod over sadistic guards, and blames the system for tearing his heart and soul out. Rocky has all the brazenness of *The Public Enemy*, the bold aspirations of *Little Caesar* and the animal magnetism of *Scarface*. Without the heroic Father Connolly to contravene his depredations, Rocky might well have been a throwback to earlier pre-Code gangster film traditions.

Angels With Dirty Faces does draw on two diverse strains in the crime film. It hammers at the social causes of crime, but never allows the idea of determinism to preempt the real possibility of moral choice. The prototypes for this film must include *Dead End*, director William Wyler's version of Sidney Kingsley's play as adapted by Lillian Hellman. This was the first feature for the Dead End Kids, a loveable group of ragamuffins who became a major cultural phenomenon of the forties. Contemporary audiences devoured the antics of these lower East Side hooligans in an endless smorgasbord of "B" features. The Dead End Kids, individually and collectively, were reshuffled and regrouped as the East Side Kids, the Gas House Gang, the Bowery Boys, and other clans too numerous to name. Most of the time their antics were the heart of the film and not a secondary motif as they are in *Angels With Dirty Faces*. In *Dead End* the kids met Baby Face Martin (Humphrey Bogart), and there was no priest around to balance his asocial gospel. The kids dream wistfully of escape from their ghetto prison, on "the wings of an angel," a reference which is no doubt the basis for the otherwise unexplained title of Michael Curtiz's film. Escape is but a dream in *Dead End*, however, and Peter Biskind in his *Seeing is Believing* cites a fascinating letter from Joseph Breen to Samuel Goldwyn requesting that the class antagonism and social determinism be toned down: ". . . be less emphatic, throughout . . . in showing the contrast between the conditions of the poor in tenements and those of the rich in apartment houses." Specifically, Breen recommended that Gregg Toland, the cinematographer, not show "the presence of filth, or smelly garbage cans, or garbage in the river into which the boys jump for a swim." The final print did, nonetheless, make clear the inevitability of crime in the ghetto and the almost certain doom awaiting the aptly named Dead End Kids. The last scene shows their adulation for Bogart, his money, and his life; no Father Connolly leads them in a novena for the souls of the faithful departed.

Angels With Dirty Faces contains many sequences that could have fit equally well in *Dead End;* screenwriter John Wexley had, after all, served his apprenticeship in the Workers' Theater. Jerry and Rocky never kid themselves; they know that "the breaks" are all important. Consider the romantic interest, for example; Laury Ferguson (Ann Sheridan) lost her first husband in a shootout because "he wanted to give me more than a taxi driver could." She loves Cagney now and assails Pat O'Brien's stodgy morality for ignoring the forces that destroyed him: "It's not his fault, Father. He was just a kid who made a mistake and got sent to reform school. They made a criminal out of him. But he's not bad, not really bad." The film reinforces her analysis with its harrowing montage of William Sullivan beginning in the Warrington Reform School for petty larceny, graduating to the county jail for assault and battery, and then hitting the big time of the State Penitentiary, where the audience sees a demonically possessed Cagney defiantly rolling a cigarette. It has all the terrible inevitability of Hollywood melodrama a la Warner Brothers. To Laury's charges, Father Connolly offers confirmation, not contradiction. In essence, the priest absolves Rocky of everything: "I'm not blaming Rocky for what he is today. But for the grace of God, there walk I. . . . I'd give my life if I thought it'd do any good. But it wouldn't." Audiences surely couldn't condemn what has been sanctioned by a feisty man of the cloth.

Only the sternest heart would fail to be moved by Rocky's own rationale; his peroration after being condemned to die is an emotional keynote in the film. As Rocky sees it, he and all his compatriots have always been hounded, "hounded from the minute we were born . . . hounded when we were hungry and wanted to eat . . . hounded when we didn't want to live no more in those dumps . . . hounded when we couldn't get the fine things all around us . . . and took 'em for ourselves." For all this sociological theorizing, *Angels With Dirty Faces* does inculcate some sense that free will separates priest and hoodlum. In a revealing comic exchange, Rocky asks Jerry how he found his vocation. Jerry muses about a day long ago when he was riding on the top of a bus and happened to look down as the bus passed a cathedral. This epiphany changed him forever. Rocky immediately wisecracks that he too had a vision on top of a bus once, but it "got me six years." Colin McArthur in his analysis of crime films, *Underworld USA*, puts a great deal of importance on these *Manhattan Melodrama* (1934) situations, where one brother or friend becomes an establishment figure and another an outlaw, though he admits that "seldom in the pre-war period" was it "made explicit" that the evil of one and goodness of the other "are the result of moral choice rather than social conditioning."

Angels With Dirty Faces clearly suggests that moral choices are grievously influenced by sociological pressures. Its attitude toward juvenile delinquency presupposes that only human contact and new heroes can save ghetto youth from a life of crime. Jerry asks Rocky to act yellow so that this next generation might have a chance. There's a deep fatalism to all the Hollywood priest-bad boys stories that posits a lot of suffering. In the 1904 *Land Beyond the Sunset*, for example, the Fresh Air Fund boy who listens to a priest's story about a fairyland beyond the sunset dies and his boat disappears into infinity. And in *The Hoodlum Priest*, a semi-documentary account of Father Charles Dismas Clark's work with juvenile offenders in Saint Louis, the focus is on the saint of the impossible, Dismas. For all his efforts, Clark loses many battles, and the film concludes with the grisly execution of one of his most interesting charges (Keir Dullea). Father Clark (Don Murray) hammers hard at the partiality of justice and the inequity of society. His most impassioned outbursts recall his youth in the coal mines where his father was a Molly Maguire and the Irish were hanged for being Irish. Father Clark proudly declares that he has always spent his life with outcasts, and his Jesuit superiors sanction his focus on good thieves by dramatically releasing him from all other duties so he can devote himself to his "cons."

Father Connolly in *Angels With Dirty Faces* is a parish priest incardinated in New York, and his ministry to the Dead End Boys is only part of his broader sacerdotal duties. Many chapters in the Hollywood catechism feature priests in more specialized roles. Instead of contending with evil throughout the whole film, these priests come in late in the action, on death row, to balance accounts and tack on a moral message to placate the Production Code and the Legion of Decency. One remarkable feature of these cinematic last rites is the herculean effort to distinguish between the will of God and the sanctions of man. These intense forays into ethics constantly juxtapose the natural order and God's plan. The bleak cell in death row is balanced by a nurturing faith in Divine Providence; the harsh bars on earth constantly contrasted with Heaven's mercifully wide gates. Most importantly, however, God's judgment is defined as quite distinct from the sentence of the court.

Sometimes the morality in all this becomes demonically tangled, and the effect on the narrative can be substantial. Film scholar Gerry Mast attacks, for example, Fritz Lang's poetic rendition of the Bonnie and Clyde saga, *You Only Live Once* (1937) because he believes its conclusion undercuts the whole film. In Lang's story, ex-convict Eddie Taylor (Henry Fonda) kills Father Dolan (William Gargan) in an escape from prison; Fonda refuses to believe Father Dolan who has come to tell him that the real criminal has been found and he is a free man (a typically Langian irony). In the final sequence of the film, the fugitive Taylor is mortally wounded just as he prepares to cross the border, and, with angelic music swelling in the background, the audience hears Father Dolan intoning his judgment: "The gates are open." All through the film, as Mast notes, Lang emphasizes the lack of justice in American society, the intense prejudice against ex-convicts, and the crushing poverty that festers into criminality; yet the last thirty seconds of action, Mast feels, undercut it all. *You Only Live Once* stands as his prime example of "a generally fine movie that suddenly and shockingly breaks its spell by introducing some element that contradicts itself."

Many other critics have sensed this tension in Lang's film. Lang's temporal order is, in the words of Richard Pells in his *Radical Visions and American Dreams*, a darkling plain where characters are "trapped and manipulated by environmental forces over which they have no control—fate, chance, heredity, inexplicable accidents, social laws, human intolerance, [and] private compulsions." Yet Lang's films frequently suggest an eternal order that is quite different. Faced with this contradiction, interviewer Peter Bogdanovich asked Lang whether the priest's words in *You Only Live Once* were meant as an ironic note or as the truth. Lang's answer was published in *Fritz Lang in America*, a fact Mast curiously ignores. For Lang, the ending was "the truth"; as the German expressionist director explained to American director Bogdanovich, "I was born a Catholic. . . Catholic education (and probably any education which has to do with ethics) never leaves you. I think it was the truth for those people—the doors are open now—it was not ironic." Not everyone could accept this Catholic resolution, of course, and author James Baldwin is even less sympathetic to visions of salvation than Gerry Mast. In his scintillating collection of film criticism, *The Devil Finds Work* (1976) Baldwin returns film criticism to the high literary standards of James Agee at his best. Baldwin's reaction to *You Only Live Once* defines the problem with priests, confessions, absolutions, and heavenly hosannas so closely associated with gallows, electric chairs, and gas chambers. As Baldwin sees it, Eddie cannot trust Father Dolan because he has "no way of knowing with whom the priest is playing ball at this moment." Besides, Baldwin continues, "the film's last line, delivered (in the dying prisoner's memory) by the priest" is not true to reality: "I knew damn well that the gates were *not* open, and by this time, in any case, the lovers were dead."

Similar contradictory responses and impulses haunt any interpretation of the death row sequence of *Angels With Dirty Faces*. Jerry Connolly asks Rocky Sullivan to feign cowardice so that the newspapers will label him yellow; as a result, hero-worshipping youngsters will despise his life-style and perhaps change their own. Rocky (perhaps symbolically) thrice rejects that request verbally, arguing that "You're asking too much." The priest doesn't deny that in human terms the sacrifice is too great, but he calls for Rocky to seek a courage of the kind that's "well born in heaven, not the courage of heroics or bravado, the kind that you and I and God know about." Rocky does crack, Jerry smiles heavenward, and most movie viewers, convinced of Rocky's courage and cognizant of his not very well disguised "heart of gold" when it comes to the Dead End Kids, conclude it's all a charade. However, the other possibility is equally logical; Rocky may have died a coward. In all his public pronouncements about the film, Pat O'Brien declared he didn't know whether Rocky was actually afraid or if he were doing a favor for a pal. Cagney in his autobiography makes a virtue of the mystery: "I think in looking at the film it is virtually impossible to say which course Rocky took—which is just the way I wanted it. I played it with deliberate ambiguity so that the spectator can take his choice." In the film the newspapers denounce Rocky's cowardice; Father Connolly convinces the boys it happened just as the reporters said, and the only happy ending comes in a dramatic ascension up the stairs out of the gang's underground clubhouse into the bright lights of the streets, a symbolic procession to a heavenly city suitably accompanied by alleluias and promises of novenas for "a boy who couldn't run as fast as I could." These prayers for Rocky's soul never quite overwhelm, however, the somber scenes of his death. Nathan Glazer and Daniel Moynihan, in their detailed exegesis of the impact of immigrants on urban America, *Beyond the Melting Pot*, comment at length on *Angels With Dirty Faces* because they feel that whenever Hollywood tried to "synthesize the Christian religion, they found it most easy to do in the person of an Irish priest," and when it came to portraying "the tough American up from the streets," the image was again Irish and often Cagney. To these academic sociologists, Cagney was a "quintessential figure," full of vitality, but also clearly "doomed." Cagney, they note, usually dies at the end of his films, and, in their opinion, "the contrast with Chaplin tells worlds." In the Hollywood catechism, spiritual salvation usually comes at the price of physical extinction. Wittingly or unwittingly, Hollywood trumpeted the New Testament lesson that the Kingdom of Heaven was not of this earth and that man must lose his life to find it.

Director Tay Garnett's *The Postman Always Rings Twice* (1946) stands as a sterling example of how the convention of death-bed conversions and religious illumination can be grafted on the most unlikely material. James Cain's original novel, a hard-nosed, nihilistic study of greed and lust, contains few hints of meaningful moral regeneration. When Frank, its protagonist, tries to figure out why he is being executed for the accidental death of Cora, his confederate in an earlier slaying, his mind just "goes blooey." Screenwriters Harry Ruskin and Niven Busch brook no such confusion; Frank (John Garfield) accepts the schema of divine retribution his confessor has provided on death row, using his own metaphor about the postman with an important letter who rings twice to make sure we don't miss him. John Garfield as Frank dramatically sorts it all out for himself and for audiences looking for the compensation the Production Code demanded: "Father, you were right. It all works out. I guess God knows more about these things than we do. Somehow or other, Cora paid for Nick's life with hers and now I'm going to." Frank's "somehow or other" suggests the murky workings of the Hollywood catechism in its death row chapters.

Frank doesn't even expect salvation for his contrition; he begs indulgence, instead, imploring Father McConnell (Tom Dillon) to "send up a prayer for me and Cora, and if you could find it in your heart, make it that we're together, wherever it is." Love may conquer all and defy heaven and hell, but, as Gabriel Miller observes in *Screening the Novel: Rediscovering American Fiction in Film*, Frank's leap to faith does result in a rather bewildering conclusion. Frank's face is, in Miller's words, "bathed in an almost mystical light" as he stares heavenward in thanksgiving. Literary critic Miller is staggered by the imagistic reversals implied here: "It seems that Cora's

76

radiant whiteness, once a symbol of mysterious, compulsive evil, now represents her (or is it God's) love and forgiveness." For Miller, this is an "incongruous" end for a tale of jealousy, bondage, and doom. For screenwriter David Mamet, who re-adapted James Cain's novel in 1981 for Bob Rafelson's steamy version of *The Postman Always Rings Twice*, the idea of death row confessions and salvation was quite dispensable. Rafelson's vision of Frank Chambers (Jack Nicholson) and Cora Papadakis (Jessica Lange) emphasizes groping, pawing, and clutching, but ignores the metaphor of its title totally. There is no Postman here, no talk of Divine Providence, and no heavenly light.

The two versions of Charles Nordhoff and James Norman Hall's novel *The Hurricane*, one by John Ford (1937) and the other by Jan Troell (1980), provide further evidence in the evolution of the Hollywood catechism over five decades. Ford's film, scripted by Dudley Nichols, seems intent on demonstrating that priests are bound by the law of God and not the laws of man. Father Paul (C. Aubrey Smith), a wrinkled veteran of the theological wars, puffs most knowingly on his pipe, trusting his illative reasoning when it tells him not to rest content in his colonialist role as a courtroom counsellor and prison house confessor but to resist an unjust regime. When he confronts Terangi (Jon Hall), a much abused native who has killed a guard and is running for his life, Father Paul does more than aid the fugitive to escape; he also offers ecclesiastical sanction for Terangi's just anger: "How can I be your judge? You've sinned, but others have sinned more against you. You weren't meant for evil; you were made to do evil. How can I judge?" Any further moral complications for his own acts of civil disobedience, Father concludes as he peers heavenward, are "between me and somebody else." Later in the film, Father Paul repeats his stirring call for civil disobedience in the cause of justice, with a defense of a boy who will not inform on Terangi: "There are stronger things than governments in this world. Something deeper, more real. This child has that in his heart. Though you torture him, he wouldn't speak. . . . and I shall bless him for it." Contemporary audiences were accustomed to this *epikeia* from Catholic priests; Father Flanagan, Father Charles Dismas

Clark, and others in their confraternity could look into a boy's eyes and see the spark of God's grace hidden to the sanctimonious.

Curiously, Lorenzo Semple's script for Dino De Laurentiis's mega-buck disaster, *Hurricane* (1980), seems out of touch with this Hollywood vision of priests and fugitives. Father Malone (Trevor Howard) in this redaction brays with the heaviest Irish brogue ever allowed on a serious sound track, but he functions for the most part as an Ann Landers of island etiquette. When Matangi (Dayton Ka' Ne) kneels and confesses his love for Charlotte Bruchner (Mia Farrow), Father Malone trivializes the whole idea of a sacrament by joking, "Now, it's decent of you to tell me; there's not a soul on this island that hasn't noticed you've been playing the fool and making cow eyes at the captain's daughter." In the place of *cura animarum*, Father Malone offers advice more suitable to a columnist in a Catholic high school newspaper: "Don't despair, there's hope for you. If foolishness were a mortal sin, hell would be full up and overcrowded. Now say a good act of contrition and forget the girl." One finally wonders if Father Malone isn't intended as a parody of discalced missionaries trying to replace ancient fertility myths with puritanical and hygienic modernity. This Father Malone cannot help Matangi escape; that task falls to the more humanistic Dr. Bascomb (Max von Sydow). And this Father Malone cannot offer his benediction to Matangi; he deflects the boy's attempted confession with a most unpastoral rebuff: "Don't be excusing yourself to me . . . speak to God." Malone consistently ignores the forces of both man and nature. During the climactic storm, the doctor jests that "Father Malone's preaching may be weak, but his building is solid rock." The pun on Peter, the rock of faith, and the Catholic Church may be unintentional, but the message in the subsequent action is clear. The natives are saved when they leave the inflexible stone church and cling to the trees which sway to the will of nature. Father Malone's last feverish gesture, holding his chalice up in defiance of a tidal wave, seems insane, not inspired; pathetic, not efficacious.

The longest and most detailed sequence of a priest on death

row contains a similar renunciation of priestly powers, albeit much more subtle. Director Robert Wise's acid tale of Barbara Graham's execution, *I Want to Live*, spends much of its duration in a cell next to a gas chamber and features a psychologically aware priest, Father Devars (John Marley), who tries to comfort "Bloody Babs" (Susan Hayward) with a medal of Saint Jude, "the patron saint of the impossible." His morality is relativistic enough to comfort the most despairing soul; he reminds his ward that "none of us are wholly innocent or guilty in the eyes of God." Unfortunately, the dramatic structure in the film begins to hinge on the postponements in the execution. The longer the inevitable is delayed, the more Barbara fidgets with her newly acquired medal until finally her death sentence seems a repudiation of Saint Jude and of the power of prayer. Like Cagney, Susan Hayward was doomed; her plea, "I want to live," an impossible dream. Neither of these Catholic criminals ever had the right "breaks" here on earth; the recompense, the Hollywood catechism taught, had to come in heaven.

The same sense of doom and of heavenly recompense also hangs heavy over Hollywood's visions of immigrant labor agitators, their unions, and their pastors. Unions were key institutions in the assimilation of immigrants, but labor organizations often violated civil law and sometimes defied Church dictates. The interactions of Old World cultural loyalties and New World aspirations, of religious fervor and terrorism, of informers and parish priests generated several of Hollywood's most interesting portraits of American Catholicism. The issues in these films are just as stark as death row confrontations: death lurks in every mineshaft and on every pier. Only now there are families involved, too, emaciated women desperate for food, sick children in need of medicines, and young lovers anxious for a better life. There are company goons, double agents, divided loyalties, and moral dilemmas. More often than not, priests are forced to be partisans and to take sides in the fray.

One of the earliest examples of these labor strife epics, *Black Fury* (1935), treats the Slavic coal mining communities in Pennsylvania. Based on the true story of an immigrant family, the Shemanski family, as portrayed in an important novel by Justice Michael Musmanno and the play *Bohunk* by Harry Irving, this film was banned in many cities because it so clearly pictured labor-management strife. In Michael Curtiz's film, Joe Radek (Paul Muni), a simple minded hulk, dreams of the day he will "go by the priest for to be married, then raise pigs and kids." His girlfriend Anna (Karen Marley) wants more, however, than to stay and be "another wornout miner's wife, pinching and starving, and trying to raise a lot of kids." She runs away with Slim Johnson (William Gargan), an Irish cop. In his drunken despair Joe inadvertently plays into the hands of the Industrial Detective Service, a racketeering operation that prompts workers to strike and then charges employers for breaking the strike and the union. Modern audiences may be aware that much of the social commentary in the film is defused by using this third party to absolve management and workers of any real responsibility for class warfare, but contemporary audiences were mesmerized by the picture of la or agitation, scabs, and terror bombs. In an unconscious extension of the social theme, a racketeer named McGee (both the cops and the criminals seem to be Irish) links the mounted police the capitalists employ to the Cossacks when he gleefully notes that "Them Hunkies sure have a healthy respect for a cop on a horse, something psychological they brought over from the old country."

The miners eventually rally around Radek, who has seized the mine and threatened to blow it up. Even Anna returns to help. Joe's eventual victory is celebrated with the re-opening of the mine and the fruition of his dream. When his supporters congratulate Joe, they assure him, "Now you can raise those pigs and kids," and Joe agrees, "You betcha your life." The link between Catholics, menial labor, and large families is quite natural in the Hollywood catechism. Catholic intelligence always seems an inverse function of physical size and athletic prowess. Papists are the original "niggers" of American cinema. As Professor Arthur Schlesinger, Sr., declared to Catholic historian John Tracy Ellis (in a private conversation quoted in *American Catholicism*): "I regard the prejudice against your church as the deepest bias in the history of the American people." This prejudice against immigrant Catholics was so pernicious because it was so pervasive. Only the most stupid hoods in *Black Fury* engage in consciously ethnic slurs; the owners, the bosses, and the president of the Federated Mine Workers of America, "Fighting Johnny Farrell" (the bellicose Irish again) engage in a more subtle discrimination. They all treat the workers with consummate condescension, manipulating them as though they were an inferior race of childish alcoholics, quick to fight, quick to shift allegiances, and quick to fornicate, but very slow to understand. Several sequences in *Black Fury* reinforce these prejudices. Often, the economic issue seems to revolve around little more than whether the boys will be able to pay their bar bills.

The most blatant examples of ethnic condescension come, however, in Hollywood's images of filmdom's "apostles" of feuding, fighting, drinking, and wenching, the Irish. The two major Hollywood films treating Irish unions and immigrant labor exploitation develop the topic in markedly different ways, but each results in some high drama and a powerful commentary on the Catholic Church in America. Martin Ritt's *The Molly Maguires* (1970) turns a dark page of Pennsylvania history into a somber but thoughtful film, while Elia Kazan's *On the Waterfront* (1954) transforms contemporary headlines into an action-packed character study lauded as one of the finest American films ever made.

Martin Ritt's largely ignored and underrated *The Molly Maguires*, a chronicle of an ill-fated uprising in the anthracite fields of Schuykill County, emphasizes the Church's role in opposing secret groups and labor violence. Father O'Connor (Phillip Bourneuf) sternly rejects any rationale for violence. Going to O'Connor's church and listening to his harangues is, as company spy James McParlan (Richard Harris) remarks, "a lively matter" and dangerous for "a brave man." Screenwriter Walter Bernstein probably found his justification for this portrait in the letter from seven local priests opposing the Molly Maguires published in the *Freeman's Journal* on October 10, 1874, and in the pastoral condemnation issued by Bishop Frederick Woods.

As Thomas McAvoy reluctantly admits in *A History of the Catholic Church in the United States*, the hierarchy's attitude did much to convince critics that "the church was unsympathetic to labor and to the sad conditions of laborers in the mines." For all his focus on the evils of violence, however, Father O'Connor does care about his parishioners. He seems deeply moved by their suffering; at a critical juncture, he even warns Jack Kehoe (Sean Connery), who everyone knows is a Molly, that there is "an informer" in their midst. That treacherous informer spells death for the Molly Maguires, but his perfidy makes their terrorist activities look just by comparison. Once again, Bernstein's script rings true to history. Local clergy may have condemned the Molly Maguires, but American Catholics at large wouldn't ignore the injustice in their executions. As Henry Brown observes in his article "A History of the Catholic Church in the United States," the whole incident became "most important in turning the Catholic press to an awareness of the social problem and led to the first major Catholic questioning of the laissez-faire philosophy of government."

Elia Kazan's *On the Waterfront* combines a hymn to a socially aware Church with an impassioned apologia for informers. This defense of the stool pigeon is, in large part, self-defense, a skillful rationalization which equates the amoral hoods on New York City docks that Terry Malloy (Marlon Brando) denounces with the Hollywood "communists" denounced by "friendly witnesses" at the House Un-American Activities Committee hearings, including director Kazan himself, probably the most sycophantic witness ever called, script-writer Budd Schulberg, and actor Lee J. Cobb (ironically called Johnny "Friendly" in *On the Waterfront*). The script was based in part on a series of Pulitzer Prize winning stories by Malcolm Johnson, highlighting the work of Jesuits Philip A. Carey and John M. Carridan, but it was the personal magnetism of Father Carridan, "the waterfront priest," as Budd Schulberg reveals in his afterword to the Southern Illinois Screenplay Library edition of *On the Waterfront*, which kept the project going even after the noted producer Darryl Zanuck rejected the whole concept as "exactly what the American people don't want to see." Schulberg makes no secret of Father Carridan's charisma; Schulberg, who calls himself a "liberal freethinker," came to cherish the Church this "tall, fast-talking, chain-smoking, hardheaded, sometimes profane Kerryman" represented, finding in Father Carridan the perfect "antidote to the stereotyped Barry Fitzgerald-Bing Crosby 'Fah-ther' so dear to Hollywood hearts." Father Carridan was no crooner dismissing life's problems with puckish smiles. As Schulberg recalls the fiery Jesuit, he was brimming with talk of revolution and reconstruction, of social justice and Christian charity, of union power and labor racketeering. Father Carridan was so effusive and iconoclastic, Schulberg recalls, that Kazan once took his screenwriter friend aside and asked him, "Are you sure he's a priest?"

In the film, Father Barry's (Karl Malden) passion mounts slowly, but eventually it does reach intense levels. Father Barry is learning as much as his charges; their interaction enriches each of them. At the beginning, the obliging priest comes merely to offer Extreme Unction; unconsciously, he has allowed the rectory to become his refuge from the world just as the nuns in Tarrytown have provided an artificial haven for the sister of the deceased, Edie (Eva Marie Saint). When Father Barry earnestly assures Edie that "I do what I can. I'm in the church when you need me," Edie's bitter response starts him on the arduous road to sanctity: "Was there ever a saint who hid in the church?"

From this point on, Father Barry grows in stature; instead of quiet prayers and studied avoidance, he takes his ministry to the streets. Schulberg's script and Kazan's realization of it both emphasize the symbolic import of Father Barry's actions, identifying his basement chapel with the catacombs, and his dockworkers with the early Christian martyrs. They also emphasize the division in the contemporary church over social activism when they picture the other priest in the parish warning Father Barry that because the dockworkers' problem is "a police problem, not ours," his religious superiors will ship him off to territories unknown and unnamed (the script says "Abyssinia").

Father Barry disregards all these practical considerations,

however. Seemingly, the Holy Spirit has touched him, and his preaching becomes more and more inspired. His gift of tongues is most evident in his version of the Sermon on the Mount, a moving sermon of the docks made the more heroic because he is pelted with garbage when he tries to convince his flock that ". . . Christ is always with you—Christ is in the shapeup—He's on the hatch—He's in the union hall—He's kneeling here beside Nolan."

One need not take Father Barry's lesson on faith, either. If ever there was a clear Christ figure in film, it's Terry Malloy in *On the Waterfront*. The film details his agonizing decision to take up the cross and emulate the Redeemer. At the beginning of the film, Terry seems the least likely candidate for apotheosis imaginable; he tells Edie that his philosophy is to "Do it to him before he does it to you" (still another hoodlum inversion of the Golden Rule). When she reminds him that "Our Lord said just the opposite," Terry answers her with his immutably perverse logic: "I'm not looking to get crucified. I'm looking to stay in one piece." By the middle of the film, under Father Barry's tutelage, Terry is weighing the consequences of denouncing Johnny Friendly and other hoods. When he complains to his spiritual advisor, "If I spill, my life won't be worth a nickel," Father Barry poses the key question for any Catholic activist in a corrupt society, "How much is your soul worth, if you don't?" Terry makes the hard choice and turns stool pigeon, only to be brutally beaten by union goons. He rises from this agony, however, and in Schulberg's words, "driven on by Father Barry's will," Terry leads the men back to work, free of the bondage of the mob. His beating and the long walk back to the docks are an unmistakable reenactment of Christ's Passion on Calvary. The filmmakers have managed to create a modern day Messiah out of a rather dimwitted, somewhat punch-drunk informer. Terry Malloy emerges in this film masterpiece, as Gordon Gow observes in his survey of *Hollywood in the Fifties*, as "a loser of the twentieth century whose passion burns to the spectator's heart with purer fire than was ever kindled by Hollywood representations of Calvary."

Demonology was much more common than Christology in

Hollywood's post-Production Code portraits of the Italians from the *mezzogiorno* and their peculiar agonies with the Mafia. Once the stuff of powerful, complex films like *Little Caesar* and *Scarface*, these *paisanos* suffered a cruel fate in the decades after the establishment of the Legion of Decency. Once the laughter died down from *Little Giant* and *Brother Orchid*, producers resurrected the Mafia in innumerable "B" movies, churning out mechanical variations on a few hackneyed themes. In these low budget but popular programmers, the staple of Saturday matinees and the invariable second half of the action-packed double features, moral recompense was paramount: the lights of the San Gennaro Festival pointed the way straight to hell.

Despite the mindless predicatability of low budget gangster films, adventure hungry filmgoers enjoyed these forays to the ethnic stronghold of the Black Hand, the Organization, the Cosa Nostra, the Gang, the Camarra, the Underground, the Mob, the Brotherhood, the *Unione Sicialiana*, and the Mafia. Organized crime under any sobriquet seemed to be spawned on Mulberry Street and its environs. Tourists still come to New York to steal a few minutes in its coffee shops and dream of nefarious plots and larger-than-life evil. The streets of Little Italy, after all, are like a second home for these American pilgrims; they've probably seen as much of them on television as they have of any locale in America.

Hollywood's Little Italy was a bizarre holy land populated by demons, a slice of the Big Apple barely concealing its worms. Behind every plaster-of-paris statue of the Madonna there lurked a Sicilian hitman intent on his vendetta; every set of rosary beads shared a pocket with a stiletto; and every household shrine contained at least one votive candle burning for a *mafiosi*. Hollywood's images of Italian culture stressed the olive complexions, the fierce loyalties to ancient traditions, and the mystical communion of silence—*omerta*. In a predictable irony, the more films concentrated on this unbreakable code of silence, sealed with the "kiss of death," a code which made the organization unknowable, the more American moviegoers and television addicts wanted to see the Mafia and its soldiers on screen. Virtually any Italian gangster of note could count on several lavish film biographies and a television series or two. Al Capone, Joe Valachi, Lucky Luciano, and Joe Columbo became full-fledged media superstars.

Most of these gangster potboilers exploit Catholic rituals purely for local color. Priests and processions, cassocks and capes become just so much oregano and garlic in these repetitious and routine rehashes of tired formulas. To satisfy indiscriminating tastes, all that seemed required was a little violence and a recognizable gangster ambience.

Despite the degeneration of the genre, a few later films, notably the works of Martin Scorsese (a Catholic from Little Italy) and the *Godfather* films of Francis Ford Coppola (a Catholic from Detroit) did use this Mafia milieu to make very telling points about the Italian-American conscience. In the mid-sixties, taking bold advantage of the new liberality in films ushered in by the shift from a Production Code that assumed every film was intended for the whole family to a system of industry ratings that labelled films as suitable for general audiences, suitable for mature audiences, and suitable for adult audiences, Scorsese and Coppola employ their guns and gunmen to speak of sin and guilt; in very different ways, these two sons of Catholic immigrants redefine the gangster film as a powerful critical focus for their art.

Francis Coppola's two Academy Award winning dissections of the Mafia, *The Godfather* (1972) and *The Godfather, Part Two* (1974), both draw heavily on traditional materials and rework them masterfully. Screenwriter Mario Puzo was especially cognizant of the prejudice against Italian immigrants and while his revisionist approach to the gangster movie stresses the successes of the Corleones in eliminating their enemies and consolidating power, he never forgets the basic antagonism between the WASP power structure and these Catholic upstarts.

Senator Pat Geary (G. D. Spradlin) tells Michael (Al Pacino) quite forthrightly in *The Godfather, Part Two* that Italians, despite their fancy suits, stylish haircuts, and large business investments, will never really be accepted in America: "I don't like your kind of people . . . trying to pass yourself off as Americans. I'll do business with you, but the fact is, I despise your

86

masquerade, the dishonest way you pose yourself and your whole fucking family."

Geary's attack is just a modern variant on all the old prejudices. As Mario Puzo observed in his collection of essays on Italian life in America, *The Godfather Papers*, peasants like the Andolini family from the village of Corleone were hated even in their homeland: "These peasants were looked upon by the ruling classes and most northern Italians as uncivilized animals; indeed the government in Rome kept separate statistics on them, much as we Americans keep separate statistics on blacks." In America, Puzo continues, newspapers called these new immigrants "the scum of Europe," arguing that they should not be admitted because they were "too violent, too dark, too drunken, and too sexual." Italians found it almost impossible to escape these stereotypes, which were reinforced in one Hollywood melodrama after another.

Coppola's epic has to be seen in the context of these well-established "B" movie conventions. Marlon Brando's landmark performance as Don Vito Corleone, one of the finest characterizations in the history of American film, works so well because it is a summary and revitalization of every hackneyed image of the Italian gangster in every film which has preceded it. In his book length appreciation of *Marlon Brando*, Rene Jordan isolates many of the "minute touches" that make Don Corleone so real: "the defiant-apologetic shrug," "the hands that helplessly shoot up," "the evanescent whiff of an *a* at the end of each noun," and "the cracked voice [which] suggests untold maladies, deeply inhaled Sicilian cigarettes." The heart of the achievement is, however, as Jordan notes, Brando's ability to find "the essence at the bottom of the heady caricature." Coppola's basic concept refurbishes the old tradition and establishes a daring new one. Where the old films had been told from the point of view of the establishment, Coppola's epic is told entirely from the point of view of the crime family; where old films had found their resolutions in the victory of the forces of law and order, his saga celebrates the survival of the Mafia; where old films had preached Christian doctrines of right and wrong, the morality of Coppola's film seems largely tied to what sociologists call "amoral familialism" but what Italians call *"l'ordine della famiglia"*; where earlier films showed the declining fortunes of mobsters, Coppola's films showed the establishment of an empire; and where old films had struggled mightily to show the distinction between private enterprise and racketeering, Coppola's masterpiece purposefully and effectively establishes an unmistakable link between the rise of the Corleones and the rise of American capitalism. In a famous interview with Stephen Farber, published in *Sight and Sound* in the winter of 1972, Coppola revealed: "I've always wanted to use the Mafia as a metaphor for America. . . . Both are totally capitalistic phenomena and basically have a profit motive. Of course, it's a romantic conception of the Mafia." It proved so romantic and so revolutionary that Coppola had many Americans identifying "the family" with their family.

Coppola's most daring revolution comes in his picture of the Roman Catholic Church. Conventional Mafia films had either used Catholicism as one more element in the local color or occasionally shown the Church as providing succour for those opposed to the forces of evil. In Coppola's *Godfather* films, the Church constantly appears at the center of the action. Time and time again, the worst crimes are linked with the most solemn religious rituals. To take but a few examples, Vito's older brother Paolo is killed during the funeral procession for his father; the young Vito (Robert DeNiro) kills Don Fanucci (Gaston Maschin) during a religious festival; and Fredo Corleone (John Cazale) is executed as he says the "Hail Mary." Combined with the images of a Don dispensing favors during his daughter's wedding, and of his son and successor discussing bribery at a First Communion, these scenes would be enough to establish a clear pattern. The Catholic Church and especially its Italian clergy, Coppola suggests, remain curiously oblivious to the activities of their parishioners; the churchmen and their flocks are content with public displays of sanctity at prescribed intervals. Both the priest celebrant and the lay participants enjoy the rituals but ignore their spiritual import. Earlier films may have excused the gap between action and significance as a reflection on the breakdown in communication between an Italian laity and an Irish clergy, but Coppola pictures parishes with Italians in charge on both sides of the altar rail, yet they seem to have thrown the religion out and kept only the majestic forms. Coppola obviously wants Americans to believe that for Italian gangs, Church ceremonies are charades, empty rituals. The sacramental forms in the *Godfather* films do not touch human lives. The mobster's observance of time-established rituals does not bring sanctifying grace.

In Coppola's epic presentation, the Italian gangster is a singularly bold and self-righteous hypocrite. The crowning demonstration of this disjunction between professed Catholicism and real spirituality comes in the baptism which fittingly concludes his original chronicle of *The Godfather*. Most critics would agree with Frank McConnell's assessment in *Storytelling and Mythmaking* that this scene is "one of the most overwhelming bravura sequences in American film," a finale no one will ever forget. Coppola is careful to have his priest confect the sacrament in all its pomp and dignity; the prelate solemnly intones his Latin in a baptism notable for its high Church formality. The *redditio* of creed is especially striking. As the priest booms out his query to Michael, who speaks for his godson, "Do you renounce Satan?" and Michael boldly asserts "I do renounce him," the film cuts to a chain of well-planned, professionally executed, and terrifyingly brutal murders which settle all of Michael's affairs and secure him as the overlord of crime. The slayings are especially gruesome versions of traditional gangland executions. Any afficionado of "B" movies will recognize every single situation as a standard feature in Saturday matinees. One victim is shot in an elevator, and another immobilized and gunned down in a revolving door. The three other targets are all engaged in the activities Hollywood long associated with Italian gangsters: One is being shaved at his barbers, a second massaged in a steam room, and the third frolicking in bed with a whore. What makes these gangland murders especially shocking is the disturbing counterpoint provided by the constant intercutting to the images of a solemn baptism and the priest's ritualistic questions and Michael's un-wavering lies "And all his works?" "I do renounce them." "And all his pomps?" "I do renounce them."

In *Mean Streets*, a small production filmed the same year (1972) as Coppola's epic, Martin Scorsese explores the disturb-ing interaction of Catholicism and crime even more rigorously. Martin Scorsese is a graduate and former professor at the New York University film school, so, as David Denby observes in his *Sight and Sound* evaluation (Winter 1973) of *Mean Streets*, Scorsese's film must be seen as "the culmination of the lonely-streets-and-sullen-bedrooms style of student films produced in the last decade at New York University." *Mean Streets* must also be seen, Scorsese insists, as part of an uncompleted religious trilogy, containing *Who's That Knocking at My Door?* (1969) and the never filmed *Jerusalem, Jerusalem* (excerpts from Scorsese's film treatment for *Jerusalem, Jerusalem* have been published in Mary Pat Kelly's indispensable collection *Martin Scorsese: The First Decade*). These two films, *Mean Streets* and *Who's That Knocking*, and Scorsese's descriptions of the unrealized project offer a sustained analysis of Italian-American Catholicism which is operatic, disturbing, and masterful. Ex-seminarian Scorsese has thought long and hard about sex and guilt, sin and responsibility, repentance and salvation; his dark night of the soul has brought harrowing visions of contradictions and complexities to the screen. All of Scorsese's later projects about troubled souls, *Taxi Driver*, *Raging Bull*, and *King of Comedy*, have their roots in his anguished, stylized, provocative earlier works. Scorsese is the tortured poet of divided allegiances, the visionary of an urban nightmare, a tormented ethnicity, and a boundless guilt. His films, like the stories of Kafka, are dis-turbingly sexual, embarrassingly personal, overpoweringly vi-olent, and intensely religious.

Mean Streets is basically one long examination of conscience by its protagonist, Charlie (Harvey Keitel), a sensitive man trapped in a brutal world, a religious man surrounded by in-stitutionalized depravity. Charlie wants desperately to be good, to find comfort and forgiveness in church; but all he can find in religion is guilt, guilt over his work for the Mafia and guilt over his sexual urges. Charlie knows in his heart that "You don't make up for your sins in Church. You make up for them in the streets or at home," so he tries to work out a temporal salvation through his loyalty to two friends, Teresa (Amy Robinson) and Johnny Boy (Robert De Niro). This trinity is eventually crushed by their environment, but not before Charlie's religious agonies have made some stunning cinematic revelations about sublime religion and mortal men. Scorsese makes Charlie the perfect embodiment of Eric Hoffer's thesis in *The True Believer:* "a sublime religion inevitably generates a strong feeling of guilt. There is an unavoidable contrast between loftiness of profession and imperfection of practice. And, as one would expect, the feeling of guilt promotes hate and brazenness." Ex-priest James Kavanaugh spoke to this same phenomenon, but put it in a specifically Catholic frame of reference in his *The Birth of God*, in which he details the endless cycle of guilt and confession, confession and guilt that seem to be Charlie's fate; Kavanaugh argues that the average Catholic learns from his youth "the agony of guilt" and this guilt "never leaves him." Kavanaugh specifically blames the guilt on the sacramant of Penance: "While he [the average Catholic] has heard that confession is a sacrament of gentle mercy, it is often a tense ritual of anxiety and guilt. . . . Theoretically, he knows what confession *should* mean in terms of confidence and peace, but practically it *does* mean a life immersed in guilt." Charlie is addicted to his daily *examen* exactly because real salvation seems impossibly remote. Charlie wants more from his Catholicism, more suffering and more relief. He holds his hand in the flame of a votive candle to taste the horrors of hell, yet he remains absolutely incapable of tasting the joys of heaven. Charlie's Italian-American Catholicism, with its dark cathedrals, brooding statues, and grotesque crucifixes, promises too much and delivers too little for him. Unlike the hoods in *The Godfather*, Charlie cannot just walk through the ceremonies for the sake of appearances; Charlie wants the appearances to be real.

Charlie is Martin Scorsese's inspired vision of the new middle-class American Catholic ethnic. He has seen the New Deal of Franklin Delano Roosevelt come and go; he has seen Al

Smith's dream fulfilled and watched a Catholic say his beads in the White House. And like the disillusioned reformer who was surprised that America didn't ascend to heaven on the wings of Prohibition, this immigrant has learned that the ascent to power in America didn't hasten any Second Coming.

THREE

The Clerical
Melodrama:
hierarchy, rectory, and convent

Pope Pius XII: "By the way, do you remember a movie
                  called *Going My Way?*"

Mervyn LeRoy: "Of course. One of my friends, Leo
                  McCarey, made it."

Pope Pius XII: "I have a print of it. Don't you love that
                  scene where the priest takes a little
                  drink?"

Conversation reported in
Mervyn LeRoy: Take One.

The Motion Picture Production Code, which governed the industry from the mid-1930s to the mid-1960s is very explicit on the matter of religion, which is treated as paragraph eight of the "particular applications." Three major strictures apply: first, "no film or episode may throw *ridicule* on any religious faith"; second, no ministers of religion "in their characters as ministers of religion" should be used as comic characters or villains; and third, religious ceremonies should be "carefully

and respectfully handled." The Code even provides an underlying philosophy for its sanctions; ministers must not be ridi-
culed or used as comic characters and villains "simply because
the attitude taken toward them may easily become the attitude
taken toward religion in general," and because "religion is low-
ered in the minds of the audience because of the lowering of
the audience's respect for a minister."

In practice, the sanction against evil or comic ministers
became a benediction for virtuous and gleeful clerics. If one
couldn't laugh at the religious, one could laugh with them.
And if clergy couldn't be evil, they could be supernaturally
innocent. The priest became a new unearthly creature, full of
smiles and cheery lessons, singing songs of innocence to confound the world of experience; nuns worked their own magic
by flying or, at the least, singing in perfect key. In the Hollywood catechism, ecclesiology became an important branch of
melodrama, and the screen was flooded with old priests who
could learn new tricks, young priests who could croon fortunes
away from skinflints, and beautiful nuns troubled by handsome
young doctors or by slight touches of tuberculosis. Miracles
abounded in the Hollywood catechism; there were improbable
marvels by and for the multitudes; statues that bled, cried, or
walked; chapels built single-handedly against all odds; children
saved from the ravages of polio, vice, and ignorance; and even
big, hairy, floppy-eared dogs snatched back from the pounds.
There were new, dangerous, expensive operations to restore
speech, sight, or gumption, all paid for by anonymous donors,
and there were sweeping indulgences to chase away the blues
of any kind.

At the center, there was Bing Crosby, the best known fictional priest in America and the official ambassador to the world
of Hollywood catechism. His portrayal of Father Charles Francis
Patrick O'Malley in Leo McCarey's *Going My Way* (1944) and
its sequel, *The Bells of St. Mary's* (1945), became an important
icon in American culture. Crosby's puckish charm struck a re-
sponsive chord in a war weary America. His bold optimism
and unflagging faith in the powers of good kindled a real popular affection for this archetypal man of the cloth. Crosby made

O'Malley's Roman collar a powerful and positive icon, under-
mining anti-Catholicism at the very primitive level where prejudices are formed, the level of memory, association, and emotion. Crosby and his director, Leo McCarey, linked religiosity
and emotionalism; their spiritual exercises rehashed the conventions of the melodrama. *Going My Way* and *The Bells of St.
Mary's* offered one-dimensional character types, easy to understand and respond to, overblown and clearly delineated
emotions, and dramatic confrontations between virtue and vice
that resulted in clear, satisfying triumphs for the pure-of-heart.
The films were simple and sentimental, poetic justice informed
every frame, and audiences loved these visions of a sugarcoated
universe where everything always worked out the way one
hoped it would, where congruism was the reality. When anyone in America thinks of Catholics in film, Father O'Malley is
invariably the first name to come to mind. The members of the
Academy of Motion Picture Arts and Sciences probably wiped
a tear or two from their eyes, lifted a silent toast to good old
Saint Dominic's, and hummed a bar or two of an Irish lullaby
when they gave Crosby the Oscar for best actor, McCarey the
Oscars for best writer and director, and *Going My Way* the Oscar
for best picture in 1944.

    Going My Way must be seen as the culmination of a long
line of Irish films, mostly funny and all emotional. The Irish
were Hollywood's Catholics *par excellence*, full of whiskey and
faith, and prone to fighting, politics, and vocations. Interestingly, sociologists support Hollywood in this vision. As Catholic Andrew Greeley notes in his *The American Catholic: A Social
Portrait*, the American Catholic Church is in large part an Irish
Church: "The Irish constitute fifteen percent of the Catholic
population, thirty percent of the clergy, and over half the hierarchy." The identification of the Irish and the Church is so
common that Lawrence Fuchs argues in his *John F. Kennedy and
American Catholicism* that "to many Americans" Irish and Catholic are "almost synonymous." And in considering Irish-American social mores, Catholic Daniel Moynihan (now an Irish politician) and Nathan Glazer sound more like screenwriters than
social scientists in their *Beyond the Melting Pot* when they term

the Irish "the playboys of this new Western World" and discuss the race's many hedonistic accomplishments. The Irishman's prowess as lover was legendary in the nineteenth century, they note, and "by the turn of the century it had become equally clear that none could run like them, nor fight like them, nor drink as much, nor sing as well." The Irish, be they Shantytown or lace curtain, made their mark wherever they went, and Hollywood was happy to record and embellish it.

Director Sidney Olcott made his career providing Irish immigrant melodramas with ethnic themes, like *The Lad From Ireland* (1910), *Rory O'More* (1911), and *The Gypsies of Old Ireland* (1917). Around the same time, Chauncey Olcott, "the servant girl's Caruso," made a similar career of being, in the words of his biographer David Carroll, *hibernicis ipsis hibenor* ("more Irish than the Irish"), lifting his glorious tenor in blarneystone renditions of "My Wild Irish Rose" and "When Irish Eyes Are Smiling." These ethnic diversions continued for decades, and Irish pastors like Father McGowan (Daniel T. Sullivan) in *Cecilia of the Pink Roses* (1918) became stock characters, counselling lovers, soothing disillusioned immigrants, and looking after assorted widows and orphans. All these films about the Irish veered wildly from comedy to pathos, and urban poverty and politics loomed as major issues. In *Little Old New York* (1923), for example, life on the Bowery mixed Irish ballads, fistfights, lost inheritances, and a whipping post. In *The Lights of Old Broadway* (1925), a color sequence details an Irish uprising put down by police with firehoses. Explicitly religious conflicts often played an important role. In *Knights of the Eucharist* (1922), for example, an Irish boy dies defending his church from desecration by the Ku Klux Klan.

The biggest hits, however, were the innumerable variants on Ann Nichols's play *Abie's Irish Rose* (first staged in 1924 and filmed many times, most notably by Victor Fleming in 1929 and by A. Edward Sutherland in 1946). Jewish-Irish romances and their ethnic and religious complications proved a staple of early cinema. In their history of motion pictures, *Light and Shadows*, Thomas Bohn and Richard Stromgren suggest that "the portrayal of Jews in silent film is virtually one long Jewish-Irish joke," citing examples as early as the 1903 short, *Levi and Cohen,* *"The Irish Comedians,"* and including *Levi and McGinnes Running for Office* (1914) and the whole, seemingly endless string of "Cohen and Kelly" comedies which began in 1926 and continued well into the sound era.

Irish Catholics were displeased with these films, and, as Thomas Cripps observes in his essay "The Movie Jew as Image of Assimilation," they mounted "effective pressure campaigns which restructured the old stereotypes." As Cripps views it, the new Irish stereotype made them "assimilationist" heroes. Irishmen were presented as the foreigners who made it as "genial cops, winsome brawlers, blustery priests, and wardheelers with hearts of gold." Some indication of the power of these stereotypes can be found in director Henry King's *In Old Chicago* (1938), one of that decade's most expensive films. This rollicking story of the O'Leary brothers (Tyrone Power and Don Ameche), their romances, their feuds, and their infamous cow, ends in a recreation of the Chicago fire; but it has its heartwarming beginning in an image of Irish immigrants coming across a desolate plain. Pa (Paul Hurst) dies (the symbolic death of Old World values) but not before he implores his clan to make "their mark on the city" and to bury him on the outskirts of town to "let Chicago come to me, that couldn't come to it." In their dramatic rise to political power, the O'Learys have more than their share of beers, dancing girls, bribes, and brawls. The Irish of the "Patch" confront the Reform party, the brothers have an epic fistfight, and Mom (Alice Brady) constantly reminds everyone, "We O'Learys are a strange tribe," as she downs her beer with gusto. For a while, it's the "O'Learys against the world," but in the end, the fire draws all the immigrant factions together in their promise to build an even better city. The Irish won't be defeated, the clan is assured, because "there's a strength in us, what we set out to do, we finish." This same image of rough and tumble Irish politics and stubborn energy informs director John Ford's *The Last Hurrah* (1958), an elegiac tribute to the best of the old political bosses, Frank Skeffington (Spencer Tracy), drawn from Edwin O'Connor's fine novel, but clearly based on Boston's Mayor Curley, who sued to keep the film from being shown. Skeffington and the cardinal (Donald Crisp) are warriors from the old school, with what Phillip T. Hartung termed in *Commonweal* "more Celtic charm than a carload of leprechauns." They made audiences mourn the passing of patronage and clubhouses.

In *Going My Way*, this old Irish tradition is embodied in the spunky but rather ancient pastor who has given forty-five years of unstinting service to Saint Dominic's Church (the patron saint's name is a sly commentary on Irish-Italian relations in the immigrant church). Father Fitzgibbon (Barry Fitzgerald) has been at Saint Dominic's since the church was founded, and he knows every flower in the garden, every soul in his parish, every stone in the church. His is an Irish parish right out of the Hollywood tradition; Saint Dominic's is in the bad section of town, overburdened by a mortgage, crowded by unruly youths, and host to a plethora of small moral dilemmas. Like the "Patch" in old Chicago, Saint Dominic's is also doomed to the ravages of a fire which tries the mettle of its priests.

Father Fitzgibbon knows he's aging, but he refuses to give in to time. The old priest doesn't realize at first that the bishop wants some new blood at St. Dominic's and that the old order is to be replaced by the more athletic, musical, and cheerful Catholicism of Father O'Malley. The clash between their two styles of saving souls, Fitzgibbon's patriarchal authority and O'Malley's avuncular charm, stands out among the welter of themes in *Going My Way*. Director McCarey obviously cherishes the protection implied by Fitzgibbon's all encompassing concern, but he also salutes the individualism and the sense of personal responsibility O'Malley tries to instill in his charges.

In place of the traditional romantic triangle of Hollywood films, with two beaus courting a young lady, McCarey's triangle has Fitzgibbon and O'Malley squaring off for control of a parish. McCarey quite skillfully explores all the subtle nuances in their battle without ever obscuring their fundamental agreements and their common heritage. The crotchety Fitzgibbon has a hard time believing the bishop would "do a thing like this to me" when he meets his new young assistant clad in a Saint Louis Browns sweatshirt, yet his question sets the tone for all their

98

future encounters: "Young man, may I ask is this the official garb of the priests in Saint Louis?" The studiously polite but pointed question is funny, not very subtle, yet still civilized. The conflicts in *Going My Way* will share these traits: battle in the film is always pointedly clear yet amusingly inconsequential enough not to demean either priest. The audience is lured into laughing with both clerics; there is no malice. As Fitzgibbon tells Crosby, "I don't dislike anyone; I just disagree with you." Out of these disagreements, McCarey has spun a wonderful web of amusing incidents.

One fine example of McCarey's technique is his skillful use of an athletic motif. When Father O'Malley arrives, Fitzgibbon is most disconcerted by the golf clubs, tennis racquets, and fishing poles his smiling new curate introduces to the rectory. One of his most humorous one-liners charges that the golf course is "nothing but a pool room moved outdoors." By the end of the film, the old codger is trudging around the greens, complaining but enjoying. When he hears that Crosby will be moving on to another parish to rescue another old "fuss-budget," Father Fitzgibbon employs a sports metaphor to signal his acceptance of everything O'Malley stands for. Bishops who send new prelates to aid old priests are, he opines, "like umpires, you have to have them to call the close decisions." All the decisions are close in *Going My Way;* these are both obviously dedicated men seeking salvation for their flock in different ways. McCarey's humor has none of the sharp edge of a satirist like J. F. Powers, whose National Book Award winning religious novel *Morte D'Urban: A Novel of a Priest* (1956) mocks *Going My Way* in its pivotal scene in which there is a hilarious golf match between Protestants and Catholics that concludes its mock heroics with the dashing Father Urban being beaned by a golf ball. The bishop who hit the wicked shot deems it "an act of God, if ever I saw one," but Father Urban finds this interpretation "probably heretical in its implications since it made short work of him as a responsible instrument of God's will in an orderly universe."

McCarey's tale of two quite different Irish priests features fewer theological questions and jokes, yet it provides many insights into the day-to-day workings of the basic unit of urban American Catholicism, the parish. *Going My Way* powerfully illustrates the central role parishes play in the life of Irish Catholic Americans. Priest-sociologist Andrew Greeley, in his *The Most Distressful Nation: The Taming of the American Irish,* isolates the parish as the "symbol of loyalty" around which immigrants clustered in an unfriendly America. Greeley explains that for his generation, the Irish parish was "the center of our lives" inasmuch as it "provided us with education, recreation, entertainment, friendships, and potential spouses. It was a place to belong. When asked where we came from, we named the parish rather than a street or neighborhood." *Going My Way* pictures such a parish at work; the different approaches of the priests touch the lives of quite a large number of people.

Several of these human interactions define the tension between the priests as they elicit chuckles from the audience. Take, for example, the problem of juvenile delinquency. As presented in *Going My Way,* errant boys are little more than restless pranksters out on a lark. Theft is their game, but it could be replaced easily by baseball, movies, or a stint in the church choir. Father Fitzgibbon seems oblivious to boyish misadventures; at one point, he even accepts their illicit plunder, a turkey. Father O'Malley can't resist teasing him about the purloined poultry, and a fine comic exchange follows. Fitzgibbon admits, "I gave the boys my blessing," and O'Malley quickly rejoins that "They gave you the bird." This carefully established pun and the double takes which follow it are typical of McCarey's style and the skills he acquired working with such great improvisationists as Laurel and Hardy and the Marx Brothers.

It should be noted, however, that Fitzgibbon's myopia and the boys' studied deception ring true to the image of an antiquated priest that ex-priest James Kavanaugh draws in *The Birth of God.* The authoritarianism of traditional religion is, Kavanaugh suggests, too outmoded to function in the modern world, and its spokesman "cannot be treated like other men" because he is "the lawgiver, the symbol of tribal law in a society that has outgrown both his product and his approach." As a result,

Kavanaugh suggests, the traditionalist is "treated with a deference that is offered to the old and senile or to the obviously neurotic." Fitzgibbon's age and his authoritarianism are unalterably linked in *Going My Way*. He is lovable but doddering; his creed is admirable but a trifle too inflexible. As James Agee notes in his famous review of *Going My Way*, Barry Fitzgerald's portrayal of the aged Father Fitzgibbon is a marvel of observation which captures all the contradictions in aging: "Father Fitzgibbon might have been any brogue-rippling old male biddy. But as Fitzgerald portrays him—senile, vain, childish, stubborn, good, bewildered, stupid—he is the quintessence of the pathos, dignity, and ludicrousness which old age can display." By extension, the portrayal also captures the dignity and ludicrousness of Father Fitzgibbon's rigid religious philosophy.

Father O'Malley is, on the other hand, the essence of youth and modernity. The boys trust him because he "didn't rat" to the police about the stolen turkeys, took them to ball games, bought them hot dogs, and treated them to movies. His Catholicism is practical, up-to-date, and infectious. Instead of proscribing, Father O'Malley lures his boys into the church and treats them to the beauty of the *Ave Maria*. He does not try to impose morality but labors instead to draw out the best in his young charges. O'Malley sees no demons to be tamed and obviously agrees with the assessment of his opera diva friend: "They're angels who've got something you lose when you get older." When he tries to explain his vocation to skeptics, Father O'Malley eschews sermons rife with hellfire and damnation; instead, he sits at a piano and tries to make music out of the joy he finds in religion: "I get a great happiness out of helping people. Religion doesn't have to be this [he pounds out a doleful theme], taking all the fun out of everything; it can be bright, bringing you closer to happiness." Father O'Malley will soon have all his parishioners swinging on a star.

A similar contrast in clerical styles and in basic religious philosophies can be seen in the different approaches of the two priests to the teenage runaway Carol James (Jean Heather). Carol is obviously tired of old-fashioned prescriptive morality, lamenting that her parents don't like her hair, her lipstick, her boyfriends, and "something or other" about her burgeoning bosom. Father Fitzgibbon ignores her pleas for personal liberation and a meaningful career, and he sternly admonishes her: "Nonsense, being a wife and a mother will do for you just like it did for your mother." Father O'Malley, on the other hand, tries the friendly approach, offering the white lie that his parents "learned a lot" in the years between his eighteenth and twenty-first birthdays. When this indirection fails, Father borrows ten dollars from his pastor and lends it to her. Later in the film, when he happens on the apartment she shares with the banker's son, he expresses his disapproval in similarly indirect ways, inspiring the young lovers with his buoyant philosophy. Soon thereafter, the young couple discover their own religious resolve; O'Malley marries them, and they enlist in the war effort. As they remark, Father O'Malley gave them a "nice thought" about "going my way"; in their eyes, he's "quite a fellow." By extension, his version of Catholicism is quite a religion.

Father O'Malley's many wonders are obviously meant to suggest an aura of sanctity informing his humanity; his victories seemingly confirm the teleological argument for God's existence. When the old Saint Dominic's is destroyed by fire, his song-writing abilities finance a modern renovation (McCarey's physical parallel to the young priest's renewal of Father Fitzgibbon's ministry). His vigor renews the bank's faith in the church and a new mortgage is issued forthwith. His boys rival the Vienna Boys Choir for charm. And to top his miracles off, he brings Father Fitzgibbon's long lost mother to America to help celebrate Christmas. During the reunion, Father O'Malley slips quietly out the door, picks up his suitcase, and starts going his way again.

The climactic reunion of the Irish mother and her son the priest is prepared for earlier in the film, when the two priests first let their guards down and begin to reconcile their differences. In the privacy of his bedroom, a contrite Father Fitzgibbon offers his young antagonist "a wee drop" from a bottle of Old Bushmills he keeps hidden in a music box behind *The Life of General Grant* on his bookshelves. This bottle, he explains, constitutes his link to Ireland, his family, and his Catholic heritage: "Every Christmas since I left Ireland, my old mother sends me one of these. With a little abstinence it becomes my calendar. I get a little behind at Lent, but it comes even at Christmas." Father O'Malley relishes the chance to share his precious liquor and to toast motherhood; the contrast between the two priests established throughout the film is maintained in this scene by O'Malley's admission that his mother died when he was quite young. As the two men drink, the affinity between them is suggested in Fitzgibbon's fond memory that his mother "always had a song in her heart," and O'Malley's rendition of one of their shared songs, "Too-Ra-Loo-Ra-Loo-Ral." This Irish lullaby affirms their cultural affinities; their differences are like varied stained-glass windows in the same cathedral, like different pews in the same Irish aisle of the Roman Catholic Church.

Individual reactions to such emotional resolutions of differences and to *Going My Way* vary greatly, even among the faithful. For some churchgoers, the film provides a fervent reaffirmation of the Catholic faith. Their reaction mirrors the assessment of Al Smith as reported in Frank Graham's *Al Smith, American: An Informal Biography*. Al Smith, years after his defeat as the first Catholic candidate for the presidency, arranged a special screening of *Going My Way* for himself and a group of young priests. According to Graham, Smith "enjoyed it immensely, now laughing, now watching with tears in his eyes, now laughing again as the story unfolded." When the show was over, an exuberant Smith told all assembled that "It reminded me of the days when I was a boy at St. James." For many viewers, *Going My Way* confirmed their memories and reinforced their beliefs. For still others, it introduced them to the emotional side of the Hollywood catechism, with human priests solving human problems with a song in their hearts. Some Protestants even went so far as to complain to the Production Code Office that Catholic clergy were being given preferential treatment in movies and that there should be Protestant equivalents to *Going My Way*.

Yet there were also serious Catholics in the 1940s and there are many concerned Catholics today who see in *Going My Way* a dangerous set of prejudices and preconceptions; they see the film as a pernicious chapter in the Hollywood catechism. Gary Wills articulates the basic criticisms in his *Bare Ruined Choirs: Doubt, Prophecy, and Radical Religion*, a very provocative and insightful work about the agonies of contemporary American Catholicism. Wills condemns the film in sweeping, uncompromising terms: "It was, for all its schmaltz, surprisingly true to Catholic life, and to Catholic blindness about that life. The film celebrated all the Church's faults as if they were virtues—right down to Father O'Malley's practiced golf game." Wills's argument depends, of course, on an individual's response to the American variant of Catholicism.

Some of the features most frequently cited as weaknesses in the film echo the standard attacks on American Catholicism. There is, for example, the emphasis on money and buildings. As Wills notes, *Going My Way*, "under its cassocks and other disguises," is "the classic melodrama based on mortgage foreclosure." There appears to be a good deal less concern in the film about spiritual life than there is about the physical survival of Saint Dominic's. From the very beginning, there is less talk of the devil than there is of the Knickerbocker Savings and Loan Company. Even the jokes seem double-edged. The banker laments to the pastor that for him it's all business, but "with you, it's different; you haven't got anything and you don't want anything, and people respect you for it. But I'm not in your business, and if I haven't got anything and don't want anything, I'm a bum." As the film progresses, it becomes clear that both priests do care about something—their beloved St. Dominic's—and they do worry about their fate if it is destroyed.

The dramatic resolution in *Going My Way* hinges much more on O'Malley's financial successes and the acquisition of a new mortgage than on anything else. The big question seems to be saving the physical plant at Saint Dominic's. This fixation on real property seems an unconscious variant on a famous joke about New York's Cardinal Spellman that was printed in *Fortune* magazine and recounted by Nino Lo Bello in his exposé, *Vatican U.S.A.* Spellman, the joke goes, went to heaven, and when quizzed by Saint Peter about his life, responded that he was "a simple parish priest who had served nearly two million souls"; Saint Peter checks but finds no dossier under the name Spellman. A little anxious at this turn of events, "Spelly" (the affectionate nickname his friends used) then tells Saint Peter about his numerous religious books, but still no luck. Finally Spelly talks about the fifty churches, two hundred schools, and innumerable hospitals, homes, and orphanages he supported. This time Saint Peter returns with a smile: "Come right in, Frank, we had you under real estate." For many critics, the joke had a bitter ring of truth, and *Going My Way* just pointed up how the American Church was prone to glorify property.

A corollary to the fixation of real estate, according to Church critics, is the disproportionate attention paid to the activist life in American Catholicism and the almost total disregard for the contemplative. In *Going My Way*, Father Fitzgibbon has a special affection for his garden and recommends it to Father O'Malley. Almost immediately, however, he has second thoughts and asks most pointedly, "You do meditate, don't you?" Meditation, the core of the spiritual life, ritual and prayer take up little screen time in *Going My Way*. Marriages, baptisms, masses, and confessions all take place off-screen. Both pastors are caught up in the welter of material concerns involved in keeping St. Dominic's afloat and in the parade of parishioners looking for advice. Add to this Father O'Malley's youth groups, social outings, choir practices, theater friends, and enthusiasm for sports, and there is little time for his breviary, let alone serious theology or prolonged spiritual exercises. His choice of the active life over the contemplative one is characteristic of the American Church. In fact, Gene Kellogg in his study *The Vital Tradition* finds more Americanism than traditional religiosity in activism: "What such priests and their lay companions were actually doing was giving a Catholic slant to particularly American characteristics, the desire for swift pragmatic action with visible results, the respect for hard work and material accomplishment." Theologian Jordan Aumann is equally critical in his article "Activism and the Interior Life," an important chapter in a very important book, Louis Putz's *The Catholic Church*

U.S.A. Aumann charges that American priests have made "the apostolate an end in itself" and that there is in American Catholicism "a marked tendency to an activism which is detrimental not only to the Church in America but also to the spiritual life of individual Christians." This criticism has its parallel in another joke Nino Lo Bello recounts in *Vatican U.S.A.* Supposedly, when Supreme Court Justice William O. Douglas was on a plane that seemed about to crash, a distraught passenger called out for someone to do something religious; Justice Douglas thought for a second and then took up a collection. In *Going My Way*, one of the few scenes that takes place inside the church at St. Dominic's involves an awkward sermon by Father Fitzgibbon, who begs for alms. Father O'Malley has pre-arranged for his song royalties to be put in the collection plates by his music publishers, and the mechanics of collection provide some highly comic moments. Afterwards, as the money is counted, a euphoric Father Fitzgibbon chides himself and his bishop for ever believing that he was slipping as a preacher. Successful money-raising and successful evangelism are for him very much the same.

This unrelenting focus on material goods and practical considerations almost disqualifies *Going My Way*, author James Agee argues, from the category of religious film at all. As Agee sees it, the film avoids all the hard questions of the religious life; in Agee's opinion, *Going My Way* "would have had more stature as a 'religious' film if it dared suggest that evil is anything worse than a bad cold." Agee's metaphor of a "cold" proved especially prescient. When Hollywood decided to capitalize on the success of *Going My Way*, producers brought the Barry Fitzgerald-Bing Crosby team back in *Welcome Stranger* (1947); only this time, the Nicene Creed had given way to the Hippocratic oath, and Barry was an aging doctor and Bing his young protégé.

Critics of *Going My Way* would see in this shift a substantitation of their charges. The Hollywood catechism seemed to suggest that saving a soul was pretty much in the same league as setting a broken bone and that the devil and evil were no more subtle than germs. Materialism and worldliness in *Going My Way* swept aside any more profound meditation on the nature of good and evil.

Such reductionism prompted the Christian philosopher and film critic Michael Leach to talk about a "pornography of piety" in his *I Know It When I See It: Pornography, Violence, and Public Sensitivity*. If the religious can attack pornography for its deceits, Leach argues, then they must be consistent and attack "family films that misrepresent the family, marriage, politics, war, or even religion." When Leach explores this "pornography of piety," he finds a noxious example in *Going My Way*. Leach admits that he still cries when he sees Barry Fitzgerald "waddle toward his ancient mother" and that he loves all the characters in the film, but he nevertheless asserts that "these movies present seductive shadows, not real people, are one dimensional in their treatment of religion, and could be called 'religious mirages' depending on your point of view." Film historian Ivan Butler sounds many of the same criticisms in his survey of *Religion in the Cinema*, but his general tone is much harsher. For Butler, *Going My Way* is more offensive than pious; for this critic, *Going My Way* "leaves a nastier taste in the mouth than the worst Biblical blockbuster excesses."

Most Americans didn't share Butler's distaste for *Going My Way*, however, so in 1945 Leo McCarey brought Bing Crosby back to the screen in a Christmas release of *The Bells of St. Mary's*, scripted by Dudley Nichols and featuring Ingrid Bergman as Sister Mary Benedict, a new authoritarian Catholic about to be mellowed by Father "Chuck" O'Malley, who was himself getting mellower by the year. Bing has some new songs in this outing, including "Aren't You Glad You're You," an ode to doing your own thing and going your own way, and "The Bells of St. Mary's," a piece as nostalgic and emotional as any Irish lullaby; but he also relies on the old standby "Ave Maria," which Bing himself sings this time. Bergman has only one song in the melodrama, but she does an accomplished comic pantomime in a scene where Sister Benedict develops her boxing skills and instructs her favorite student in fisticuffs. All the music and buffoonery, and the magic of the Bergman-Crosby team made *The Bells of St. Mary's* a sequel with more box office clout than the original.

The Bells of St. Mary's is heir to many of the plot devices, comic twists, and thematic dissonances of the original. Once again the main problem is a building. The present schoolhouse has "grown old doing good," and the sisters dream of inhabiting the new skyscraper across the way, a building owned by a contemporary Scrooge, Mr. Horace B. Bogardus (Henry Travers). The nuns' prayers, a heart palpitation, and Chuck's foreboding snatches of *"Ora Pro Nobis"* quickly dispense with Horace's "humbugs" and prove every bit as effective as Dickens's three ghosts at changing a miser into a philanthropist. Mr. Bogardus gives the building to the nuns, consoling himself in the good it will do his heart and the tax advantage it will accrue. The Catholic drive for property is so strongly expressed in *The Bells of St. Mary's* that some critics are embarrassed by its excesses. Normally sympathetic James Agee admitted he was "just plain horrified by the way the sisters hound an old nabob into beneficence." Critic Richard Corliss uses the whole episode as an excuse for some anti-clerical barbs in his *Talking Pictures*. In Corliss's view, Bing Crosby "pulls off a land-grab scheme" for the Church and for Sister Benedict that is "less than heartwarming for any infidel aware that the Roman Catholic Church was New York's largest landowner at the time." Corliss finds the whole episode so distasteful that, despite director McCarey's obvious intentions, Corliss feels that "in this struggle between Church and Capital, the capitalist can't help but be the sympathetic party."

The Bells of St. Mary's also has that sports motif so familiar in Catholic films. When the nuns chatter away outside his window, Father O'Malley comes bursting out to ask, "What's the excitement? Notre Dame win another one?" The sustained metaphor, however, is a boxing match between two boys, Tommy and Eddie, which provides fine opportunities for a sparring match between the pragmatic Father Chuck and the intellectual Sister Benedict. The two religious antagonists banter pointedly about the nature of life. Father O'Malley lauds Tommy because he's a "good fighter" and in a "man's world," sometimes "you have to fight your way through." Sister Benedict deflates his male ego by questioning how well the men are doing in running their world and by proposing that it's better to think your way through than to fight. Round One ends with her best line: "You look after Tommy and I'll look after Eddie who lost the fight because he listened to me."

The next rounds are fought in Father O'Malley's ring as the mother superior converts to his tactics. She studies up on the manly arts and works out most gingerly with Eddie. All goes well for a while, and then she takes a haymaker from her pupil when she "walks right into the payoff." The educated Eddie proves more than a match for Tommy, but Father Chuck has his satisfaction in watching Sister Benedict look out a window at the fight and urge her champion on with body English. Her satisfaction comes in the subsequent verbal exchange; when the priest talks of "an improved man," the nun quotes some mushy prose that the soft-hearted cleric wrote for a female student and reminds the somewhat crestfallen Father O'Malley that "We try to raise masculine men even with our limited knowledge of the outside world."

Where Father Fitzgibbon and Father O'Malley differed on pastoral styles, here nun and priest differ on academic standards. Chuck is of the "let-them-all-through" school of pedagogy, while Sister Benedict calls for unalterable standards. Since he is *de facto* principal of the school, she agrees to defer to his authority and pass the child in question, Patsy (Joan Carroll), but even then "the grade would remain the same." Father O'Malley warns her "This is serious," but she remains unrelentingly stern. Father would, of course, never force anyone to do anything, and it takes a McCarey plot artifice to resolve the issue in the way the audience wants. As it turns out, Patsy failed because she wanted to be with Sister more, and when Sister learns this, her inflexible, even-handed code demands that Patsy be graduated and forced to move on to Catholic High School. It's typical McCarey. Crosby has his say and wins the audience's sympathy, Bergman maintains her principles as she learns new lessons, and the child gets her diploma.

This focus on academic standards in the Catholic school system is quite daring, since the whole concept of separate parochial schools often raised angry voices in America. Many distinguished educators had attacked Catholic schools for their separatism and for their lax standards, yet in McCarey's film, there never seems to be a doubt that Catholics belong in Catholic schools. Even Mr. Bogardus, when he suggests that St. Mary's be torn down and the land used as a parking lot for his building, doesn't suggest a public alternative; he tells Father O'Malley that the children could go to the "modern, up-to-date" Saint Victor's. His flattering descriptions are no doubt another attempt to bolster Catholic education by suggesting that St. Mary's rundown condition is an anomaly.

The real proof of the efficacy of the Catholic school system comes, however, in the transformation of Patsy, a poor student from a broken home with a large chip on her shoulder. Father O'Malley promises Patsy, "We'll take good care of you," and his pledge seems a gross understatement by the end of the film. Patsy wipes her makeup off, takes the "rat" from her hair, and learns all the virtues of honesty, chastity, purity, and justice. When Sister Benedict gives her failing marks on her exams, Patsy is stoic, a veritable martyr to her own love of St. Mary's. Her street urchin's English is so improved in a matter of months that she can correct even her teacher's subtle faults. Meanwhile, Father O'Malley takes the time to reunite her mother and father with his skillful rendition of "The Land of Beginning Again." He dismisses their anxieties about Patsy's marks with the convenient equivocation that her grades "were exceptional; there wasn't a child in the class anywhere near her," and the result is a picture-perfect graduation full of smiles, tears, and hugs. In *Going My Way*, Father O'Malley only had his boys singing in the choir; in *The Bells of St. Mary's*, his wayward girls graduate with dreams of a vocation.

Sister Benedict (whose very name raises allusions to marriage) does everything she can to remind Patsy of the joys of

110

earthly love, admonishing her that the convent is no escape from the world and counselling that a young girl must experience a "first prom," a "party dress," and a "ball" before she can truly decide to be a nun. The problem is that all this advice is coming from the radiantly beautiful Ingrid Bergman. When Father O'Malley arrives at St. Mary's (the Blessed Virgin) parish, his housekeeper warns, "You'll be up to your neck in nuns," the same nuns, she feels, that drove the last pastor, Father Fogarty, to Shady Rest in a wheelchair, mumbling pathetically to himself. In fact, Father is really bothered by only one nun, a nun whom James Agee felt came painfully close to twittering her eyes in scenes with Crosby. Agee was not alone in recognizing the sexual tension in a film about two young, healthy, vibrant personalities, both pledged to vows of chastity. Bing Crosby is such a charmer and Ingrid Bergman such a beauty that *The Bells of St. Mary's,* inadvertently or not, had to suggest a deeper dynamic. Francis Ford Coppola obviously was attuned to this subtext, when he pictured Kay (Diane Keaton) and Michael (Al Pacino) in *The Godfather* leaving a Radio City Music Hall Christmas show featuring *The Bells of St. Mary's.* Kay first asks Michael, "Would you like me better if I were a nun?" Her following question is "Would you like me better if I were Ingrid Bergman?"

A subtle hint at this need for deeper communication between Sister Benedict and Father O'Malley comes in the bizarre plot twist that concludes *The Bells of St. Mary's.* Sister has to be transferred because she has tuberculosis, but her doctor advises Father O'Malley not to tell her of her illness because it might discourage her and impede her recovery. The priest knows this unexplained transfer will lower her esteem for him, since she will probably assume it is his revenge for her defiance and inflexibility. But the noble clergyman does tell the noble lie, and the noble sister does the noble thing when she prays in chapel for the strength to accept her fate: "Dear Lord, remove all bitterness from my heart and help me to see Thy Will in all things; please, please help me." Once all this self-sacrifice and stoicism is justly appreciated, Leo McCarey lets their humanity shine through and wrings a few tears from his audience. Father

O'Malley does the good bad thing and tells the heartbroken nun the truth. She melts in gratitude, assuring the worried pastor he has made her very happy, and pledging to return to her duties after a speedy recovery. As she leaves, Father O'Malley tries to remind her that if she needs anything, he's always there; she smiles and echoes his famous slogan, "Just dial 'O' for O'Malley." This last overwrought scene provides, Richard Corliss notes, "a prime example of Nichols's (and McCarey's) cynical shuffling of emotions for an effective fade-out."

Bing Crosby and Ingrid Bergman, who were good pals off screen, had their own idea for a fade-out, which the singer details in an anecdote published in his "authorized biography," *Bing,* by Charles Thompson. Crosby and Bergman thought that the religious adviser for the film, Father J. J. Devlin, who was employed by the studio to assure that the production did not offend the Church, was much too "dour"; to the two stars, the priest was another Father Fitzgibbon, "a very serious, quite humorless, but nice man." So after the real final sequence was set, Crosby and Bergman conspired to do another take especially for Father Devlin's benefit. This conclusion, Bing Crosby notes, took greater cognizance of the fact that "throughout the film there'd been a note of something more than just a priest-nun relationship." As cameras rolled and Father Devlin watched, Father O'Malley reached for Sister Benedict, took her in his arms, and gave her a powerfully erotic kiss of clearly immoral duration. The effect, Crosby recalls gleefully, was more than they had hoped for: "Father Devlin was ashen. He was shaking and his eyes were standing out a foot. Then, of course, everybody laughed and he saw it was a gag. He was so relieved, but for a moment it was really something."

The final chapter in Bing Crosby's escapades as a priest wouldn't come until 1959, in Frank Tashlin's *Say One for Me,* a lightweight musical showcase for the talents of Debbie Reynolds and the songs of Sammy Cohn and James Van Heusen. A slight name change to Father Conroy of Saint Joseph's Parish couldn't disguise how tired Bing Crosby's impersonation of a young cleric had become. Father Crosby was rightfully the stuff for parody now, as Dean Martin and Jerry Lewis showed in *At*

War With the Army (1950). Their takeoff on *Going My Way* in this film ranks among the all-time gems of screen art. As Crosby, Martin has all the studied casualness down pat, including the one hand that dangles nervously while the other digs deeper in a pocket, the rumpled clothes, the pipe that is always slightly out of control, and the dreamy eyes that never quite come into focus. As Fitzgerald, Jerry Lewis shuffles along determinedly, totters unsteadily, blinks in incomprehension, and clears his throat all the time. Both comedians clearly relish their hilarious dialects, chockful of Irish phrases, circumlocutions, and rhythms, all delivered with brogues dense enough to befuddle a leprechaun. And for all the exaggerated "Top of the morning" and "Oh my boy" fun, Martin does manage a passable rendition of "Too-Ra-Loo-Ra-Loo-Ral" before the boys belt down a few stiff jolts of Irish whiskey and dry their tears in black handkerchiefs. Almost two decades later, Rod Steiger would build on Lewis's caricature to create his own masterful parody of Barry Fitzgerald in *No Way to Treat a Lady* (1968). In this product of the ratings era, comedy gives way to murder. Dressed as Father Fitzgibbon, Steiger cons his way into a widow's house and strangles her. Audiences everywhere gasped at this unexpected turn of events, for the earlier stereotypes were a deeply ingrained part of American culture.

Unfortunately, Bing Crosby fails to see the caricature implicit in Frank Tashlin's resurrection of an Irish priest, Father Conroy, and the crooner plays his role straight in a film intent on more self-conscious fun. Father Conroy manages to seem both incongruous and anachronistic in *Say One For Me*, a better title for which might have been *The Perils of Holly*, in honor of Father Conroy's youthful and vivacious charge. Most of the film's better sequences concentrate on the many challenges that performing at the Black Garter Club poses to the virtue of Debbie Reynolds, a lively, beautiful, talented, and virginal trouper trying to make enough money to support her father's convalescence at the Home for Old Actors. Debbie clops around the stage in underwear, a swimsuit, and much less; promises erotic delights in torch songs remarkable for their smutty lyrics; and make a scantily-clad pilgrimage to lounge on every tabletop in the seedy night club. Offstage, of course, her Murphy bed stays locked in the closet, her rosary beads and daily Missal get regular workouts, and her persistent suitors are likely to find themselves locked outside her door. *Say One For Me* reworks an archetypal theme of the fifties: male wolf meets female lamb and is finally devoured by marriage. In this particular farce, Robert Wagner serves as an ersatz Rock Hudson and Debbie Reynolds becomes the ersatz Doris Day. Bing Crosby is the pious onlooker, the guardian of maidenly virtue, and the prod to male moral regeneration through marriage.

Screenwriter Robert O'Brien makes Father Conroy's participation in backstage antics dramatically feasible by locating St. Joseph's right in the heart of the theater district; it's an ersatz Saint Malachy's, a "players' parish," a model Catholic branch of the Actors' Guild. Father Conroy, the "theater priest," wallows in modernity and concern. His masses include a 2:00 A.M. special for his unique flock; his associates include bookies, bartenders, cabdrivers, and theatrical agents. Father Conroy recasts his sermons in the jargon of the trade; his Bible rests on top of his copy of *Variety*. Even his housekeeper at the rectory sometimes wonders if he's really an ordained priest at all.

Many of the cinematic conceits in the film revolve around Father Conroy's easy assimilation of sanctity and showtime. One of his earliest sermons, for example, sounds like a Johnny Carson monologue in its gentle call for regular church attendance: "If you run into any of the absentees, tell them Father Conroy will be very glad to see them at his late, late, late show." This salvation-show business link finds fuller development in the person of "the television monsignor," Francis Stafford, who visits Father Conroy and asks his help in producing a gala telethon to benefit aging and infirm performers. Monsignor Stafford, a Bishop Fulton Sheen sound-alike, makes even Father Conroy seem shy and retiring. The implication is clear: successful priests have to understand mass media and adapt to the times.

One sad variation on this show business and sanctity motif involves Father Conroy's ill-advised theft of a joke from the ne'er-do-well who is stalking Holly and big-time bookings with equal ardor. The plagiarism, though well intentioned, justifies

114

the seedy performer's charge that Father O'Malley is just "a Milton Berle with candles," and embroils Crosby in one of the least successful quests for a joke ever shown on screen. Father Conroy, it seems, feels morally obligated "by his Church" to make restitution in kind, one good joke given to replace one good joke stolen. This bizarre permutation of Catholic teachings keeps Father Conroy up at nights reading Gordon's *Book of Jokes*, and he fails abysmally in his attempts to be a new Bob Hope. Father Conroy even tries some of his material out in the pulpit, a sad commentary on the state of preaching in Catholic churches. Holly laughs uproariously at all Father's jokes; in the rest of the pews, there is a terrifying silence.

In *Say One For Me*, screenwriter Robert O'Brien too often contents himself with stylized one-liners and unimaginative reversals of the old cliches. Father Conroy's characterization is all *shtik* and no substance; it's as though Robert O'Brien thought humor would come automatically if he just negated the old conventions. Take, for example, the business of priests and "the Fighting Irish." Father Conroy roots for Notre Dame, indeed bets on Notre Dame, but they lose to Army, and he owes two jokes instead of one. Or consider O'Brien's reworking of the cliche that the priest was God's version of Joe Palooka. In *Say One For Me*, the night Father Conroy prepares to visit the Black Garter in street clothes, his housekeeper reminds him about the last time he took his collar off. Father rubs his jaw ruefully and recalls, "Oh, yes, he was a wife beater and, and a priest beater—ohhh! You can't win them all." Finally, there's that old tradition about priests and the bottle. A bartender friend does tell Father Conroy that he's sorry now he didn't listen to his mother's advice and become a priest since he would have had "better hours and heard fewer confessions," but that's as close as priests and serious drinking ever come in *Say One For Me*. In his forays to the nightclub, Father Conroy, even out of his cassock, proves the most noticeable teetotaler since Carrie Nation came in with her ax. Back at the rectory, his housekeeper chides him because he accepted the gift of a bottle of Benedictine from a parishioner, but he is the soul of probity and tries to convince her it's moral because the liquor is made by monks.

When Monsignor Stafford pays a surprise visit, the embarrassed lady hides the infamous bottle under a pillow; the priests agree that this special occasion justifies something out of the ordinary and she must retrieve the bottle so the two men can pour themselves a very wee drop. At Father Conroy's pace, his Benedictine might well be a perpetual calendar.

All these labored jokes fall as flat, however, as Crosby's feeble efforts to restore the stolen jest. And while Father Conroy does work many of his old miracles, making cynical drunks believe in a beneficent God, baptizing bastards cherished by chorus girls, staging star-studded telethons, guarding Holly from seduction and disillusionment, and converting an opportunistic masher to a life of self-effacing stardom and marital bliss, the audience knows that the pretentious last title card of the film "The Beginning" conceals the truth. *Say One For Me* clearly demonstrated that it was time for Bing Crosby to retire his cassock. Too many members of the audience were beginning to agree with the alcoholic songwriter's plaint, "I like you, Father, you're so obvious, so obviously good. But what do you do with all the people you save? You must have trunks full." Even the newlyweds feel that they can outsmart the Old Irish Catholic pastor. There is a good deal of condescension in their final agreement not to tell Father Conroy that they've earned a shot at stardom in Florida and that they really didn't lie to him because "he gets such a big charge out of forgiving people."

Director Leo McCarey proved even slower than Bing Crosby in understanding how dated his formulation of the Hollywood catechism had become. Catholicism was entering a period of cataclysmic change, a change that would soon be reflected in films, when director McCarey tried to reset *Going My Way* in China and to transform St. Dominic's parish into a missionary outpost overrun by the Red Army. *Satan Never Sleeps* (1962), released in the first year of the Vatican Council, mingles politics, romance, and religion in an untidy and unsatisfactory way, and results in a film almost as unpalatable as Father O'Banion's (William Holden) much maligned Irish-Chinese Stew.

Director Leo McCarey's fanatical anti-Communist zeal has its effect on every frame of *Satan Never Sleeps;* McCarey makes the vituperation of Senator Joseph McCarthy, the prototypic anti-Communist Catholic, seem tame by comparison. McCarey's yellow hordes of communist villains spend all their time shouting political slogans, desecrating churches, destroying hospitals, burning books, terrorizing nuns, stealing food, raping peasants, humiliating the elderly, machine-gunning parents, and torturing priests. Their reign of terror is such an endless nightmare of ignorance, sadism, and anarchy that all the old priest (Clifton Webb), who has spent twenty-five years in the missions, can hope for is that they "roast in hell." To make sure that everyone understands that all Communists are bad and that the Cold War is worthwhile, director McCarey introduces an English-speaking Russian addicted to snide comment and violence; this grotesque martinet condemns his Chinese minions for being "too soft" on religion. Even Colonel Ho San (Weaver Lee), the leader of the Chinese marauders, can't stand this worm from the Kremlin, so he defects, embraces Catholicism, and spirits the woman he raped, their child, and the priests to Hong Kong and a world where "a son and father can talk freely." To snatch victory from seeming defeat, McCarey has Ho San explain to the priests that their official expulsion "is a proof of your success and their fear of you."

Intertwined with all this rabid propaganda, there is a very silly love story in *Satan Never Sleeps.* A village girl (France Nuyen) idolizes Father O'Banion and vows to marry him; when he protests on the basis of his vow of celibacy, she casually suggests that if he were to become a Protestant minister, everything would be fine. In one particularly saccharine sequence, she leaves a bell by his bed so he can summon her for lovemaking. Needless to say, he knocks the bell over by accident and is misunderstood by both the girl and by his fellow missionary, who exclaims that "In all my years, I have never encountered a priest like you. You have entered a new dimension to the priesthood." Eventually this love interest only serves to make Ho San's rape of the girl more dastardly. As in Victorian fiction, this one act of rape results in a baby boy, who melts Ho San's heart and starts him on the road to Catholicism, capitalism, and Hong Kong.

Meanwhile, the two priests are acting out their own roadshow version of *Going My Way*. Scene after scene of their encounters rework incidents in the original film. O'Banion's attire, his informality, his purported romance, his temper, and his execrable cooking all distress the older priest. By the end of the film, however, the crotchety missionary must admit that O'Banion has "been of some help" and that he's even developed "a sort of reserved fondness" for the young prelate. A measure of this fondness comes when the sickly old priest sacrifices his life so that the others in his escape party can survive.

Surprisingly, the religious issue in *Satan Never Sleeps* gets pretty muddled. For all his desire to laud his Catholic martyrs, Leo McCarey seems troubled by the pacifism Catholicism implies. McCarey doesn't have time to develop the idea of just wars and other such theological niceties, so he just has the unregenerated Ho San slap ex-Marine O'Banion hard enough, often enough, and insultingly enough, until O'Banion puts aside principle for a second and delivers a devastating blow to the solar plexus. At first, the old priest is elated, shouting out his approval, "Congratulations! If ever a blow was delivered on behalf of the Almighty . . ." but just then O'Banion interrupts, 'Was it, Father?" After some sober reflection, both clerics see the error of their ways. They lament the "big black mark" that will come from "a church resorting to violence against an officer of the Red Army," and they agree that if "the Church had come first" O'Banion would have controlled his temper. Because this scene plays so poorly and the whole tenor of the rest of the film is so rabidly anti-Communist, it's hard to believe that anyone—especially Leo McCarey—could have wanted Father O'Banion to turn his cheek for more insults and blows. McCarey has such clear problems with these special responsibilities of priests, that Robin Wood's argument in his article "Democracy and *Shpontanuity*: McCarey and the Hollywood Tradition," published in *Film Comment* (January 1976), is quite convincing. According to Wood, the film is "riven with internal ideological conflicts" and "Catholicism is shown in almost as unfavorable a light as Communism." The value most affirmed in *Satan Never Sleeps*, Wood correctly asserts, is "democratic individualism" and not monolithic orthodoxy.

Religious orthodoxy proves the most difficult feature of Roman Catholicism for Hollywood to picture accurately in its catechism. The commitment to something "One, Holy, Catholic, and Apostolic," the fixity of dogma, the bold assertion of Papal infallibility in matters of belief, and the abiding reverence for centuries of tradition make Catholics unique and difficult to portray. This difficulty is especially marked when Hollywood deals with the clergy, and the problems go far beyond Production Code structures. To suggest the differences between Catholicism and Christianity at large, between Holy Orders and ordination, between priest and minister, Hollywood usually depends on one of the three major vows of Catholic religious orders—poverty, chastity, or obedience—as a focal point to explore the Catholic *Weltanschauung* and the gestalt of rectory and convent. Poverty, chastity, and obedience serve as Hollywood's keys to this separate kingdom, a mystical domain at once American and Catholic, a vineyard in this world but not always of this world. Hollywood's image of the mysteries of faith usually begins with a vision of a Catholic cleric renouncing the material trappings of this earth, foregoing the pleasures of the flesh, or submitting to the discipline of God's will.

The most sweeping clerical renunciation of worldly wealth comes in Michael Anderson's hyperbolic *The Shoes of the Fisherman* (1968), a film almost as overstated as it is long. This bombastic recasting of Morris L. West's simplistic best seller features Anthony Quinn as the pious cleric Kiril Lakota, who is ransomed from the Gulag Archipelago, rushed to Rome to receive his *biglietto*, then seated in Conclave when the pope (John Gielgud) dies unexpectedly. During the vote, Kiril's gruff, tenacious sanctity and his luminous humility mark him for election as the first non-Italian pontiff in four centuries, Pope Kiril I. In a comic-strip style summit meeting with the Russian premier (Laurence Olivier) and the Communist Chinese Chairman Peng (Burt Kwouk), Kiril averts a famine-induced Sino-Soviet nuclear war by pledging all the Church's resources to the alleviation of hunger. Back at Saint Peter's Square, Pope Kiril thrills the world and silences doubters when he declares that the Roman Catholic Church will use its land, buildings, and works of art for "the relief of our hungry brothers." None of this dramatic renunciation of wealth occurs in West's original novel, and it clearly seems designed to balance the endless tracking shots through ornate chapels, fabulous art galleries, and lavish cathedrals of the Vatican, all the detailed reenactment of elaborate ceremonies, and the many closeups of luxurious Church vestments. Kiril sacrifices all this glorious legacy and all the wealth it represents to feed his brothers; Kiril's rediscovery of the Church's sacred duty is affirmed when a once dissenting cardinal poignantly avers Kiril's authority and wisdom: "This is Peter and I stand with him." For those sympathetic to Catholicism, Kiril's sweeping gesture provided one more image of a Church that transcended the trappings of liturgy to embrace the creed of charity, "the shoes of the fisherman." Less sympathetic viewers probably agreed with Renata Adler in her *A Year in the Dark* that this religious epic was "daring and almost anticlerical" in its finale. In Adler's vision, when the pope gives everything to the poor and embraces poverty, ". . . its effect on screen seems intended, almost inevitably, to make you think, why not?" This problem of divergent reactions haunts any recitation of the Hollywood catechism. Where some see prayer, others see foolish babbling. Where Adler sees a repudiation of the real Church in an idealized vision of a fictional pope, others find a glorification of Catholic social action in a cinematic hyperbole.

One purposeful ambiguity in *The Shoes of the Fisherman* deserves note. Actor Oscar Werner brings Germanic charm, boyish enthusiasm, and dramatic intellectual anguish to his portrayal of the physically ailing Father David Telemond, a theologian under investigation for heresy. Telemond's life and predicament are clearly a commentary on the works of Pierre Teilhard de Chardin, the Jesuit philosopher-scientist-theologian whose book *The Phenomenon of Man* was all the rage among Catholic intellectuals. At one point in *The Shoes of the*

Fisherman, Father Telemond even describes his theology in what could easily pass for a simplistic summary of the real Teilhard de Chardin's work: Telemond rhapsodizes about a great becoming, in which man is thrust by evolution towards a new perfection with "the cosmic Christ." The actual Teilhard de Chardin and his "Christ who is to be" was recognized around the world as the inspiration for the *Aggiornamento*, the renewal to universal Catholicism, which the Vatican Council hoped to bring about. In this context, it is interesting that while Pope Kiril loves and protects Telemond, choosing him as his secretary and turning to him for advice, Kiril the man finds in Telemond's work "very little of the Christian faith as I know it" and Kiril's Papal Commission rules that his teachings on good and evil are full of "omissions and grave errors." This intriguing plot line is terminated rather than resolved when Father Telemond dies from a cerebral hemorrhage and the question of his orthodoxy becomes less pressing than the impending Sino-Soviet showdown.

Most questions and complications in films about Catholic priests, their vow of poverty, and the Church's material assets are less cosmic, vexatious, and intellectual. Normally Hollywood films picture the Church as needing material things to do its good deeds, focusing on an impoverished priest or two doing the best they can to keep the wolf away from the door and the poor in their parish fed. Many small films work interesting variants on this theme. Michael Curtiz's *Trouble Along the Way* (1953), for example, manages to combine the plight of Saint Anthony's College with football and John Wayne. This sentimental mélange of social workers, little girls, eccentric clergy, and football action, chronicles the misadventures of a college rector (Charles Coburn) whose superiors in the Province instruct him to balance the books or close the school. In his desperation, he convinces a shady ex-professional football coach to build a profitable sports program; Wayne obliges, but breaks every recruiting rule in the book, bringing the "trouble" to this collegiate version of *Going My Way*. When Saint Anthony's manages (with the help of an obliging Cardinal) to schedule games against Notre Dame, Villanova, and Holy

Cross, Wayne laments, "Couldn't he have booked one Protestant school for a breather?" Wayne's dishonest tactics are eventually repudiated, and the contrite college president reminds the coach that you can't save Saint Anthony's by "destroying what it stands for." The money-conscious superiors in the Province also rethink their tactics, reaffirming their commitment to intangible values beyond "the mentality of the cash register," and they reassure Coburn that it "would be a great shock not to hear your annual report of a deficit" at Saint Anthony's. *Trouble Along the Way* makes an endearing virtue of the impracticality of the religious life. The college president likens himself to the old chapel bell in his final speech, a bell which is "picturesque but not very useful." Just then the chimes almost confound him by ringing right on time, but, in a wonderfully evocative visual, this timely chime is undercut by the erratic motion of the hands on the clock which eventually fall down and cease to function. There seems to be as much chance of that clock working as there is of the president ever balancing the books.

Director Irving Pichel's *The Miracle of the Bells* tries to intertwine the traditional theme of a poor pastor (Frank Sinatra) in an impoverished mining community with an exposé of publicity stunts and Hollywood hype, but the script by Ben Hecht, based on a best-selling novel by Russell Janney, quickly bogs down in sentimentality and tears. The casting of Frank Sinatra as the parish priest does suggest, however, that the Roman collar was becoming an important costume for male peformers; the cassock was emerging as another Hollywood icon like spurs, a policeman's cap, an army uniform, or a trench coat. One put on a particular posture, demeanor, and code of ethics with each, and each performance in this costume became a reinforcement of a cinematic tradition. Cowboys leaped to their saddles and twirled their guns, soldiers hovered in foxholes but automatically jumped on live grenades, cops were always eager for a chase, and priests were good-hearted fellows, quick with prayers and handouts, always giving and rarely getting. More and more beginning actors, like Gregory Peck in *The Keys of the Kingdom* (1944), discovered that the path to Hollywood

122

stardom often involved some time in the Catholic missions. Actually, Frank Sinatra's performance of a frail man—who, though he loves beauty and loves God, is being crushed by a world of ugliness and suffering all around him—is one of the highlights of *The Miracle of the Bells*. He cannot make audiences ignore, however, the implausibilities in the plot nor the crass exploitation of Saint Joan, Christmas Eve, moving statues, and mysterious fatal ailments. *The Miracle of the Bells*, it should be recalled, prompted James Agee to declare himself "the founding father of the Society for the Prevention of Cruelty to God."

The theme of priests and money, of clerical piety and earthly power, did generate one truly distinguished Hollywood film, however, an understated masterpiece that renders both God and Caesar their due, director Ulu Brosbard's *True Confessions* (1981), based on John Gregory Dunne's novel, and co-scripted by Dunne and his wife, Joan Didion. Every element in this film bespeaks its quality, including the exquisite photography of Owen Roisman, the evocative music of Georges Delerue, and the transcendent performances of the three principal actors: Robert DeNiro as Father Des Spellacy, the young monsignor who "looks like a leprechaun and thinks like an Arab"; Robert Duvall as his jealous brother Tom Spellacy, a hardnosed cop driven by the fear that his mother loves Des more; and Charles Durning as Jack Amsterdam, a celebrated "Layman of the Year," who hasn't been to confession in twenty years. Robert DeNiro and Robert Duvall, two of the most accomplished and exciting contemporary screen actors in Hollywood, bedazzle with their energy, verve, and intensity. Their dialogues reek of anguish and self-recognition; the two brothers look deep into each other's souls as they relive a harrowing tale of betrayal and redemption, plumbing it for its lessons and revelations. Theirs are death-bed confessions, for Des Spellacy's "arteries to the pump are shot," and he has only a little time left to reveal God's Providence to the troubled Tommy. Tom has come to beg forgiveness for ruining his brother's clerical career years ago; from Des, he hears a tale of spiritual illumination he may be too blind to fully understand.

Every major element in *True Confessions* shimmers in the

glittering ambiguity of the title, part pulp magazine, part Catholic sacrament, and part human compulsion. Basically the movie is a tabloid thriller about a "virgin Tramp" with "a nice set of Charlies" and a rose tattoo on her buttock who drifts into porno films and prostitution only to meet the wrong "john," a sadistic freak who saws her in half and rams a "candle up her joy trail." But the film is also a series of true confessions, in restaurants and in confessionals, in police stations and in churches, in whorehouses and rectories, during which a priest discovers real sanctity, a cop learns about retribution and redemption, and a hypocrite learns about scandal and true religion.

Father Des Spellacy's discoveries pinpoint some basic contradictions in an American priest's life. Des seems the perfect prelate, the cardinal's right-hand man on the way to his own cappa magna. The worldly monsignor knows everything and everybody in town. When Jack Amsterdam offers the diocese free land for a school in his Rancho Rosa housing development, this shrewd analyst warns Cardinal Danaher (Cyril Cusack) that this magnificence comes only because the city has already refused to build a school there, so families aren't buying, and the banks are getting ready to foreclose. He suggests that the Church ask Amsterdam to build the school for them at his cost. Des puts a price tag on everything, from golf balls to a "Layman of the Year" award; his dishonest associates pay in cash for a cloak of Catholic respectability. This young prelate has his regular day at the country club, his regular lunch at a posh restaurant populated by insiders and the movers and shakers of the city, and his regular after dinner speech delivered with a flair any politician would envy.

Yet Father Spellacy knows something is wrong with his life. His radio Rosary Hour doesn't satisfy his spiritual needs. His emptiness propels him to Father Seamus Fargo (Burgess Meredith), an irascible Irish priest who denounces Des to the Cardinal time and time again as a "better accountant" than priest. Des knows Father Seamus has something to teach him, and almost compulsively, he makes all his sacramental confessions to this gruff, ornery traditionalist who proudly barks that young priests "whose eyes twinkle all the time" are morons. Father Seamus tells the truth, but Des recoils from it. In Seamus's eyes, Des's error is clear: "You like power. You like to use power, I told you that." The young priest constantly takes refuge in the same rationalization: "How could you get things done without using it? Our business is saving souls and we need a place to do it. Somebody's got to take care of that." When Des asks his confessor, "What other choice is there?" Father Fargo counsels: "I don't know, but don't sell yourself short."

Des's spiritual regeneration and final absolution result, paradoxically, from a combination of Seamus's example and Tom's frenzied attack on the hypocrisy of a Church that toasts whoremasters and power mongers. Seamus is eased out of his parish for his belligerent nonconformity; the Cardinal wants young priests "who will do as they're told—for the good of the Church." Seamus chooses to end his days in a remote rundown chapel deep in the desert, a purgatory on earth where the temperature hovers around 100° and the cars whiz by on the highway without a second's hesitation.

Father Spellacy chooses that same unlikely haven after his brother files a spurious murder charge against Jack Amsterdam, an indictment that results in scandalous newspaper revelations about Catholic notables consorting with whores, pornographers, and murderers. Tom's motives for exposing this corruption are quite complex. He knows the actual killer was a sadistic freak who died in a car accident, but he wants to degrade Jack Amsterdam, a hypocrite who deals as much in human flesh as he does in construction. Amsterdam seduced the young murder victim, Lois Fazenda (Amanda Cleveland), an innocent who came to the city full of poetry and seeking stardom, and turned the girl (whose favorite movie was *Going My Way*) into the Virgin Tramp. When he was bored with her, Amsterdam passed her along to all his friends, then introduced her to the sleazy film producer who killed her. In part, Tom also wants revenge on Amsterdam for corrupting him; years ago, Tom was the police bagman collecting protection from Amsterdam's whorehouses. Tom wants revenge for Brenda, too, one of Amsterdam's old madams, who finally felt she had run out of options and killed herself. But Tom also wants to hurt his brother Des, his mother's favorite, by proving once and for all that this priest with racketeer friends is just as human and just as flawed as he is; Tom wants to expose Des as just another bagman, with a Roman collar instead of a police shield. Tom's police partner understands fully that this arrest and the scandal it will precipitate is Tom's nasty way to "settle an old score," and he berates Tom for his stubborn desire to besmirch Des: "What are you trying to prove? That he's just like you? He is; he's your brother."

When the two brothers meet for the last time in the desert, the scandal has run its course and the radio drones on about a visit to California by President Kennedy, the Catholic President. Now their confessions to each other are all that matter. Tom, a laconic man, struggles to tell his dying brother that "It's all my fault, Des, every bit of it. I'm sorry." Des absolves Tom by sharing his deep consolation in his discovery of the real meaning of priesthood, the love of God: "No, Tommy, you were my salvation. You made me remember the things I had forgotten. I thought I was someone who I wasn't." Des has even picked out his burial plot, right next to the unassuming tomb of Father Seamus Fargo. The worldly Tom still doesn't seem to understand Des's peace; it is a consolation he cannot comprehend, and he mumbles on about being "out here in the middle of all this sand" and "one place being as good as another" for a corpse.

True Confessions comes closer in this sequence than does any other Hollywood treatment of a Catholic priest to defining the conflict between an active life in the world and the interior spiritual life. Father Des Spellacy's torturous journey from youth to experience, from city to desert, from a position of high esteem to anonymity, from affluence to abstinence, from pleasure to penance, embodies his spiritual voyage from darkness to light, from damnation to salvation.

An opposite odyssey is presented in *Monsignor*, easily the trashiest movie of 1982. New York reviewers were in their sardonic glory with this bloated monstrosity: Vincent Canby of the *Times* saluted it as "the perfect junk movie for our time," and Kathleen Carroll of the *News* proclaimed it "one of the most embarrassing fiascos in the movie business . . . a prime example of Hollywood schlock masquerading as a bold work of art." As Ms. Carroll notes, in screening rooms everywhere anonymous wags were searching for more appropriate titles, ranging from "The Godfather Goes to the Vatican" to "Father Dearest," a reference to another failed work, *Mommie Dearest*, by the same producer, Frank Yablans, and the same director, Frank Perry.

Monsignor presents the clerical career of Father John Flaherty, a super-priest played by none other than superman himself, Christopher Reeve. Father Flaherty, heeding the call of his archbishop to "Let all evil thoughts die in you so that you may enter into a new life," proves more successful killing Nazis as an army chaplain (a violation of the Geneva Convention) than expunging his worldly desires. This immoral worldliness elevates him immediately to the top echelons of the Vatican, where his mentor, Bishop Walkman (Robert Prosky), is full of advice on the "real life politics in the Vatican." With cunning akin to that of Shakespeare's Polonius, Bishop Walkman gives the young priest on the rise an assortment of *do*'s and *don't*'s: "Smile," "Keep your mouth shut," "Follow orders," "Remember you're an American," and "Don't be a wise ass." Finally Walkman sums it all up in one sentence for Father Flaherty: "You've got faith, brains, and balls; use them discreetly."

Girded with these new cardinal virtues, Flaherty fills the Vatican coffers with money from the black market, links the Curia to the Mafia, and allows his gangster friend to wager Vatican millions in the world currency market. For his diversion, Father Flaherty seduces a comely Carmelite postulant, Cara (Genevieve Bujold), who's happy to doff her clothes and swill champagne with the handsome Lieutenant Finnegan (one of Father Flaherty's disguises and aliases) on their very first date. As she tugs her clothes off in an R-rated striptease, Cara warns her lover that "God gave me a strange gift. He made me attract love affairs that quickly become disastrous"; this is Cara's rationale for being a postulant so long and not a novice. Her superiors don't think her reasons for leaving ordinary life are "profound enough." Cara's big clothed scene in *Monsignor* comes at a papal audience when, amidst all the pomp, she sees Father Flaherty in his other disguise, the robes of priesthood.

Eventually the bubble bursts, and the currency market collapses. Flaherty's associates are assassinated by the mob, and he begins an exile at a monastery, where he is supposed to find silence, meditation, and the Holy Spirit. But there will be no illuminations for Father Flaherty; *Monsignor* is too much a soap opera to end off in an isolated chapel with discoveries of inner peace. The stewardship of Vatican fortunes goes to a new pope, one of Father Flaherty's closest intimates, who welcomes him back and embraces him as "My Son," while the film glides to its final image, a closeup of the cross. Cheap ironies, dramatic reversals, and sensational revelations are the stuff *Monsignor* is made of. One cannot fail to lament with the trade reviewer for *Variety* to see the talents of outstanding screenwriters like Abraham Polonsky and Wendell Mayes go so sadly awry. As the reviewer suggests, these veteran writers seem to have overlooked a "most gaping fundamental flaw," the total lack of motivation for Father Flaherty's becoming a priest in the first place. In *Monsignor*, Flaherty is, as the *Variety* reviewer notes, "a totally worldly adventurer interested in carousing and sampling all the pleasures of the flesh. In no way does he seem like a man of God, and matters are hardly helped by Reeve's smirking, upstart manner. . . ." *Monsignor*, a sleazy, tasteless film, insults religion and clergy without providing any real insights. Its excesses finally call attention to themselves, and its artificiality, exaggerations, and sniggering tone become ridiculous. Frank Perry, once a director of real importance, was rapidly becoming a camp hero. Audiences everywhere brought metal clothes hangers to *Mommie Dearest* and pounded them on their seats as Faye Dunaway ranted and raved as an overblown Joan Crawford. If *Monsignor* had stayed in distribution long enough to make it to neighborhood screens, it too could have been an occasion for audience participation. It is the kind of movie sophisticated audiences love to hate.

Junk movies like *Monsignor* prompt audience participation in altogether different psychic ways, as Vincent Canby notes in his essay review of the film for the *New York Times* "Fresh Fodder for Reflection: the Savory Junk Movie" (31 October 1982). Canby postulates that "Junk movies tell us a lot more—more effectively—about the secret fantasy lives of Americans." Carmelite postulant Cara's bare breasts in *Monsignor* and her erotic frolic with a handsome priest do have an importance far beyond this one sleazy film. The Catholic clergy's renunciation of carnal pleasures and of marriage have long made priests and nuns objects of curiosity and sexual fantasy. Father Andrew Greeley, writing in *TV Guide* to prepare American audiences for the miniseries based on *The Thorn Birds* by Colleen McCullough tried to explain the endless procession of handsome clerics in perfervid romantic fiction, and his remarks aptly summarize the key elements in Hollywood's treatment of the priestly vow of celibacy: "Celibate priests are fascinating men precisely because they are men of mystery. They live different lives from anyone else because they are committed to a reality beyond this world. Their oddness is appealing, repellent, strange, and intriguing." Equally revealing, however, is *TV Guide*'s treatment of Greeley's article. Its cover for the 26 March 1983 edition features a priest in a clinch with a beautiful young girl and the caption "Priests, Sex, and *The Thorn Birds*"; in the index, the title given to the article is probably Greeley's original title, "Priests, Celibacy, and *The Thorn Birds*." Priestly celibacy in Hollywood or in televisionland virtually always becomes priestly sex, guiltily realized or disastrously suppressed. As *TV Guide* observes in bold type under its ornate illustration to Greeley's text, quoting the author out of context, "Do Priests Fall in Love? Of Course They Do." Anyone who has ever been to an American movie about priests and young women would have known that answer.

One of the more interesting examples of this overworked theme comes in Richard Boleslawski's *The Garden of Allah* (1936), based on Robert Hitchen's 1904 novel about a romance between a Trappist monk in flight from his abbey and a romantic English woman seeking an answer to life's mysteries in the desert. *The Garden of Allah* had been filmed before in 1916 and with Alice Terry in 1926, but it was Marlene Dietrich as Domini Enfielden and Charles Boyer as Brother Antoine who helped to create the definitive version in 1936. This David O. Selznick production with music by Max Steiner and Oscar-winning color photography by W. Howard Greene enraptured contemporary audiences with its star-crossed lovers, exotic locales, and portentous dialogue. Dietrich sulks regally around desert and marketplace, cloister and cafe, dramatically lamenting that "No one but God and I know what is in my heart." Boyer, for his part, squirms in libidinal agony as a belly dancer gyrates before him; makes conscience-stricken, clandestine visits to churches; and breaks into a cold sweat when he weighs his "right to live and right to love" against his "most sacred vows." Eventually, the lovers accept their fate, yield to the inviolability of his vows, and do "what must be done." Boyer returns to the monastery, assuring Dietrich that their marital bliss will come in heaven: "We are believers. We know this can't be all. It can't be. We know that in that other world—the real and lasting world—we'll be together forever." He further confuses whatever issues of *eros* and *caritas* that remain by assuring her that "in knowing your love, I have known Him." Dietrich, for her part, looks distraught and beautiful; assures him he will always be in her heart; and, as Max Steiner's version of the heavenly chorus swells in the background, she flees his arms, imploring her driver to "Drive faster, drive faster." *The Garden of Allah* made few pretenses at realism, but even producer Selznick was distressed by Marlene Dietrich's fixation on fashion, coiffed hair, and perfect makeup. One of his famous memos asked Director Boleslawski to remind Marlene that "Surely a *little* reality can't do a great beauty any harm."

When Hollywood tried to bring more "reality" to its images of priests and the vows of chastity in post-ratings-board dramas about a post-Vatican Council Church, the priest invariably bedded the girl (more likely than not a nun) and left the Church. A prime example of this modern cliché is Daniel Haller's *Pieces of Dreams* (1970), based on William E. Barrett's novel *The Wine and the Music*. Father Gregory Lind (Robert Forster) just cannot cope with his conservative superior Father Paul Schaeffer (Ivor Francis), and he is irresistibly drawn to a social worker with the body of a high-fashion model, Pamela Gibson (Lauren Hutton). Fears of excommunication cannot deter Father Lind, and he becomes Hollywood's image of the thousands of priests who left the Church between 1960 and 1980 over issues like abortion, birth control, divorce, homosexuality, papal infallability, and institutional inflexibility. Hollywood's visions of these upheavals invariably centered on celibacy. In the nineteenth century, Lawrence Fuchs notes in his *John F. Kennedy and American Catholicism*, Americans had a "pathologically prurient interest" in the "alleged sexual proclivities" of nuns and priests; and almost any work dealing with the lurid details of sex life in convent, cloister, or rectory was assured popularity. This prurient interest seemed almost as strong in the U.S. during the 1970s and 1980s. Broadway offered dramas like *The Runner Stumbles, Agnes of God*, and *Mass Appeal*, and Hollywood quickly gobbled up the rights for screen versions.

Stanley Kramer's Hollywood version of Martin Stitt's *The Runner Stumbles* (1979) typifies these dramas in its literate style, claustrophobic sets, and its pontificating tone. Catholicism is on trial in these works, and the civil charges are mere masks for more covert charges that the creed has lost touch with God, with life, and with humanity. Father Rivard (Dick Van Dyke) in *The Runner Stumbles*, pastor of Holy Rosary Catholic Church in a town where even the mines are closed, wants desperately to believe that "The Church makes order out of absolute chaos," but somehow he can never finish his long overdue treatise on "Augustinian Order: An Examination and an Extension." Sister Rita (Kathleen Quinlan) is all art, poetry, song, and charity on the surface; and although she can fool other people into thinking that "I'm a person who is a nun, not a nun who used to be a person," she knows that she joined the order to fill the void in her life and has been pretending to be religious without any sense of fulfillment because the only love and affection she ever knew was with the sisters.

Neither Father Rivard nor Sister Rita has found solace in their vocation. Despite all their hysteria, however, and their crushing sense of guilt, and their burning desire to hold on to religion and their vows, the two tortured souls do eventually seem very close to finding fulfillment in each other. But just when they declare their love, a scandalized housekeeper kills Sister Rita; the feeble-minded but devout woman believes the demon who seduced a priest must be destroyed, the serpent of concupiscence must be crushed. Rivard is left alone, shattered. He leaves his order and rails at Rita's graveside to God himself: "What kind of God are you? I loved her. I loved her. I don't have the Church anymore. What do you want from me? Tell me." The little boy who walks over at this moment and hails Rivard with a "Peace be with you Father" gets an automatic *"Pax vobiscum,* James," from the defrocked pastor, but the end of the film is far from Hollywood's standard of happiness. The solution to the dilemma of Father Rivard and Sister Rita involves too much *deus ex machina* and too little of God's peace to be consoling.

Some of the most disquieting portraits of priests in the Hollywood catechism concern the question of obedience and submission to "Holy Orders." Not every celluloid cleric may be as involved in the niceties of Augustinian Rule as Father Rivard, but many priests in films do become entangled in a conflict between their conscience and the Church's rules or between their responsibilities to promulgate Church dogma to their congregations and their own desires to remain popular with parishioners. Priests often are pictured as whiplashed by both pressures: a hierarchy that demands one course of action and a constituency that requests a different ministry.

In Mervyn Le Roy's *The Devil at Four O'Clock,* for example, Spencer Tracy has travelled far from the optimistic days of *Boys' Town* to a weary outpost in the south Pacific; old age, alcoholism, and despair wrack Father Matthew Doonan, a short-tempered Irishman who has been ostracized by his congregation because he founded a lepers' hospital on their island. The judgment on his last flock comes when a volcano destroys the tropical paradise they wanted to exploit for tourism; Doonan dies in the explosion, but not before he has found faith in an encounter with three convicts who accept his hard lessons of charity and self-sacrifice.

The strengths in *The Devil at Four O'Clock* come mostly from

132

Liam O'Brien's screenplay, an adaptation of Max Citto's novel. Father Doonan is no superpriest, immune to the criticisms of the world. When the young priest (Kerwin Matthews) arrives to replace Father Doonan because of the complaints from everyone on the island, Dr. Wexler (Martin Brandt) explains that Father Doonan could not function as a priest "alone with no congregation"; it destroyed him to say Mass for just himself. For years, Wexler explains, Doonan blamed himself and prayed to God, trusted in God, that the islanders would recognize their greed and see the need for charity and his hospital. When the congregation never returned to the Church, this "good man, no saint, but a good man" crumbled and cracked open at the seams, lost his faith, and took to the bottle for consolation.

The volcano which takes Doonan's life will also restore his faith. When he convinces three convicts to help him save his lepers, he promises them a commutation of their prison terms; they all die heroically, but not before he leads them each to salvation. The film makes it clear that Doonan's own charisma has redeemed these outcasts and enabled them to "steal Heaven." One prisoner even explains, when asked about accepting that God stuff so fast, that while he may not yet believe in all the traditional dogma, he does believe in Father Doonan because Doonan "takes responsibility" and "behaves the way God oughta behave." Doonan, for his part, acknowledges that these three unlikely heroes have restored his own faith: "Priests are human. We fail just like anyone else. . . . I stopped speaking to God for a long time. That's when you three came along. I had lost my faith in God, and you fellows gave it back to me."

Director Otto Preminger tried to outline a similar movement from doubt to faith, from qualms about obedience to a certainty of vocation in his sprawling version of *The Cardinal* (1963), an adaptation of Henry Morton Robinson's best-selling novel, but as Raymond Durgnant suggests in his *Films and Feelings*, Preminger managed to create a "mountain-size framework" which generates "a mouse-size thought." Catholic historian John Cogley in his *Catholic America* describes a Catholic propensity to "ghetto culture," an unquenchable urge to have a Catholic position on 'just about everything under the sun, which leaders of the Church were usually eager to make abundantly clear." Preminger in *The Cardinal* seems intent on bringing Catholic "ghetto culture" to the screen. In three hours of screen time, Father Stephen Fermoyle (Tom Tyron) manages to skip wildly from Boston to the Vatican to Georgia, to Vienna, bouncing from one ministry to another, from one mentor to another, from one lover to another, and from one moral dilemma to another. Father Fermoyle's action-packed life was meant, according to Preminger in an interview Gerald Pratley reprints in *The Cinema of Otto Preminger*, to picture "a hero moving from immaturity to maturity"; Father Fermoyle's final enthronization as a cardinal celebrated, Preminger declared, "a mature man who knows how to combine his own feelings with the laws of the Church, and to live within the Church without giving up his own personality or hurting his conscience." If this is the intended pattern, the script—which Preminger claims in *Preminger: An Autobiography* was totally rewritten by Gore Vidal, though credited to Robert Dozier—bogs down terribly in all its details of Catholic "problems" in the twentieth century. The film seems rather out of breath, racing to show its vision of "Abie's Irish Rose" in Boston, a clinically dated dilemma over craniotomy in a soap opera-inspired hospital, a truncated "diary of a country priest" in L'Enclume, a brief encounter in Vienna, a few cross burnings in Georgia, and the rise of the Third Reich in Vienna. In all these feverishly assembled vignettes, loaded with decisions to be made and actions to be taken, *The Cardinal* struggles, as Raymond Durgnant notes, "to see all sides of the question, so disturbing everybody a little and nobody much."

A similarly contrived ambivalence mars Stanley Kramer's *Guess Who's Coming to Dinner* (1967), a so-called "problem film" about interracial marriage that quickly obscures any problem by making the white reticence to embrace this black son-in-law incomprehensible. The handsome Sidney Poitier is the most eligible bachelor in the world with his medical degrees, charm, and United Nations credentials. Kramer equivocates about the religious position on racism by introducing a Catholic monsignor (Cecil Kellaway) as a friend but not a pastor to the non-

134

Catholic family in question. This artifice avoids the question of conformity to doctrine; Father Ryan isn't functioning in any official capacity when he teases Matt Drayton (Spencer Tracy) and Christina Drayton (Katherine Hepburn) about their hypocrisy. James Baldwin was quite sensitive to this trickery when he made the fine distinction that in this film the priest seems "truculent" but not "militant." The question is of more importance than it may seem. Andrew Greeley quotes several studies in his article for *The Secular City Debate* (1966), edited by Daniel Callahan, to show that "the strongest predictor' of an attitudinal change on race was how a respondent answered the question, 'Did your minister (or priest) preach in the last several months on racial justice?' " Father Stephen Fermoyle could carve out stirring victories against the Grand Dragons, Hydras, Furies, Exalted Cyclops, and King Kleagles of the Klan in *The Cardinal* and Monsignor Ryan could chuckle self-righteously in *Guess Who's Coming to Dinner*, but their lessons were circumscribed by context. During the critical years of civil rights activism and of clerical civil disobedience, Hollywood did little to show Catholic officials joining the march on Washington or protesting with Dr. Martin Luther King in Selma. The Hollywood catechism found it easier to hum "With God on Our Side" when the battle was over or when the moral problem was less controversial, like hospitals for children with Hansen's disease.

Sometimes Hollywood pictured problems of clerical obedience to Church teachings that were too esoteric for non-Catholic audiences to appreciate fully. An important example of this involves a highly acclaimed Catholic director, Alfred Hitchcock and his neglected mystery *I Confess* (1953). Hitchcock told Francois Truffaut years later, in an interview reprinted in the French director's homage, *Hitchcock* (1967), that *I Confess* should never have been made because its plot hinged so heavily on the confidentiality in the sacrament of Penance. As Hitchcock observed: "That's the trouble with *I Confess*. We Catholics know that a priest cannot disclose the secret of the confessional, but the Protestants, the atheists, and the agnostics all say, 'Ridiculous! No man would . . . sacrifice his life for such a thing'." *I Confess*, based in part on the actual case of Father Anthony

Kohlmann, features some of Montgomery Clift's most accomplished acting as Father Michael Logan, a priest trapped in a web of blackmail, murder, and coincidence. Circumstantial evidence links the priest to a crime committed by the sexton of his church, but Father Logan cannot clear himself without implicating the man and breaking the seal of the confessional. For Catholic critics like Claude Chabrol and Eric Rohmer, major filmmakers themselves, Hitchcock is working with a most important theme; as they write in their extended analysis *Hitchcock: The First Forty-Four Films*, "We find ourselves confronted not only with an allegory of the Fall, but with a tragic situation worthy of that adjective and having as its mainspring . . . the traps of sacrifice and sainthood." Catholic critic Neil Hurley also finds much to discuss in *I Confess* in his survey of "The Cinematic Transfiguration of Jesus." For Hurley, Logan is an "explicit Christ Figure," whose walk through the streets and alleys of Montreal is a veritable *via crucis*, forcing audiences to trust "the images" and not the "external evidence." Most audiences and critics, however, were annoyed by the mechanical plot contrivances of *I Confess*, which depends on a rather poorly explained blackmail threat concerning a night Logan spent in the country with a married woman before he was a priest, a blackmail scheme instigated by the very same man the sexton kills. The narrative gets so convoluted that the conclusion involves a jury verdict of innocence, a judge's declaration of "total disagreement" with the verdict, a courtroom audience's hissing and catcalls of "Take off that collar," a mad chase, a clumsy shootout, and some death-bed revelations. Even the last shot of the film seems contrived, with Father Logan cradling the killer in his arms in Pieta-like fashion and finally completing his absolution of the killer with a blessing and an *"Absolvo te."*

Hitchcock's attempted glorification of confession and of a priest's devotion to its forms might well be contrasted to Burt Reynolds's vitriolic and blasphemous caricature of the priesthood and deathbed confessions in his frivolous and dour comedy *The End* (1978). The twenty-five years between Hitchcock's mystery and Reynolds's comedy witnessed cataclysmic changes in the Catholic Church. Malachi Martin titled his history of the evolution of Catholicism in this period *The Decline and Fall of the Roman Church* and posited that "the most surprising and puzzling development in the last twenty years has been the sudden and undoubted decline of the Church of Rome in its ecclesiastical organization and ideological unity. The sheer suddenness of this development makes the decline catastrophic." In his sometimes simplified but always interesting account, Martin lists a host of issues beleaguring the Church, including abortion, contraception, divorce, secular education, homosexuality, euthanasia, and genetic engineering; and he catalogues a chorus of dissatisfied parties, including women who wanted to be priests, priests who wanted to be married, bishops who wanted to be regional popes, theologians who claimed absolute teaching authority, Protestants who claimed equality, homosexuals and divorced people who demanded recognition, Marxists bewildered by political conservatism, and traditionalists angered by liturgical changes. Sociologist Andrew Greeley foreshadows much of this analysis in his *Come Blow Your Mind With Me: Provocative Reflections on the American Scene*, in which he speaks angrily of disintegration and confusion in American Catholicism. The American Church, Greeley charges, could not assimilate all the new ideas of the sixties, and as the "old values failed and the old structures crumbled, even those who had introduced the new values were not sure of themselves or in what direction they were both going." The result, Greeley opines, is an American Church in "a double crisis" with both beliefs and organizational patterns in great disarray.

Sensing this upheaval in the American Church, pollsters were everywhere, and Leo Rosten summarized their findings in his encyclopedic *Religions of America: Ferment and Faith in an Age of Crisis*: "a majority of Catholics in America no longer seem to share the hierarchy's moral and spiritual vision." Three quarters of Americans, Rosten reported, thought religion was "losing its influence," and over eighty percent of the Catholic laity favored married priests; a majority of Catholics thought the Church would have to change its position on divorce, birth control, and abortion. Less than half attended Mass regularly, and less than a third had been to Confession in two months. Even fewer believed in papal infallibility.

This restiveness in the laity came at the very same time vocations to the priesthood were falling. In the ten years after the Second Vatican Council, almost 5,000 diocesan priests, one eighth the total, resigned from the priesthood. Almost a third of all nuns left religious life, and more than half the seminarians ceased their studies. Hundreds of seminaries shut down. By 1983 there were fewer than 12,000 students studying for Holy Orders, and only about half of those were expected to make final vows. The average age of a Catholic priest had risen to 56; by the year 2000, statistics suggested, the average would be 73.

Burt Reynolds makes black comedy out of the upheaval in American Catholicism in *The End*, picturing a Church in utter disarray. Reynolds, the number one male star at the box office in the late seventies and clearly the most widely acclaimed champion of American machismo since John Wayne, is a most unsympathetic critic. The sacrament of Penance as seen in *The End* is undoubtedly the most extended smutty joke in the whole of the Hollywood catechism. Reynolds's humor is much more sacriligious and profane, for example, than any of the celebrated icons of post-Production-Code anti-clericalism like Woody Allen's priest who hawks Holy Smokes in *Bananas* (1971), or Joan Rivers's mechanical pope in *Rabbit Test* (1978); it lacks the lunatic touch of Marty Feldman's bug-eyed, money-hungry friar in *In God We Trust* (1980) and the surrealistic detachment of Mel Brooks's Busby Berkley inquisitors in his *History of the World, Part I* (1981). Reynolds's humor seems bad taste for the sake of bad taste, a kind of smart alecky naughtiness that delights in dragging serious topics down to its sophomoric level.

Sonny Lawson, the protagonist in *The End* (played by Burt Reynolds) has a mysterious blood disease and is told he's dying (contemporary gossip columns had headlined Reynolds's mysterious ailment the year before), so Sonny sets off, like a cut-rate contemporary Everyman, to find the meaning of life. Quite by accident, since such a modern Casanova and cynic as himself would never intentionally seek solace in a church, Sonny drives by a church, and, on a lark, dashes in for some of that old time religion. Inside he finds the "bare ruined choirs" Gary Wills writes so poignantly about, a large cathedral with few worshippers (all immigrants or old), where Latin hymns have given way to an Hispanic rhythm. Screenwriter Jerry Bolson and director Reynolds undoubtedly wanted to remind the audience that given the demographics of American Catholicism, the Mass should be said in a different vernacular, Spanish, and offered mostly in old age homes.

Walking past dozens of empty pews, Sonny finally discovers a boy kneeling alone, an Anglo who seems out of place in this environment, and he asks him, "Excuse me, kid, do you know where I can talk to a priest?" Robby Benson turns around, with a twinkle in his eye and a smile on his face that needs no Father Seamus Fargo to decode. This kid is a moron, who cements the impression of imbecility by tripping over a kneeler and banging against the pew as he mutters, "I'm a priest." Sonny cannot believe it, so the boy apologizes, "Really, I am." Prolonging the joke so that even his most dim-witted fans can appreciate the satire in the fact that the priesthood is reaching this low in the barrel, the bewildered Sonny remains incredulous and hesitant, "Oh no, I believe you—I think." Father Benson (Is the use of the actor's name an insider's joke?), flustered at his inability to even look adult, let alone mature and religious, digs for his wallet, assuring himself and Sonny that his driver's license does say he is a priest.

Sonny is so non-plussed by Father Benson's youth and general demeanor that the questions turn to the priest's qualification, not Sonny's problems. Quizzed about his vocation, Father Benson says he entered spiritual life directly after high school and that his calling to Holy Orders was "more like a whisper, nothing like you see in the movies." Sonny is hardly consoled, and his fidgeting prompts Father Benson to suggest that he wait for the older priest who will be on duty in the afternoon, Father O'Hara. The big recommendation for Father O'Hara is that "He's old—he's old" and that "A lot of people say he looks just like Barry Fitzgerald, you know, kindly with a little twinkle in the eye." Sonny can't wait, though, and when Father Benson finally figures out how to open the confessional door, the parody of the Sacrament begins. Sonny has mortal sins to confess, not the "crummy little sins" seminarians practiced with to perfect their confessional manners. Father Benson is obviously flustered; he has had little experience in the confessional and even less in the world. Sonny begins by admitting that he hasn't been to confession in twenty-two years, ever since "I discovered fu-- [he stops himself] sex." Father Benson muses, "That's when we lose a lot of them." By now, Father Benson is getting rather warm under the collar at the anticipation of some licentious revelations, some candid peeks at the life of a grownup, and he removes his Roman collar and plays with it for the rest of the scene. Within seconds, he's engaging in his own version of Browning's "The Soliloquy of the Spanish Cloister," confessing that every day he questions if he made the right decision becoming a priest. Father Benson feverishly explains that "Becoming a priest can keep a person from committing a sin, sure, but it can't keep a person from, from lusting after women, craving alcohol, dreaming of screwing a business partner, contemplating going out every night." Every imagined sin drives poor young Father Benson into such a delirium of desire that even Sonny cannot stand it and interrupts the agitated cleric: "This is *my* dime, not yours."

Though it hardly seems possible, the humor takes an even darker turn. When Sonny inquires if "jacking off" is still a sin, Father Benson, at this point so overwrought that he's talking more to himself than anyone else, murmurs something rather incoherently, but the more cogent parts of his babbling ask, "Is that still your biggie?" and admit, "It's mine." This young priest, mired in dreams of bigger sins but given only to self-abuse, cannot contain himself when Sonny confesses that he has spent much of his married life "copulating around"; when Father Benson urges him to quantify his acts of adultery and Sonny replies about 200, Father Benson explodes in envy: "Jesus Christ —two hundred times! Wow! All right!" The scene ends at this point, largely because it has no place more to go. Sonny drifts off, unshriven, to seek therapy in other places.

Having dismissed the Church as a serious sanctuary for modern man and besmirched its clergy with images of immaturity and imbecility, Reynolds dismisses them as childish masturbators not worth another thought.

The End is remarkable for the savagery of its attack, but it does mirror an unsettling tendency usually more associated with Hollywood's images of nuns than with images of priests. Hollywood often finds it difficult to treat nuns like mature human beings. In the Hollywood catechism, nuns are often denigrated by the very process of idealization. They become so holy and so unworldly and so impractical and so pious and so virginal and so innocent and so bubbly and so cheerful that they cannot be taken seriously. There are few serious movies about conventual life, and religious sisters are much more likely to be found in B movies, relegated to the ranks of orphaned children, cripples, shaggy dogs, and wounded animals, or off singing, flying, or strumming a guitar. Films about nuns rarely attempt to make audiences think; their sagas are normally melodramas designed to make audiences feel and feel and feel. Hollywood uses nuns' vows as focal points; poverty, chastity, and obedience remain the major issues. But the complications in pictures about nuns are less likely to be serious considerations of the active versus the spiritual life, belabored forays in guilt and repression, or essays about social upheavals, and are more likely to be miraculous, heartwarming tales of financial miracles worked against all odds, stirring musicals about uneasy novices whose temporary vows evaporate and free them to love their benefactors, or comedies about nuns who doff their old habits to join a youthful revolution go-going around a juke box and sitting in at the local courthouse, draft board, or chemical plant. The Hollywood catechism especially favored the preliminary vows of novices and postulants; with temporary vows, movies could have their moral cake and eat it too since religious issues could be enjoined without involving everlasting difficulties.

Films that begin with a few impecunious nuns adrift in a strange culture constitute a prime and lively staple of the Hollywood catechism. A strange accent, even stranger clothing, a modest demeanor, a vow of poverty, and a set of rosary beads clearly signal any regular popcorn muncher that the impossible will soon transpire, that hard hearts will melt, that construction will run way ahead of any earthly schedule, and that good works and tearful gratitude will abound.

Henry Koster's *Come to the Stable* (1949), based on a story by Clare Boothe Luce and starring Loretta Young (Sister Martin) and Celeste Holm (Sister Scholastica) in roles that garnered them Oscar nominations, provides a sterling example of this genre. These French refugees from the Order of Holy Endeavor unleash what the local bishop calls "an irresistible force loose in New England." They've come to build a hospital *ex voto* to thank America because its troops spared their abbey in an artillery barrage during the Second World War. Signs are not propitious for their success: a gangster owns the land they want and the local wealthy playboy doesn't want a hospital disturbing his rustic retreat, but these two nuns have all they really need, a supply of Saint Jude medals. *Come to the Stable* is another of Hollywood's homages to this "patron saint of the impossible," for it turns out that the gangster's son was killed near the French convent, and, of course, his tearful father will gladly give up his hideout for a hospital if the sisters just put a stained-glass window in their chapel for Luigi Rossi, Jr. And the wealthy song writer just needs a jolt of good old Gregorian Plain Chant to see the errors of his ways. Pad this mixture out with a black butler (Dooley Wilson) who clumsily sneaks support to the nuns, a sister who once played tennis in the French Open, a mother superior who drives like a demon making U-turns onto the front steps at St. Patrick's Cathedral, Damon Runyon gangsters who use their Saint Jude's medals to break the bank at gumball machines, some picturesque Christmas masses, spirited cake sales, and an eccentric local artist who specializes in religious tableaux, and one has the kind of corn Hollywood usually associates with nuns. Reactions to such silliness vary, of course. In a dialogue at the chancellory, the bishop in *Come to the Stable* muses aloud that "Sometimes the blind faith of such sisters is really . . ."; as he gropes for a word, his monsignor prompts, "Disturbing," only to be rebuffed by

142

the bishop's final choice: "Indeed not—sublime, magnificent."
Most film critics leaned more to the monsignor's point of view.
Ivan Butler in his survey *Religion in the Cinema* reflects the
worldly consensus: "The most caustic criticism [of religion in
films] probably does less harm to the object of its attack than
this sort of pink-lampshade cosiness."

Ralph Nelson's *Lilies of the Field* (1963) also suffers from
excessive cuteness and belabored improbabilities. This time the
nuns are German, and what they want is a chapel. Their reluctant savior comes in the person of a black Baptist, Homer
Smith, played by Sidney Poitier in an Oscar winning performance. Homer and Mother Maria (Lilia Skala) are engaged in a
war of wills, and he has about as much chance of winning as
his pocket-sized Bible has of outweighing her heavily illustrated
Gutenberg version. Homer's chapel soon rivals the famed "miraculous staircase" in Santa Fe, drawing the whole community
together in recognition of their common spirituality. Even the
nuns discover their affinity for Negro spirituals. The whole
project has such an infectious, Pentecostal energy that Nelson
concludes with an "Amen" rather than the normal "The End."
But while the film surely is winning in its way, there is the
undercurrent present that the nuns would be lost without a
Protestant male laborer to save their vision and realize their
dream. Alone they are holy but ineffectual. It takes Homer to
do the heroics; the nuns are "inspiring," probably the most
notable characteristic of the sisterhood in the Hollywood catechism. In American cinema, movies about nunneries tend to
be inspirational pictures reeking of Ivan Butler's aptly phrased
"pink-lampshade cosiness."

Even Hollywood's treatment of nuns troubled by earthly
desires and uncomfortable with their vows of chastity usually
seem rather ethereal and unmitigatedly romantic. Genevieve
Bujold's nudity in *Monsignor* dramatically reversed a long tradition; usually even a postulant's problem with chastity was
more discreetly presented. Thus, in the most commercially successful depiction of nuns ever filmed, *The Sound of Music* (1965),
everyone could sing about "the problem with Maria," since it
clearly had more to do with open meadows, curlers under her

wimpet, and girlish high spirits than any longing for a brave, handsome military commander like Baron von Trapp. When the plot crystallizes, and Maria admits that she "could hardly breathe" in the Baron's presence, the Reverend Mother quickly brings everything back to a spiritual plane: "Maria, the love of a man and a woman is holy, too. You have a great capacity to love. What you must find out is how God wants you to spend your love." Maria has made no final vows, and the shrewd abbess sends her off to "live the life you were born to live." From then on, the film is a merry chase across the Alps, full of "Edelweiss," "The Sound of Music," and "My Favorite Things." The von Trapps climb every mountain while buffoonish Nazis bumble around like hapless stooges and errant schoolboys. The whole German high command seems little match for a few giggly nuns who steal the alternator and battery cables from their jeeps and then run to the mother superior to confess their mischief. A film like *The Sound of Music*, with its popular success, exists, as George Amberg notes in his introduction to *The New York Times Film Reviews*, "virtually outside the realm and reach of aesthetic valuation" since "the reviewer-critic can merely observe, but not affect, the phenomenon of the triumph of the worthless." Hollywood's inspirational story of heartwarming nuns and the optimism of Richard Rodgers and Oscar Hammerstein's musical provided just the tone audiences wanted and kept business churning at the box office. *The Sound of Music* proved so immensely successful that many Hollywood cognoscenti would agree with James Pratt, who said in an interview for Mike Steen's oral history, *Hollywood Speaks*, that this Julie Andrews extravaganza, which defied critics and studio prognosticators alike by dominating the box office, marked the beginning of a new era for the studios, a period marked by an almost suicidal urge to make a "blockbuster."

Most Hollywood treatments of nuns and their commitment to chastity work on considerably smaller canvases and play to much smaller audiences than *The Sound of Music*. Usually, in fact, the moral conflict is presented within the conventions of some well-known genre, like the historical epic, the war film, or the Western. More often than not, nuns who break their vows will be caught up in some dimly recollected foreign war like Carroll Baker in *The Miracle* (1959) or adrift on the Western prairie like Leslie Caron in *Madron* (1970), and divine intervention will kill off the lover and resolve the problem, leaving the nun to return to her God. A major variant on this formula is the nun who isn't really a nun but merely a woman disguised as a nun. Clint Eastwood's *Two Mules for Sister Sara*, for example, begins with the graphic rape of the "dance hall" performer, Sara (Shirley MacLaine), who, after lengthy visuals of her nude predicament, scrambles into the robes of a nun. Her rescuer, Hogan (Clint Eastwood), tells Sister Sara that he cannot forget "the first time I saw you and you were almost naked." His longest speech in the film, in fact, is a rhapsody of his desires: "I cannot forget that [nudity], sister, my beautiful sister. Every night when we bed down together next to each other, I think of you that way. I want to reach out and touch you and hold you and feel you." Hogan only has to wait until they're in the clear and laden with treasure for Sara to shed her habit and join him in the bath. *Two Mules for Sister Sara* never violates, however, the tradition of the nun who is beyond the call of the flesh. Dressed as Sister Sara, MacLaine behaves like the perfect cliché when she's in Eastwood's presence. When her dauntless hero probes her vocation with leading questions like "Haven't you ever wanted to be a whole woman, have a man make love to you, and have children?" even a dance hall girl knows the catechism by heart, and she answers, "I've chosen a different way of life." Undeterred, Hogan presses the issue and asks about those "feelings I'm sure God gave every woman." The phony Sister Sara is quick with her response, "Well, we're human, of course; when we get those feelings, we pray until they pass." Convinced of her piety, Hogan laments, "I sure would have liked to meet up with you before you took to them clothes and them vows." Hogan's elation is unbounded, and Eastwood's image is saved when the cowboy discovers it's only "them clothes" he has to worry about and that Sara is just another belle from the saloon.

Male image frequently plays as large a role as religious restraint in Hollywood's vision of the temporary vows of chastity. Studios often display an almost perverse desire to demonstrate that their Romeos can compete with God himself and to prove that, as the Beatles once claimed, their entertainers are more popular than Christ. An early example of this—the 1930 melodrama *Call of the Flesh*—pits the matinee idol charms of Ramon Navarro, his Valentino-like hypnotism, against an older brother's demands that his sister renounce the world and fulfill her mother's dreams by entering the convent. Maria, a novice at the Convento de Saint Augustin in Seville, is enraptured by "what sweet songs the world makes," and Navarro's renditions of "Questo o quella" from *Rigoletto* and "Vesta la Giubba" from *I Pagliacci* carry the day. To calm any fears that Church laws are being violated, there is a mother superior on hand to remind Maria's brother and the audience that Maria has taken no vows and that "the Church asks nothing of her children but duty . . . to ruin the lives of two children who might serve in other ways is no part of God's plan." Even contemporary reviewers noticed how mechanical this benediction was, and the critic for the *New York Times* chided the work of writers Dorothy Farnum and John Colton, opining that "the happy ending cannot be said to be accomplished by any show of skill."

Director William Graham's *Change of Habit* (1969) makes its lack of skill evident from the very beginning, yet this project, Elvis Presley's thirty-first film, does manifest the Hollywood fixation of having a nun, in this case Sister Michelle (Mary Tyler Moore), faced with the choice between her calling to be the bride of Christ and the attraction she feels for altruistic Dr. John Carpenter (Elvis Presley), who runs a clinic in the poor section of town and relaxes by singing in a rock and roll band. All of Elvis Presley's films project a rather frivolous, slapdash air, and *Change of Habit* is no exception. However, the core of the plot does revolve around the nun's shifting allegiances, and the last sequence literally flashes back and forth between Elvis and the cross as Sister Michelle ponders her choice. The film ends with no decision: Mary Tyler Moore is sitting in the chapel, Elvis is rocking the cathedral to some rockabilly music posing as a folk mass, and the credits roll on. The audience knows, however,

146

that Mother Superior has told Sister Michelle, "You've got to choose the kind of love you want, physical love or the love you can find only through prayer. From my own experience I can tell you nothing is more painful than no decision."

For all its frivolity, *Change of Habit* does capture some interesting resonances of the turmoil American Catholicism was facing during the Viet Nam years. Its opening sequence, for example, a sexually charged production number, has three young nuns stripping off their protective habits and putting on sheer underwear and clearly feminine garb as they prepare for ministry in the ghetto. Sister Barbara (Jane Elliott) remarks that she never realized how safe she felt in the habit until she took it off. Sister Michelle reminds her colleagues that the habit was just a symbol of authority like a policeman's uniform, but she also stresses a militant feminism in their experiment: "We've got to escape the old order, got to be accepted as women first, then as nuns." The people they minister to have some trouble with these new female invaders; they mistake the three attractive strangers for new prostitutes on the beat. And Father Gibbons (a diminutive Fitzgibbon?), the Irish priest who has spent forty years in this ghetto only to discover a sad truth about his parishioners, "They're Catholics, but it's too bad they're not Christians," denounces these "secret agents" from the Little Sisters of St. Mary. Interestingly, Father Gibbons (a rich portrait by character actor Regis Toomey) focuses most on the unseemly sexuality of "nuns in silk stockings" and "flapper skirts on the brides of Christ," and swears they will get no help from him in promoting a carnival for the patron saint of Puerto Rico, a man who, Gibbons opines in an interesting ethnic riposte, "never drove a single snake" out of the island. By the end of the film, even the bishop retreats and demands that the nuns take their makeup off and put their habits on. Sister Barbara refuses and leaves the order, telling Sister Michelle: "I haven't given up the fight. I've organized political action committees. We've scored two victories already, and now is no time to stop." Sister Michelle is very sympathetic to Barbara's choice, and although she has yet to give Dr. Carpenter her answer to his plea that they "try to find a way" to express their love, she has made it very clear that although she is a nun, she is "still a woman," and he has reminded her quite forcefully that she can get a "release."

Questions of leaving the religious life and accepting more worldly roles are often posed in Hollywood's treatment of nuns. The vow of obedience a nun took was always viewed as subject to dispensation. Once a Trappist, always a Trappist might be an axiom in *The Garden of Allah*, but once a Sister of Mercy always a Sister of Mercy was not a corollary. One wonders if this was a reflection of Hollywood's male chauvinism or a recognition of the sacramental nature of a priest's commitment, inculcated by numerous religious technical advisers. Frequently, the issue was clarified by clearly identifying the wavering sister as a novice or postulant, but there are numerous cases of nuns who seemingly have taken final vows but are still troubled by questions of obedience to Church dictates.

One comedy that deals with such a nun's bridling at Church disciplines, James Nelson's *Where Angels Go, Trouble Follows* (1968), veers quite disturbingly from serious issues to the most adolescent humor and clumsy slapstick. This hastily assembled sequel to a forgettable but popular vision of teaching sisters and their troublesome prepubescent charges, *The Trouble with Angels* (1966), aspires to more than the boarding school antics of its hackneyed and saccharine original. While the sequel does pause to show the "angels" (the heavy irony is indicative of the level of humor) cavorting in the dark funhouses and on the death defying roller coasters of Dorney Park, sneaking through the dormitories of a boys' college, taming steers and cowboys at a rodeo, and all lathered up when they get caught in a car wash gone haywire, the film also introduces as its protagonist Sister George (Stella Stevens), a comely feminine version of the dragon-killing cult hero of leftist causes everywhere, who has been sent to test the mettle of the mother superior of St. Francis Academy for Girls (Rosalind Russell), self-proclaimedly "the one dragon she isn't going to slay."

Sister George and Mother Superior banter about some of the most important issues confronting the contemporary nun, and the disproportion between the issues they raise and the filmic presentation of them would be most disconcerting if it were not so clear that the release print of *Where Angels Go, Trouble Follows* is little more than a rough cut, a hurried assemblage of widely disparate material in a desperate attempt to string some episodes together in the loosest of picaresque structures.

Sister George does get the chance, however, in the midst of the caravan's stop at St. Francis' School for Boys, to tell its rector, Father Chase, that the Church could well become totally irrelevant to the modern world if it sits around waiting for "hardening of the arteries." For her part, Sister declares: "I want to make a meaningful contribution with joy. If I conduct myself like a twentieth-century woman, I don't want to be patronized by people who say 'Look at that darling little nun; she's just like a real person'." Sister George proudly affirms that in her nun's role she must remain "a real person with flesh and blood, feelings and convictions." Challenged by Father Chase's assertion that this makes her vocation look like little more than inspired social work, Sister George quickly responds that "Faith, like love, should be shared, not hoarded. There's a new wind going through the church." Overhearing this exchange, Mother Superior, in the snide style Rosalind Russell brings to the role, rues the young nun's activism, curling her lip and sardonically suggesting that "A new wind is fine, but we can do without a typhoon."

Mother Superior, as portrayed by the arch Miss Russell, has a disconcerting propensity for nasty asides and bitter humor. In a key exchange, when the nuns leave the hospitality of Saint Francis, she etches a most unsympathetic portrait of a nun too sure of her own virtue. Sister George calls to Father Chase, suggesting they meet at a pray-in, and Father Chase jokingly calls back, "I'll see you there, I'll be wearing black," a humorous comment on the uniform of the new anti-war avantegarde. Mother Superior whispers that their clothes should be "more like red," but when asked by Father Chase, "What did you say," she retreats to the tidy white lie, "I said I'm ready to go." When Sister George calls out, "I'll pray for you" and Father Chase responds, "I'll pray for you," Mother Superior again secretly relishes her sanctimoniously condescending aside, "Somebody better." Miss Russell's unfortunate decision to assume this acerbic and shallow tone for the mother superior undercuts what could have been a most interesting scene later in the film when Sister George lashes out at Mother Superior for wallowing in the whole "nun mystique." Sister George, embittered by Mother Superior's charges that she has trivialized her calling by descending to the girls' level where she is, her superior allows, "a smashing success," cannot restrain her natural anger; and the young nun denounces her superior for enjoying her smug holiness: "You enjoy the whole nun mystique, don't you, Mother? Because it places you above the ordinary, because it makes you something special?" This explosion prompts Mother Superior to warn Sister George most ominously that she shouldn't say things she might regret and to admonish her pointedly that "There are also some truths you had better face, Sister." Sister George is shaken and asks if the question Mother intends is "whether or not I'm fit to be a nun?" Mother Superior assumes all her ecclesiastical stature when she solemnly but emphatically replies, "I didn't pose the question, Sister; you did, and now you answer it."

The question of Sister George's vocation quickly blurs, however, into more antics on the set of a Western film with Milton Berle making a cameo appearance as a vain director and the girls caught up in a chase reminiscent of Mel Brooks's *Blazing Saddles*. Mother Superior finally retreats a bit and tries to assure Sister George that she's reconsidering her authoritarian and provincial viewpoints and will turn the authority at St. Francis over to someone else if she cannot escape the mentality of a cloister. Sister George is moved by all this and exclaims, "Damn, I can't find my handkerchief," only to hear Mother Superior retreat to authority again when she admonishes, "Sister, please watch your language." Screenwriter Blanche Hunalis tries to salvage what she can of her focus on the tension between the new nun and the old mother superior in a final voiceover by Miss Russell, who, in mellowed tones, explains that eventually the nuns "got involved in caring and doing, for there is a good stiff breeze blowing through Saint Francis and we have changed some of our habits." The need for this mechanical exposition says much about the lack of artistry in the film. Obviously the producers felt that any film with some more of the Angels' antics, a few glimpses of contemporary upheavals in the convent, and enough slapstick action would satisfy the undemanding audiences who made St. Francis Academy viable at the box office. It provides one more example of the propensity of Hollywood producers to treat nuns as the stuff of B movies, constantly surrounding these religious figures with a raft of broad sentiments, comic pratfalls, and easily assimilated adventures.

Perhaps the best indication of how the Hollywood catechism trivialized nuns is provided by the one exception to this long tradition, Fred Zinnemann's *The Nun's Story*, the finest film about the Catholic religious life ever made, a masterpiece in its conception and its execution. This Jewish director's adaptation of Kathryn C. Hulme's book, scripted by Robert Anderson, plumbed the vows of poverty, chastity, and obedience, revealing in the words of the book's original European title how constantly nuns live *Au Risque de se Perdu (At the Risk of Damnation)*. Its account of the events that led to a day when, in the words of the film's ad copy, "the nun called Sister Luke under special and extraordinary circumstances was forever released from all her vows" resulted in, in the words of that same ad, "the most gripping and dramatic personal story of the decade," a truly remarkable cinematic achievement filmed in Belgium, Italy, and Africa, but "mostly in the conscience of a young and beautiful girl."

Director Zinnemann knew he had unusual material to work with and important things to say. A small measure of his dedication to authenticity in his project can be found in an important chapter of Jack Vizzard's *See No Evil*. Mr. Vizzard, the religious technical adviser for the film and a longtime official at the Production Code Office, provides many of the details of Zinnemann's dealings with the Sister of Mercy in Ghent and suggests a good number of the difficulties Zinnemann faced in assuring a balanced view of conventual life. Zinnemann himself is quoted by Gordon Gow, in *Hollywood in the Fifties*, as viewing that objectivity and authenticity as central to his purpose in the film: "We all felt that we should remain objective and not favor one side or the other in the case . . . in *The Nun's Story* it was essential for us not to make a comment—to leave the comment to the audience."

Zinnemann's respect for his audience and for the talents of his star Audrey Hepburn permeates *The Nun's Story*. Few compromises are evident; Zinnemann relies on consummate artistry to carry the day. His visuals are stunning, complex, and challenging; the film is hauntingly evocative and intriguing, with bedeviling juxtapositions between everyday life and an eternal order. Hepburn's performance is all subtle nuance; a shift in posture here, a quick movement this way or that, a change in vocal cadence, a downcast eye, an unexpected hesitation, all speak volumes about the torture in her soul. Rarely has an American film so depended on one person's portrayal for its energy and subtlety. Before this film Audrey Hepburn was recognized as a popular star; *The Nun's Story* established her as an accomplished actress.

The most fascinating sequences in *The Nun's Story* treat the transformation of Gabriel, the dutiful daughter of an eminent surgeon, into a daughter of the Church, Sister Luke. Warned by Mother Emmanuel (Dame Edith Evans) that the life of a nun "In a way is a life against nature . . . a never ending struggle for self-perfection," this postulant enters a severe training program which brings her face-to-face with the many difficulties implicit in vows of poverty, chastity, and obedience. Gabriel has especial difficulty with pride and stubbornness, and her story contains agonizingly intimate questions about appearance and motivation, about doing T. S. Eliot's famous "right for the wrong reason." The religious life, the film makes clear, must be centered on more than good deeds; at the core of the nun's spiritual life there has to be a self-effacing love of God, a charity almost beyond human comprehension. As Mother Emmanual warns all the postulants, "The sacrifices that are required of us are bearable only if we make them with love. Just as in the world we can do impossible things with a glad heart for a loved one, so it is with us." The nuns in *The Nun's Story* are clearly called to do the impossible, cheerfully, for the love of God.

Zinnemann's *A Nun's Story* begins with a shot of a cathedral reflected on shimmering and moving water, and this visual suggests his central metaphor of the religious life. Sanctity, he convincingly demonstrates, is not one bold action, one heroic test, that once accomplished stands as a cathedral for all to admire; sanctity must be reflected instead in every moment of life and glimmer in everything the religious person does. *The Nun's Story* doesn't celebrate a bold martyrdom, but instead pictures the everlasting struggle nuns face to tame their desires for small material comforts and for personal recognition, to avoid the temptation to be vain about their appearance or their achievements, and to bind their will to God's will. Author Hulme had described the life of the cloister as being made up of "an infinity of small things that had an importance here undreamed of in the outside world." To satisfy the demands of the order, she wrote, "each simplest act, each hidden intention had to be cut to the Rule and polished and perfected like the tiny stones of a mysterious mosaic"; the mosaic had as its controlling pattern the formation of a nun. Fred Zinnemann translates this mosaic into the drama of his film. The nun's story demands that its audience appreciate the rigors of the grand silence, the impiety of daydreaming, slammed doors, or spilled milk in a convent, the seriousness of fasting and abstinence, the renunciation of fashion and of mirrors, the need to confess impure and uncharitable thoughts, the call for a constant examination of conscience, the value of public confession and charitable accusations, the necessity for public penance in chapel, public humiliation in refectory, and the judicious use of the penitential scourge in the privacy of a nun's room. The religious life, Zinnemann shows, is not an extension of life in the world. If Gabriel truly desires to be transformed to Sister Luke, she must embody the biblical injunction Zinnemann cites over his image of that cathedral reflected in the water, "He that shall lose his life for me, shall find it," and she must embody the mother superior's words, also spoken over that shimmering image, "Each sister shall understand that on entering the convent she has made the sacrifice of her life to God."

Sister Luke has a good deal less trouble doing charitable service in the world, comforting others in body and soul, than she does curbing her own inner demons. Her missionary work in Africa serves the community well and brings plaudits from the world, but it leaves her even more torn by doubt and despair. Sister Luke has the physical courage to overcome tuberculosis, to face privations, and to confront terrorists, but she constantly seems enmired in the same spiritual problems. The wise doctor at the hospital in the Congo (Peter Finch) diagnoses not only the small summit lesion on her lung, but he also perceives the blot on her soul. Sister Luke will never fit the mold of her order, he warns her, and the tension between what she is as a human being and what she wants to be as a religious sister may destroy her: "You're what's called a worldly nun—okay for the public, ideal for the patients. But you see things your own way." Her order, he knows, can never stand for this: "You stick to your own ideas. You'll never be the kind of nun your convent expects you to be. That's your illness; the tuberculosis is a by-product."

Reassigned to a hospital in occupied Belgium, Sister Luke finds stunning confirmation of this surgeon's analysis in her reaction to the Nazi occupation. Her physician father is killed by Hitler's forces and her brother is trapped behind the lines, but even in these dire circumstances Sister Luke knows her duty lies in the principled neutrality of her religious order. Sisters have been instructed not to take sides in the worldly conflict and not to engage in any activity for the Allies or against the Nazis; the order is above the fray and desires only that "the orderly life of the religious community is not disturbed so that our hospital work may go on without confusion." Sister Luke yields to the call of the Underground, however, repudiates her vows, and trusts to her own conscience, not the strictures of her special vocation. Inevitably, practical actions of the resistance and the spiritual devotions of the order clash, and Sister Luke must choose. The choice between her hatred for the Nazis and her desire to be a devoted bride of Christ merely culminates Sister Luke's other struggles to renounce the world and embrace heaven, to subject her individual will to the discipline of

154

a religious institution dedicated to seeking absolute harmony with God's will. As Sister Luke finally explains to her Mother Superior in a scene notable for its intelligence and restraint, all her problems with her vocation, various as they seem at first, come down to one central issue: "obedience, without questioning, without inner murmuring, perfect obedience as Christ practiced it." Sister Luke no longer feels capable of sustaining this obedience; she cannot control her inner voice, her conscience asking, "Which has priority, it or Holy Rule?" Since she cannot quiet her doubts, Sister Luke asks to leave. Mother Emmanuel asks her to think longer about the decision, but this religious superior never moves from her central concept that to be a nun and to stay in the convent, "the religious life must be more important to you than your love of man."

Film critic and priest Neil P. Hurley may not agree with this statement of Catholic creed, having retitled his text *Theology Through Film* a less forbidding *Toward a Film Humanism* for its mass market edition, but he is quite correct in his observation that the final scene in *The Nun's Story*, a sober and restrained treatment of the laicization of Sister Luke, reveals Zinnemann's artistry at its peak. When Sister Luke has completed the necessary paper work in triplicate and returned her keys, she is told she must take back the dowry her father contributed when she entered the order. With cold efficiency, the nuns then direct her to a solitary cell in an isolated wing where street clothes await the former nun. Everything is mechanical, including the doors; when Gabriel is dressed, she pushes a button, and a door swings open on what Hurley aptly describes as "a forlorn alley." She walks off, and Zinnemann holds the shot for what seems like an eternity; the effect, Hurley observes, generates "the same mingled emotions of compassion and admiration felt in the key scenes of *Pickpocket* and *High and Low*."

There is no doubt that Zinnemann's accomplishment in *The Nun's Story* places him in the pantheon of world directors alongside Akira Kurosawa and Robert Bresson. Zinnemann may have felt the constraints of the Production Code Office in the person of Jack Vizzard, and he surely, as Murray Schumach details in *The Face on the Cutting Room Floor*, faced the meticulous scrutiny of the Legion of Decency, but his essential vision remained untouched. Zinnemann told Gordon Gow that one of the popes he had admired had called Catholics "spiritual Jews"; sensing the same affinity, Zinnemann attested that in *The Nun's Story* he found a great many things that touched him "very strongly." That passion and not the easy tears of sentimentality fill his screen. He manages to show the deepest quandaries in the spiritual life, to confront the large questions of good and evil that Nazi horrors raise, and still to maintain a glorious image of a mighty cathedral more beautiful for its tranquility in a restless, sometimes chaotic world.

FOUR

The War Film:
god, man, and the bomb

Colonel R. L. Scott, Jr.:   "You sound more like a soldier than a missionary."

Father Mike: "I guess there's not much difference, only in the weapons. We both fight the forces of evil and take the same chances."

Colonel R.L. Scott, Jr.:   "I guess you're right. I've never thought about it that way before. But I'm not exactly a religious guy."

Dialogue in *God is My Co-Pilot*

The onset of World War II marked, as James Hennesey postulates in his *American Catholics*, the beginning of a critical "rite of passage" for the immigrant Church. America had been founded, as Lawrence Fuchs observes, "in part out of a hatred for the Catholic world view," and for the vast majority of Americans well into the modern age, the Catholic Church was not just another Christian denomination, Fuchs notes, but a foreign faith, "a melange of decadence, superstition, corruption, and authoritarianism"; the commitment to popery resembled for these Americans, Fuchs writes, a commitment to "despotism pure and simple." World War I heroics by Catholic troops had done little to dispel these impressions; as late as the early thirties, the Ku Klux Klan still found it easy to attract recruits by denouncing the foreign allegiances of Roman Catholics. The tenor of the Klan's approach, especially in the Midwest, can be found in Robert Coughlan's widely anthologized article, "Konklave in Kokomo." As Mr. Coughlan recalls, the Klan's exhortations focused heavily on fears of the Catholic fraternal order, the Knights of Columbus, whose uniforms and rituals had a militaristic air. The Klan lashed out time and time again at the Knights as crusaders who wanted to put the pope in the White House by force of arms. The rhetoric of the Klan was, Robert Coughlan recalls, quite specific: the Klan asserted that the Knights of Columbus was a secret army that kept "their guns in the basements of Catholic churches—which usually had high steeples and often were located on the highest ground in town, so that guns fired from the belfries could dominate the streets." Despite these bizarre accusations, the propagandistic ravings of the Klan were quite effective. As John L. Thomas reports in his article "Nationalities and American Catholicism," fully one-fourth of the American men in the twenties eligible for membership in the Ku Klux Klan did join.

The abiding American fear of a foreign religious domination meshed with the broadly based cultural xenophobia and a fervent political conservatism to shape an American generation between the two world wars which was intent on preserving democracy by ignoring global issues. President Wilson's vision of a world made safe for democracy yielded to a desire for a country secure in its own democracy. This widespread, quite emotional isolationism created significant problems for the War Department and for a Hollywood pledged to support the war effort. As Sergeant Richard Griffith, who became curator of the film department of the Museum of Modern Art after the war, told Roger Manvell, for his volume *Film and the Second World War*, the task was "to turn the youth of the nation, so recently and so predominantly isolationist, into a fighting force not only effectively trained and equipped but armed too with the conviction that his country's entry into a world war was not only just but the inevitable answer to serious wrongs." In the war years, 1941-45, the film industry of the

the epic

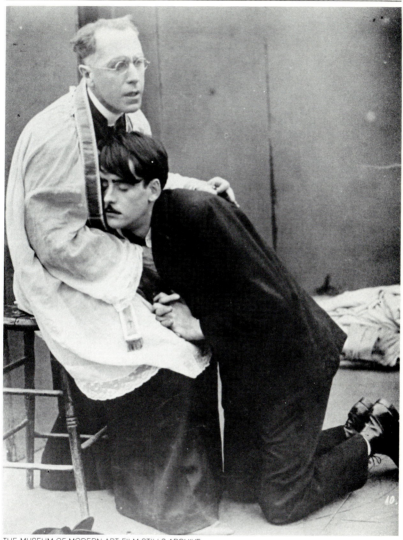

Father Farley (Reverend A. W. McClure) and the
Boy (Robert Harron) in "The Modern Story" of
director D. W. Griffith's *Intolerance,* Wark
Producing Corporation, 1916.

The Catholic martyrs climb the staircase to
the arena, death, and eternal light in Cecil
B. DeMille's *The Sign of the Cross,*
Paramount Pictures, 1932.

Eugene Pallete as Friar Tuck brings comic relief to director Michael Curtiz's *The Adventures of Robin Hood,* Warner Brothers—First National Pictures, 1938.

the crime film

Father Jerry Connolly (Pat O'Brien) and Rocky Sullivan (James Cagney) walk the last mile together in director Michael Curtiz's *Angels With Dirty Faces,* Warner Brothers—First National Pictures, 1938.

Antonio Camonte (Paul Muni), who bears a
clearly cruciform scar, defies the world with
his sister Cesca (Ann Dvorak) in director
Howard Hawks' *Scarface,* Hughes
Production—United Artists, 1932.

Father Edward J. Flanagan (Spencer Tracy)
consults with the mayor of Boys Town
(Mickey Rooney) in director Norman Taurog's
Boys Town, Metro-Goldwyn-Mayer, 1938.

Father Barry (Karl Malden) brings his "Sermon
on the Docks" to the longshoremen in
director Elia Kazan's *On the Waterfront,*
Horizon-American Picture—Columbia
Pictures, 1954.

Marlon Brando as Don Vito Corleone, one of the finest characterizations ever limned on the American screen, in director Francis Ford Coppola's *The Godfather*, Paramount Pictures, 1972.

the clerical melodrama

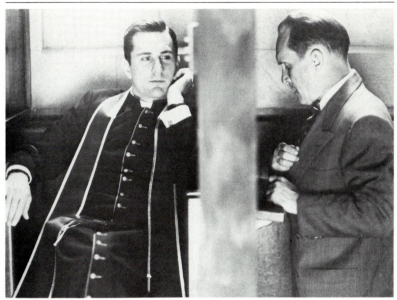

Monsignor Desmond Spellacy (Robert DeNiro)
and Detective Tom Spellacy (Robert Duvall) in
director Ulu Brosbard's *True Confessions,*
United Artists, 1981.

Father John Flaherty (Christopher Reeve) and the young Carmelite postulant he seduces (Genevieve Bujold) in director Frank Perry's *Monsignor,* Twentieth Century Fox, 1982.

An American vision of Children, Church, and Country in director Lloyd Bacon's *The Fighting Sullivans,* Twentieth Century Fox, 1944.

the war film

Catholic mom Lucille Jefferson (Helen Hayes) uses her family Bible to extract an oath of allegiance from her son John (Robert Walker) in director Leo McCarey's *My Son John*, Paramount Pictures, 1952.

Director Robert Altman envisions his own
"Last Supper" in *M*A*S*H,* Twentieth
Century Fox, 1970.

the horror movie

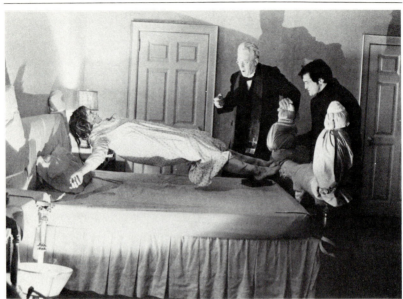

Father Merrin (Max von Sydow) and Father Karras (Jason Miller) struggle with the demon possessing Regan MacNeil (Linda Blair) in director William Friedkin's *The Exorcist,* Warner Brothers, 1973.

the romance

Tony Manero (John Travolta) tries on his
brother Frank's Roman collar in director
John Badham's *Saturday Night Fever,*
Paramount Pictures, 1977.

Diane Keaton as Theresa Dunn in director
Richard Brooks' *Looking for Mr. Goodbar,*
Paramount Pictures, 1977.

United States became a bold propaganda effort. Aesthetics became much less important than patriotism; entertainment less critical than espousal of the proper attitudes and sentiments. All America was to be humming "Yankee Doodle Dandy," and Hollywood provided the song and dance men to lead the chorus; patriots everywhere were preparing to embark for global war, and Hollywood was leading the way with heroes like John Wayne.

The era of global war also saw, John Cogley reports in his volume *Catholic America*, a similar fixation in the American Catholic Church. Catholic parish life in America, he reports, "came to something of a standstill" when young Catholics everywhere donned uniforms and more than five thousand priests volunteered as chaplains. Everything else, Cogley chronicles, was subordinated to a massive war effort. Cardinal Spellman personified the fighting clergyman, assuring troops everywhere, but especially on the front lines, that their battles were God's battles, their flag his banner, their victories his triumphs. American Catholicism, an immigrant faith, seemed intent on showing that its sons and daughters were the most loyal Americans of all, the staunchest patriots, and the bravest warriors. A critical example of this vision of the devout Catholic as super patriot can be found in Lloyd Bacon's *The Fighting Sullivans* (1944), a melodramatic homage to an actual Catholic family from the heart of Middle America, Waterloo, Iowa, who sent five brave, wholesome Irish sons to die in combat on one American vessel, the cruiser *Juneau*, which went down in the South Pacific off the Solomon Islands.

Director Bacon's sentimental account of the Sullivan boys and their progress to sainthood begins in the baptistery of a Roman Catholic Church and ends as they storm the Pearly Gates with their "fighting walk." Bacon forms key sequences from each spiritual milestone; he focuses on the sacraments as the very foundations of the American Catholic's piety. Baptism, Penance, Holy Communion, and Matrimony are everywhere in his hagiography, and his film often seems perilously close to insisting that the sacraments gave the five brothers both God's grace and an unparalleled fighting spirit.

One of their most dramatically interesting brawls comes the very day Al (Bobby Driscoll) makes his first confession in preparation for his first communion the next day. His mother has carefully prepared him for this grand occasion and warns him not to get as much as a speck of dust on his new suit. Uneasy with all this seriousness and with his new clothes, poor "Small Change" hears his brothers synchronized warning whistle as he says his penance at the main altar, and the perenially late youngest son dashes down the aisle to join them in a donnybrook. When Al reaches the heavy wooden doors of the church, he remembers where he is, hesitates for a moment, and then stops to get some holy water, blesses himself, and genuflects in the main aisle. Only with these pious formalities out of the way can he spit in his hands and jump down the church steps into the brawl, new suit and all. The brothers win, despite some rather sneaky rock throwing from the other side and a punch that gives Al a picturesque black eye.

Back at home, the boys' mother (Selena Royle) nurses their wounds and sternly criticizes their actions. She laments the brawling on the eve of a first communion, warning them that "You've got no right to be fighting and brawling in the very shadow of the church." At first she decides not to allow Al to make First Communion, but then she softens, admitting that "It's beyond me and that's a fact." She tells the boys to sneak down the back alley so no one can see the pack of hoodlums she's raised and to make their pleas to Father Francis (Roy Roberts). At the rectory, the smiling priest focuses on the aftermath of the battle, not the fray itself. He is concerned to see that no grudges remain and that the boys are reconciled with their enemies (prophetic concerns for a film coming toward the end of the world war). Assured by the boys that it's all over— "We *won*," they declare, "and that's that"—Father Francis advises them that they can go to Communion "with the best of them" and gives them all some fruit, including an apple with a worm, his comic reminder of Adam's fall and man's imperfections.

Much of the fun in *The Fighting Sullivans* reflects the worm in the human apple. Contemporary audiences had read mournful newspaper accounts of the ultimate fate of these brothers, so their story as told in the film had an *Our Town* sort of charm; all their boyish antics and adolescent crises were constantly being viewed in the context of their tragedy and their heroism. Bacon wisely decides to emphasize their devilishness and their humanity; the actuality of their valor is understood, and their ultimate sacrifice looms softly in every scene. Watching their makeshift raft sink slowly in the pond, for example, foreshadows the end of the *Juneau*, just as the mother's request that the boys swear never to go on a boat again, at least until they've grown up, assumes a poignant irony.

The whole film has a bittersweet mood, as Bacon emphasizes the laughs in crowded bathrooms, strained budgets, and family quarrels. The adventures of the Sullivans mirror a catalogue of family film clichés: daring rides on bannisters, unsuccessful fishing expeditions, mongrel dogs, smoking in the outhouse, first dances, and death-defying races. Even Al's sweetheart is introduced in a romantic fantasy about small talk in the garden, scandalous kisses, and intercepted love letters full of phrases about eyes "like deep blue lakes" and hair "glowing in the sunlight." Wartime audiences took all of this quite seriously; the reviewer for the *New York Times* lauded it as "a fond and satisfying picture" with "a simple and genuine feeling for boys and for Americans as we are."

Catholic patriotism is a given in *The Fighting Sullivans*. The boys' response to the first reports of Pearl Harbor is their familiar signal, a whistled call to combat, and it comes immediately and spontaneously. They caucus only to decide whether it will be Army, Navy, or Marines. When they decide on the Navy, they huddle with their family to get all the crying and carrying on over at once since "we've got to be down there in the morning" to sign up. Actually, the Sullivans aren't given to emotional display, so when Mom announces that she's going to church to light a candle for Jim Bascomb, a neighbor's son who was stationed at Pearl Harbor, the boys announce, "We'll all go." These boys are clearly soldiers of Christ first and their patriotism comes as a corollary to their sanctity. All their ethnicity, especially their Irish temper, become emblems of their assimilation: Sullivan spunk is a face of American daring, Sullivan familial ties a form of American loyalty, Sullivan stubbornness a tribute to American perseverance, and Sullivan blarney and brogue a part of America's poetry. Most importantly, their Catholicism is an equal partner in the emerging American trinity of faiths: Protestant, Catholic, and Jew.

Hollywood filmmakers displayed a veritable fixation on the ecumenical moral sanction for World War II. Whenever possible, chaplains from different creeds will speak of similar moral lessons and of the need to fight God's war regardless of your church affiliation. Thus, when Cecil B. DeMille re-released *The Sign of the Cross* in 1944, a prologue was added to link the Catholic martyrs who suffered under Nero to the Christian soldiers sacrificing their lives to stop Hitler. As a bombing mission prepares to strike at Rome, Captain Driscoll (James Millican) is advised that as a Catholic he could withdraw from the mission. Driscoll wants no special consideration, however, and he's quite willing to sacrifice the Eternal City, since the raid on Rome is "a job that has to be done." On the plane, two chaplains are along for the ride, Rev. Lloyd (Stanley Ridges), a Protestant, and Father Costello (Arthur Shields), a Catholic from Boston. After numerous wisecracks about the Irish never ducking a fight and disconcerting disturbances in heaven, the priest gets down to serious moralizing about it being only "one step from being a dictator to thinking you're God"; the Protestant chaplain echoes these sentiments and reaffirms the link between brave martyrs who "certainly could take it" and "you boys" today. All these warriors, they agree, are linked by the sign of the cross, an emblem, they prophesy, which "nothing could destroy."

Lewis Seiler's *Guadalcanal Diary* (1943), based on the dispatches of Richard Tregaskis, mingled its topicality and propaganda rather gracefully except in its opening minutes when the urge for an ecumenical sense comes very close to a comedy of religious malapropism. The crew on deck spiritedly sing "Rock of Ages," an exclusively Protestant hymn, while Father Patrick Donnelly (Preston Foster), an all-American fullback from Notre Dame, works the "second shift," a Catholic high mass on an ornate altar. Then one sailor turns to congratulate his friend Sammy on his fine singing, and Sammy explains, "It should be, my father is a cantor." Not two minutes into the film, audiences know that the Protestants, the Catholics, and the Jews were there; the next five minutes zoom through nationalities, home-towns, races, occupations, and social classes. By the middle of the war, America rejoiced in its totality of commitment. Almost every film featured a platoon or squad or barracks with WASPs, ethnic Catholics, and Jews, city boys and farmers, corporate executives and cab drivers, college graduates and dropouts.

The chaplains assigned to these units were frequently Irish Catholic giants with hearts of gold, dazzlingly fine psychological insights, and an encyclopedic grasp of moral theology. Hollywood glorified an almost endless parade of courageous chaplains dragging men to safety, hearing last confessions, mending broken hearts, curing battle jitters, and anointing the dead. The heroic padre became a leading icon in Second World War films; his most stirring scenes usually involved reading the Lord's Prayer over graves or leading unseasoned young recruits to military victories and spiritual maturity. Master sergeants may have aided in teaching the manual of arms, but Irish Catholic priests in uniform were the drill instructors of the soul.

Father Donnelly in *Guadalcanal Diary*, one of the most fully developed examples of this convention, can stand as a token of literally dozens of other Hollywood portraits of Catholic chaplains. Chaplains were shown landing on the beaches of Normandy, trekking across Europe, sailing in the Pacific, and flying China skies; wherever the boys were, Father Donnelly or some other surrogate of Catholicism was there. Much was made of the Irish side of their priesthood. Irish chaplains tolerated drinking, dancing, and even wenching well enough; they even countenanced doubts, fears, and tears rather well. What they couldn't stand, however, was cowardice or indecision; the lukewarm had no place in this holy war.

Father Donnelly and other chaplains oozed courage and resolve; they rarely spoke of fortitude, but they embodied unflagging faith and dedication. When his commander suggests that maybe it would be best if he didn't go with the first wave, Father Donnelly quietly asks to be allowed to go "where I'll be most needed." Hollywood chaplains rarely appear in the rear guard; their assignments always favor the front lines. In one particularly harrowing episode, Father Donnelly pauses to praise some doctors for staying on despite desperate dangers. Pausing a minute, his companion remarks that Father had also stayed. The priest humbly agrees, but he explains that he "had to be there."

Father Donnelly teaches his flock both the tricks of warfare and the meaning of the good life in God. In heavy artillery bombing, he shows them how to avoid concussions; surrounded by snipers, he shows them how to maintain their nerve. He's quick to join Corporal Potts (William Bendix) in a spirited Irish jig, but he's equally capable of sharing the taxicab driver's fears and turning his human doubts into a prayer. Corporal "Taxi" Potts's impromptu sermon in *Guadalcanal Diary* typifies Hollywood's use of ecumenical prayers in movies with a World War II setting. Obviously shaken by grief and fear, he worries aloud that "I'm no hero . . . just another guy. I can't tell those bombs to hit somewhere else. I guess it's up to God. . . I only hope He figures we've done the best we could and lets it go at that." The corporal admits this is "a funny kind" of praying, but he reaffirms that it is what he's thinking. In the silence that follows his long peroration, his sentiments are boldly seconded by Father Donnelly's forceful "Amen."

Most chaplains in these patriotic frontline fictions sanction every American bomb that's dropped and bless every bullet and grenade. There are few moral qualms about the justice of the war or about the necessity for such violence. The chaplain's sermon, more often than not, provides both benediction for the troops and solace for the audiences at home. *Guadalcanal Diary* was, in essence, an inspirational epistle from the military command and from Hollywood to all Americans. The film was in the theaters so fast that the battles were still in the headlines and the campaign's total outcome still in question. Based on the film, however, everyone could join priest and naval captain in their final sentiment: "These boys were perfectly wonderful

. . . if the millions we're training at home are like these boys, we have nothing to worry about." As Joe Morella, Edward Epstein, and John Griggs discovered in their colorful survey of *The Films of World War II*, American audiences didn't want documentaries; they wanted what later came to be called docudramas, fictions based on fact, but fictions which, in the words of these historians, "always said the right things."

Perhaps the wordiest and most sanctimonious film to come out of World War II was director Robert Florey's *God Is My Co-Pilot* (1945), a Hollywood rehash of the best selling autobiography of Colonel Robert Lee Scott (Dennis Morgan), a Georgian who flew many missions with General Claire Chennault's much celebrated "Flying Tigers." The real warrior in this tale, however, is "Big Mike" (Alan Hale), a Catholic priest whose twenty-four years in the missions prompt him to joke that "the Chinese are my people, not the Irish." Big Mike's boisterous patriotism almost beggars description; even the Flying Tigers, no slouches when it comes to commitment, come to him for pep talks. They enthusiastically build him a chapel right next to their runway so he can split his ministry between pilots and orphans. Father Mike has enough energy and zeal to make these herculean tasks seem mundane.

Colonel Scott's skills as a pilot soon become as legendary as Big Mike's evangelism, and the farmboy atheist starts to trust the Catholic dynamo. As their camaraderie grows, Colonel Scott asks Father Mike about what the aftermath of the war will be (a critical audience concern in 1945). Scott confesses that he's killed hundreds of men that afternoon and hundreds more in his tour of duty, so he wonders if he and all the other men who've killed in battle will still be the same when they get home to wife and family. Scott's fears are most profound: "Will we be hard and bitter and burned out inside? And will life be the same meaningless thing it is out here?" Father Mike answers with pastoral concern and "the right words," a non sequitur which changes the focus altogether: "You're confused, Scotty. Life is always cheap in a war, yes, but neither life nor death are ever meaningless. And a man only changes for the worst when he thinks they are." Theologian Michael Leach, commenting on this film, felt compelled by such exchanges to attack the film's one dimensional morality as a kind of "divine mirage." The filmmakers obviously didn't agree, because after one exchange, as Ted Sennett reports in *Warner Brothers Presents*, the studio technicians tried to create an unusual special effect, "a miraculous effulgence of light in the sky, a kind of spiritual revelation." Father Mike and Colonel Scott find this light when the priest tries to convince Scotty not to rest in a faith in his personal skills but to trust instead in God's Providence. Big Mike even reads a long prayer written by a British pilot killed in the war, who discovered that God provided the strength he sought, the ability to cast out fears and doubts, if only he would believe. Scotty is slow to convert, even after the divine effulgence, but by the end of the film, he too intones this prayer piously.

Colonel Scott's leap to faith comes largely as a result of the efficacy of his first prayer. Scotty has been grounded because he's too old, but he wants this one last mission, a bombing foray into Japan, as the capstone of his career. So he speaks directly to God: "I've never asked for anything. If it's your will, please let me go with them, just this one time." Big Mike overhears, and he too rolls his eyes to heaven in prayer. Just then, the commanding officer comes out and tells Scotty that the new Curtis P-40, a "plane bigger, faster, and deadlier than anything you've ever flown is waiting for you with your old crew, compliments of the old man." Even Big Mike stands in awe of this instant miracle, and before he intones that British flyer's prayer one more time to end the film, he explains to the commander and the audience that "More things have been brought about by prayer than this world dreams of." In its war movies, Hollywood dreams of an immense array of instant miracles prompted by prayer; faith in God moves huge cannons over mountains, directs grenades into pillboxes, and sustains the most hopelessly surrounded units until help can come. The right prayer could confound kamikaze pilots, panzer units, and storm troopers; the religious soldier could withstand the most heinous tortures and confound the most demonic schemes. Faith could lead aviators in on *A Wing and a Prayer* (1944), guide nuns and pilots back to Allied lines in *Till We Meet Again* (1944), and unite the Underground against *Hitler's Madmen* (1943). In the European theater, prayer sustained *Joan of Paris* (1942), while in the Pacific the link between faith and the flag propelled John Wayne *Back to Bataan* (1945).

Faith usually shone brightest when circumstances were most desperate. This convention informed the Hollywood catechism until well after the war years. In John Huston's *Heaven Knows, Mr. Allison* (1957), for example, the more isolated a pious nun and a brave marine become, the more they affirm their individual loves for Roman Catholicism and the Marine Corps. Fairly soon, they both see a virtual identity between their callings. Lost on an atoll somewhere in the Pacific, the burly, rather stupid Corporal Allison (Robert Mitchum) realizes that "You've got your cross, and I've got my globe and anchor; I've got the Corps just like you've got your Church." The demure, quite beautiful, and intellectual Sister Angela (Deborah Kerr) also concedes that Church and Corps have many things in common, and before long she's talking about her drill instructor, Sister Brigitta, as "the Holy Terror"; the sacred vows of poverty, chastity, and obedience as her "enlistment papers"; and the loss of her immortal soul as the penalty for "deserting her outfit."

Sister Angela and Corporal Allison find their common enemy in the Japanese army. Catholics are, the corporal assures her, "good marines, the best," even if they do get teased for going to the chaplain before each attack and for eating fish on Friday. Sister Angela rejoices to hear that these "mackerel snappers" serve their country and their God so well. And when the occasion arises, and the corporal hears the "voice of God" calling him to knock out enemy emplacements, Sister Angela first probes his motives, asking, "Are you sure it's God you're obeying and not your own natural desire to take part in the fighting?" and then she blesses his resolve, assuring him that God protects His soldiers. Corporal Allison's mission succeeds, his marine colleagues storm the island with little resistance, and he and the nun are carried off the island, heroes, in a solemn procession, with Sister conspicuously displaying her large crucifix. This victory suggests how important happy endings and the image of an omnipotent and beneficent God are to the Hollywood catechism. Jack Vizzard, the religious technical adviser for this film, in his firsthand account of the production in *See No Evil*, recalls that the plot for the film was a reworking of an actual incident. In reality both the nun and the corporal were killed in an ironic twist of fate. When the marines came, the two of them forgot they were wearing stolen Japanese uniforms, and as they ran to the beach to greet their rescuers, the marines shot them. Hollywood rarely showed such bitter truths; sublime virtue, bold courage, and glorious victory always went hand in hand.

Even Jack Vizzard, an ex-seminarian, was aghast at how sublime the virtue was in *Heaven Knows, Mr. Allison*. He came to the set full of suggestions for the production company on how the expiration of temporary vows and extraordinary circumstances could ease the problem with Sister Angela's chastity in the film. Director John Huston needed no such expedient, however, for he had already decided not just to abide by the nun's vow of chastity, but to make her virginity the very cornerstone of her character. The corporal might lust after Sister Angela in his heart, but his outward demeanor is all "Begging your pardon, ma'am" and nervous modesty. When he discovers Sister has yet to take her final vows, he begs her not to, declaring his love and proposing marriage. When she answers that she has given her heart to Christ, he patiently accepts her resolve, saving face by declaring that it's no good for a marine to have a wife anyway. Only once does his libido really threaten to take control, and that's after a good deal of potent Japanese sake. In his drunken despair, the corporal tells the nun how tempting her blue eyes, her freckles, and her smiles are; Huston sums the emotion of the scene up with a splendid visual metaphor when a besotten, mildly threatening Mitchum flings his pipe at the door, exasperated because he has exhausted his supply of tobacco. The soldier's impassioned rhetoric about the possiblity of being on the island for years, the pointlessness of being a nun or a marine in such isolation, and the loneliness of the two of them, Adam and Eve with nothing but the island and themselves, frightens Sister Angela; and she pushes him

168

away, running hastily into a swamp, where all the fears of her subconscious overwhelm her and throw her into a delirious fever. Corporal Allison finds her the next day, and the clearest sign of his regained composure is his exquisite care to remove the nun's wet clothes without ever looking at her naked body. When Sister Angela recovers, even she confesses that she wasn't running away from him; she knew he was no physical threat. She was running from the truth, from the possibility that she might never reach the world and take her final vows; she was running from the fear of God's silence. When her strength returns, she reaffirms her belief in Providence, reminding Corporal Allison that "Only God knows what will happen to us."

Filming a drunk scene between a sex-starved marine corporal and an anguished nun had the whole production company nervous, Jack Vizzard reports in *See No Evil*, and there were careful conferences about the degree of physical proximity, the camera angles, Mitchum's lecherous tone, the nun's reaction, and numerous other details that would concern the Production Code enforcement officials and the Legion of Decency. But finally the big day came, and everything was ready. Jack Vizzard was called to the set and the cameras rolled. Robert Mitchum as Corporal Allison stepped forward; and in response to Deborah Kerr's cue, "What are you doing, Mr. Allison?" he grabbed Sister Angela by the wrist, held her tight, and began caressing her as he cooed, "Now, Sister." His kisses became harder to avoid, so the flustered nun hissed, "Let go of me, you sonofabitch" and sank her knee into his crotch. Religious adviser Vizzard was flabbergasted, flapped his hands weakly for a while, and then recognized that John Huston had had his little joke on the censor.

During the filming of director Leslie Martinson's World War II biography of a young Catholic war hero, *PT 109* (1963), the censor more clearly dominated things. President Kennedy hovered so forcefully over this production that Julian Smith in *Looking Away* compared the White House operation to a scene out of *The Godfather*; only this time, Smith notes, it was the first Catholic president, the "capo of the Irish Mafia," delegating his press secretary, Pierre Salinger, to take care of a casting problem and some problems in a script. Kennedy had his eye on re-election, so a proper respect for his adventures in the Blackett Strait during World War II became his obsession. According to Jack Warner, whom Smith quotes, Kennedy concentrated on editing the script even as John Glenn made his historic orbit of the earth. If all these allegations of Kennedy's concern have a foundation in fact, *PT 109* stands as a clear example of how a politician can fail as a showman. *PT 109* sank slowly from sight despite its topicality; the public was unwilling to sit still for a loving ode to doing your job, a stuffy profile of modest courage intent on proving the wisdom, stability, and leadership of the young commander. Kennedy's Catholicism is carefully down-played in the film since the consensus seemed to be that it didn't win votes in a national election. In a telling exchange, a frightened sailor asks, "What can a man do, Mister Kennedy, except pray?" The young officer replies, "You can do your job, like all of us." Audiences were obviously supposed to under-stand the broader implications: Catholicism would be no barrier to an effective presidency. In Camelot, prayer could wait until the job was done.

Kennedy was not the first American president to see the movies as essential to his election, nor was he the first president to use images of war and religion in an attempt to influence public policy. One of the most popular films of the silent screen, Thomas Ince's *Civilization* (1916), an allegory set in the kingdom of Wredpryd, featuring submarines, police states, and a wom-an's brigade, contributed to Woodrow Wilson's reelection on an anti-war platform in 1916. At that juncture, the emphasis in the film was on the lessons espoused in the opening title card: "Not until Hatred, Greed, Envy is plucked from the heart of man can we hope for Eternal Peace." Christ was reincarnated in the film to preach pacifism, and Wilson himself appeared in an epilogue to thank Ince for his fine moral lesson. Within a year, Wilson and the country were moving toward war, and *Civilization* was reedited in May 1917, with new title cards, American flags, and Wilson's new plea to Congress to enter World War I. Christ now seemed the champion of war against tyrants. Commenting on these shifts in his *Religion in Cinema*, Ivan Butler felt they needed "no elaboration as a comment on the sincerity of some filmmakers" though he admitted it was unclear whether Ince approved the changes.

World War I never garnered the unanimous public approval nor the unified movie industry support that the next global war did. Movies about World War II usually reflect a consensus of opinion, but films about World War I often suggest a multiplicity of viewpoints. The place of Catholicism in films about World War I normally reflects the filmmakers' attitudes toward war and not an assessment of religious dogma at all. For those opposed to the war, the sanctity of the Church and the violence of the conflict represent two distinct, diametrically opposed universes. For those who support the war, the cross and the cannon ride the same caisson.

William Keighley's *The Fighting 69th*, released in 1940, boldly urged the United States toward involvement in the new war in Europe by recounting the glorious achievements of the Rainbow Division and its Irish Catholic contingent, who marched directly from the sidewalks of New York to the trenches of France in World War I. There was no ambivalence about global war in this slugfest. Pat O'Brien was unrelentingly pious and patriotic as Father Francis J. Duffy, the real life chaplain of the unit, who combined a scholarly interest in philosophy with the street smarts necessary to make him a battlefield legend and a political counselor to Al Smith. Father Duffy has a formal monument and his own park in the middle of Times Square, but another part of his legacy is Hollywood's deification of this Irishman as the prototype for all chaplains in its pro-war films. There's a little of Father Duffy in every brave cinematic religious mentor leading his flock to glory and salvation. In *The Fighting 69th*, most of Pat O'Brien's attention goes to none other than James Cagney. Once again O'Brien must show Cagney how to die a hero and provide a lesson to all the boys around him. As Private Jerry Plunkett, Cagney eventually learns that toughness and courage aren't enough, and that it's teamwork and sacrifice that carry the day. When the time comes, Plunkett shows he has what it takes, jumping on a live grenade so others can live. Interestingly, the biblical injunction so heavily stressed by Father Duffy, "Greater love hath no man than he lay down his life for his brothers," suits the needs of the war genre quite well. As Thomas Sobchack suggests in his article "Genre Film: a Classical Experience," the hero in war films is "always in the service of the group, of law and order, of stability, of survival not of himself but of the organization, the institutions. . . ." The villain, on the other hand, looks out only for selfish interests and personal welfare. In the Hollywood catechism this pattern forms a critical triangle that connects belonging to a Church, belonging to an army, and belonging to a nation. Eliminate any one leg in the triangle and none can stand; social maturity and religious sanctity, Hollywood suggests, have their wellsprings in a charitable concern for others. Heroes subscribe to great causes and make bold sacrifices; they work and pray and as a result become noble Americans in "one nation under God."

Anti-war films frequently must engage in the broadest social commentary to reveal how interconnected the concept of Americanism and spirituality has become. Dalton Trumbo's *Johnny Got His Gun* (1971), for example, uses the plight of a World War I casualty who has lost his arms, legs, and face, and who wants desperately to die, though army doctors take heroic measures to save his life, as a springboard to comment on all the insanities of nationalism, materialism, and capitalism. In his agonized dreams, Joe Bonham (Timothy Bottoms), the hapless victim of a land mine, imagines a Christ unlike any Redeemer ever seen before in American film. His Christ (Donald Sutherland) looks like the face on a Hallmark card, but he belongs more to the pool hall and poker table than to the chapel. Christ has but one parable for Joe: "Life is a card game, and if you stay in long enough, you lose, and once you lose, there's no way back." Even Christ has trouble with this game of life, for he admits to Joe he never has any luck hitting a 12 and that he is haunted by images of "so many dead men you wouldn't believe it." This Christ's fatalism makes bunk, of course, of the whole American struggle-strive-achieve ethic. Interestingly, all of Trumbo's heroes in the film are Catholics, and all reverse by their actions the stereotypes common to so many World War II movies. Thus, for example, there's the Irish Catholic father with the lovely daughter about to see Joe off to the war. Normally one would expect some fatherly admonitions about the fine thing he's doing and some stern caveats about his daughter's virtue and fidelity. Instead, Trumbo's father is a Wobbly, who denounces the war machine and the bankers and encourages his daughter to sleep with the boy. In bed, the young lovers frolic around nude; Joe teases her about being a "Mick" and therefore no lady, and she implores him not to go. So much for the homefront.

At the hospital, the one nurse who understands Joe (Diane Varsi) is also a Catholic, who proudly displays her crucifix and carefully recites an act of contrition. However, she's no chaste Florençe Nightingale bridled by an inflexible moral code. Her humanity overrides any creed. As soon as she understands Joe's predicament, she masturbates him to climax and then cuts off his oxygen in a compassionate attempt at euthanasia. A self-righteous army officer stops her, however, and Joe's private hell continues.

Finally, there's the Catholic chaplain (Edmund Gilbert), whose confrontation with the general hammers home the dichotomy Trumbo sees between the army and the Church. The World War I general implores the priest, "Don't you have some message for him, padre? Couldn't you tell him to put his faith in the Lord?" This disillusioned priest, however, cannot offer any of the normal pieties; instead, he promises to pray for the boy for the rest of his life. Rebuffed, the general snorts, "You're a helluva priest," a sentiment that aptly describes how far Trumbo has drifted from the normal Hollywood stereotype. The priest strikes back at the general with sharp words, "He's the product of your profession, not mine," a stunning affirmation of the distance between his Catholicism and his commander's militarism.

A similar separation between battlefield and celestial peace informs both film versions of Hemingway's World War I romance, *A Farewell to Arms*. Frank Borzage's 1932 version with Gary Cooper as Frederic Henry and Helen Hayes as Catherine

Barkley, has the young lovers, who have made their separate peace and deserted the chaos of war for the serene mountains of Switzerland, glide into heaven in its last shot as church bells herald the armistice and the dove of peace takes to wing. Their battlefield marriage vows, not one of Catholic author Hemingway's inventions, but a concession to Production Code strictures and to the Legion of Decency, are blessed by a Catholic chaplain (Jack LaRue), and their undying love opens Heaven's gates. This flight to Paradise on the wings of love is a long way from the Sullivan brothers who leave family and sweethearts behind to storm heaven.

Director Charles Vidor's *A Farewell to Arms* (1957), a mammoth David O. Selznick production featuring the producer's wife, Jennifer Jones, as the saintly British nurse and Rock Hudson as the ambulance driver who discovers the insanity of war, makes the distinction between army and Church, military orders and moral mandate, even more explicit by its addition of another scene never penned by Catholic convert Ernest Hemingway, the martyrdom of Father Galli (Alberto Sordi). When the evacuation of a field hospital is ordered, neither the anticlerical surgeon Rinaldi (Vittorio de Sica) nor the chaplain want to leave their charges. The doctor must leave, however, under his military orders, and this cynic, who has consistently attacked piety, sees the chaplain's religion in a new light. He turns to the priest and salutes his faith: "I am ordered by the military to leave, but you have much better orders to remain, Father. I salute your commanding officer." The doctor cannot live with his desertion of patients who need him, and he dies before a firing squad cursing the lunacy of the military. The priest, fortified by his creed, leads his patients in a moving proclamation of faith: they are singing the *Ave Maria* when the final barbarous artillery attack on the bedridden casualties comes. War annihilates the hospital and Father Galli, but his glorious sacrifice and the futile death of the surgeon push Frederic Henry to his final decision to renounce the arms of war and take his lover to the sanctuary of Switzerland.

While Frederic finds salvation in the arms of Catherine Barkley, many other lovers in pre-World War II romances found their sanctuary in the Roman Catholic Church. A major theme in earlier war melodramas involves the choice between life in the world of heroes and battlefields and life in the cloister, a world of sacrifice and prayer. The various adaptations of Francis Marion Crawford's immensely popular 1909 romance *The White Sister* suggest how important this theme was in American films of the twenties and thirties. Catholic mystic Henry King directed Lillian Gish in the best known, most widely acclaimed version of *The White Sister*, which was released at the peak of America's disillusionment with World War I in 1923. The plot of *The White Sister* involves an Italian heiress Angela Chiaromonte, who thinks her betrothed, Captain Giovanni Severini (Ronald Coleman in the 1923 version), has died in battle and dedicates her life to God by entering the convent. Her lover returns, however, and she must choose between God and man.

The White Sister represented a daring gamble on the part of both director King and star Gish, for the film was an independent production under the aegis of the aptly named Inspiration Pictures, and the feature's heavy emphasis on the rubric of Roman Catholicism almost blocked its distribution, since exhibitors feared a Protestant backlash. Discussing the film in her memoir, *Dorothy and Lillian Gish,* Miss Gish recalls that in the silent era, religious stories from the Bible were easily marketed, but exhibitors shied away from *The White Sister,* which she considered "the first modern story, based on Catholicism." In Gish's interpretation, the exhibitors' motives for refusing to show *The White Sister* were more economic than sectarian; she remembers that "the big companies who owned the theaters said the public could get religion free on Sundays, so they're not going to pay for it during the week." (Miss Gish's analysis suggests an interesting reversal of the earlier encounter between an impecunious exhibitor, Adolph Zukor, and a censorious priest who feared religion in the movies would challenge the Church's hegemony.) To circumvent this impasse between Inspiration Pictures and the major exhibitors, producer Charles H. Duell, director Henry King, and star Lillian Gish opened *The White Sister* themselves at the George M. Cohan Theater in New York City. The premiere was a gala affair, which the reviewer for the *New York Times*, seemingly incognizant of the behind-the-scenes difficulties, described in great detail. In the critic's words, the audience was "a most interesting assembly, which included persons prominent in society, distinguished politicians, well-known authors and writers, screen celebrities, and heads of the motion picture industry," and this opening for *The White Sister* was an occasion, the journalist opined, which "revealed the standing of the films possibly more than any other photoplay presentation." *The White Sister*, it seems, brought both American film and American Catholicism to a new social standing.

Within days, everyone recognized that *The White Sister* was box office magic in New York City, and Nicholas Schenk of Metro Pictures took over distribution. Even in its later national distribution, however, *The White Sister* was handled with special care because of its Catholic theme. Theater owners were instructed to inform local Protestant clergy about the film's inspirational tone and its markedly Catholic orientation, in the hope that local ministers would encourage their congregations not to avoid the film just because of its unique religious orientation. *The Exhibitors Trade Review* for September 22, 1923, tried to assure theater owners that this story of a soldier desperately in love with a nun is one "that will stir the non-churchman," and "to those who follow the creed of any denomination and, of course, the Catholics especially, the impress must be multiplied manyfold."

Director King had actually increased the Catholic focus in *The White Sister* manyfold. On his way to Italy to shoot the film, King happened to meet the papal delegate to Washington; after a brief chat about the film's treatment of the sister's final vows, the papal delegate arranged for the head ceremonial director of the Vatican to show the company all the intricacies of an Italian nun's traditional wedding with Christ. Lillian Gish recalls that the company was allowed to film a sacred ceremony "that had never been filmed before, with the bride in all her finery being married to the church . . . just before dawn." Director Henry King assured Kevin Brownlow in *The Parade's Gone By* that everything in the sequence was authentic; he watched

176

the papal adviser stage the ceremony and then "shot the entire thing while it was fresh in my mind, without a scene of it being written down."

King did have one big problem in his script, however. In the original novel the lovers eventually marry. As Gish recalls the project, this was "an impossible situation for a successful film": "You can't care about a character you see taking solemn vows before God at eight o'clock and then by nine changing her mind." This is especially true if the most interesting visuals in your film picture her eternal marriage to Christ. To resolve this dilemma, the film of *The White Sister* introduces an eruption of Mount Vesuvius which kills Captain Giovanni and thus frees Sister Angela of any qualms about her oath whatsoever. Victor Fleming resolved this problem of romance and vows in the 1933 version by having his star, Helen Hayes, portray an even more ethereal nun than Gish managed. This Sister Angela cannot be moved by Clark Gable as a dashing soldier intent on seducing her. As Rene Jordan laments in an appreciation of *Clark Gable,* although "the Gable blowtorch style could by then melt an iceberg," it moved this *"grande dame"* not a whit. All through the film, Jordan complains, "an invisible ten foot pole seems to be keeping them apart, even when they embrace."

The cleft between earthly love and heavenly duty, between God's peace and man's wars, also plays a central part in Ernst Lubitsch's 1932 film *The Man I Killed,* which contemporary author and critic Robert E. Sherwood hailed as "the best talking picture that has yet been seen and heard." *The Man I Killed* may not actually be quite that great a masterpiece, but it does show this German émigré who had such a great influence on contemporary filmmakers in a serious mood, arguing most movingly for piety and pacifism. Lewis Jacobs in his *The Rise of the American Film* accurately cites *The Man I Killed* as a fine example of Lubitsch's visual style, pointing to wonderful shots of "old Germans in their beer gardens recalling their past glories, with the camera gliding over their faces," "an Armistice Day parade, photographed through a one-legged ex-soldier," and an ironic "scene in a church where the camera moves past the praying officers and reveals their guns." Lubitsch's central plot concerns a dashing young French soldier named Paul (Philip Holmes), whose conscience won't allow him to forget the German soldier he has killed in combat. When the boy reveals his nagging grief to a priest (Frank Sheridan) in confession, the cleric suggests the possibility of a direct confession to the dead soldier's parents as a means of assuaging his guilt. Once he's in Germany, the plot takes a bold twist with the dead soldier's parents (Lionel Barrymore and Emma Dunn) finding a replacement for their son in his presence and with their daughter (Nancy Carroll), the dead man's sister, falling in love with him. The rather too mechanical plot artifice obviously suggests that war is the aberration; if only people truly know each other, émigré Lubitsch suggests, they would see they were all part of one family.

The Man I Killed is especially interesting because of its forceful presentation of the psychological dimensions of war and religion, its riveting attention to the link between physical violence and moral guilt, and because of its harrowing depiction of the devastating effect battlefield fatalities have on families and loved ones at home. These themes were muted if not silenced during World War II. As Judith Crist observes in her introduction to *The Films of World War II*, American audiences demanded something altogether different in the war years, and Hollywood provided the necessary comforting fantasies with predictable regularity: "for the duration the security blanket of [Hollywood's] illusion kept us warm: every boy [was] a potential hero, every mom a bundle of cheer, every girl a patient page-boyed Penelope . . . we wanted no tonings. And we got none."

After World War II, however, some tonings would come, and as Hollywood looked back at the best years of our lives, it also discovered some moral questions along the paths of glory. There was, for example, the question of the atom bomb. While screens were curiously devoid of odes to the Manhattan Project, Hollywood did generate a biography of Colonel Paul W. Tibbetts, who organized Operation Silverplate and led the Bluelight Mission over Hiroshima. Tibbetts, played by Robert Taylor in Melvin Frank's *Above and Beyond* (1952), deflects other air force officers' questions about the ethics of nuclear war by arguing that "War is immoral, not weapons" and by a skillful begging of the question, opining that "To lose this war to the gang we're fighting would be the most horrible thing we could do." The chaplain in this film blesses the crew, sending them forth "in the name of Jesus Christ," and Tibbetts himself exhorts his crew that "We've come a long way, fellows; let's pray to God we finish the job right." Yet a reporter's pointed question to Colonel Tibbetts about his slaughter of 80,000 civilians, "What do you think about it?" elicits only the commander's irate plea for a public debate of the issue, "What do *they* think about it?"

In the years after World War II, especially during bloody and unpopular military engagements in Korea and Viet Nam, serious questions would arise in American films about public opinion, government policy, and the proper role of the Catholic Church. These films about American wars, both hot and cold, would range in tone from hysterical anti-Communist tracts to irreverent anti-military satires; they would echo both Catholic senator Joseph McCarthy's bumptious rantings and Catholic priests Daniel and Philip Berrigan's silent, self-effacing blood-lettings.

The years immediately following World War II witnessed a political trial in Hollywood during which many fine talents were ruined and many other lesser lights profited from their ability to name names. Lillian Hellman genteely refers to this era as "scoundrel time"; for Dalton Trumbo, it was "the time of the toad." Richard Nixon and Chairman J. Parnell Thomas brought their House Committee on Un-American Activities to Hollywood to investigate the "Communist Infiltration of the Motion Picture Industry"; despite the assurances of the then president of the Screen Actors Guild, Ronald Reagan, that "I do not believe the Communists have ever at any time been able to use the motion picture screen as a sounding board for their philosophy or ideology," the *subpoena ad testificandum* was everywhere, artists like Bertolt Brecht and Joseph Losey left the country, and the "Hollywood Ten" went to jail. Before the Committee left Tinseltown (Chairman Thomas to eventual scandal and imprisonment; Nixon to Watergate and forced resignation from the presidency), the studios initiated a rigid ideological blacklist. As Alvah Bessie indicated in the title of his prison memoirs of the period, it was an *Inquisition in Eden*, and the forces behind much of what was happening were the soldiers of American Catholicism marshalled by Senator Joseph Mc-Carthy, the darling of Holy Name societies, sodalities, and first communion breakfasts.

Analysts and historians differ in their assessment of how much real Catholic support McCarthy mustered and how representative he was of the majority of American Catholics, but there is no doubt, as Lawrence Fuchs reports in *John F. Kennedy and American Catholicism*, that Joseph McCarthy offered some powerful illusions: "McCarthy hit every raw nerve of suspicion, resentment, and prejudice which American Catholics had developed in years of exclusion. Now, in one rich fantasy, they could knock together the heads of Communists, internationalist Jews, and Anglophile Yankees." Even historians like John Cogley, who feel that McCarthy's Catholic support was merely a vocal minority of the faithful, concedes his importance as an image of American Catholicism. In *Catholic America*, Cogley admits that McCarthy "represented to many, both within and without the Church, an almost perfect example of what was widely taken to be the authentic Catholic approach to the issues created by the Cold War." Cogley also cites "one Washington wag" whose jest summarizes much of what intellectual America thought was happening: "the Harvard and Yale sons of the Old Protestant aristocracy were regularly investigated for un-Americanism by certified products of Fordham and Notre Dame."

The result of all the "Red Scare" on blacklisted Hollywood was a flood of Cold War films pitting Catholics against Communists. The tone of these encounters is typified in Felix Feist's *Guilty of Treason* (1949), an account of the torture, brainwashing, and bogus trial of Cardinal Mindszenty in Hungary. Communists were deceivers, sadists, leather-coated Gestapo-like perverts who would stop at nothing to subvert patriotism, the family, and the Church; and the fact that they carefully left no marks on the body to reveal their basement third degrees, cold and hot alternating showers, and other sexual and psychic abuses made them even more heinous. Simplification was the order of the day in these Cold War melodramas. In *The Red Danube* (1949), directed by George Sidney, for example, an army major (Walter Pidgeon) and a Mother Superior (Ethel Barrymore) conspire to save a ballerina (Janet Leigh) from extradition back to Russia and the endless horrors that would entail. Age, grace, and beauty, the military, the Church, and art here align themselves against chicanery, perversion, and villainy. The contest is so lopsided and overdrawn that Joel Greenburg and Charles Higham in their *Hollywood in the Forties* conclude that "These crude and foolish pantomimes did the cause of anti-communism probably more harm than good." The flavor of these Cold War tracts is captured quite dramatically in the poster for Director R. G. Springsteen's *The Red Menace* (1949), which Richard Averson and David Manning White reproduce in *The Celluloid Weapon: Social Comment in the American Film*. The poster assures audiences that this project is "so shocking it was filmed behind sealed studio doors," but that it will become the "most talked about drama of our time!" Tiny portraits identify the principal players; their concise descriptions marvelously suggest the stock company in all these melodramas. The characters include, for example, Bill Jones, "the ex-G.I. who almost lost everything he fought for"; Nina, "the girl who came to breed hate but instead learned to love"; Solomon, "he gave his life rather than bend to the yoke of tyranny"; Mollie, "the seductive party girl used as man bait"; and Yvonne, "a power hungry psychopathic love-starved woman of destruction." At the center of it all there is Father Leary, "the fearless, fighting priest, who conquered evil with faith!"

The most famous confrontation between evil and faith in a Cold War film comes in Leo McCarey's much debated *My Son John* (1952). McCarey, the creator of *Going My Way* and *The Bells of St. Mary's*, had appeared as a friendly witness at the hearings of the House Committee on Un-American Activities to denounce the godless enemies of the American family. His *My Son John* was clearly a labor of love, hitting those enemies over the head, quite literally, with the family Bible. *My Son John*, as Stefan Kanfer indicates in *A Journal of the Plague Years*, remains important to any history of Hollywood film, inasmuch as it provided "a view of the primordial thought of a show-business Red-baiter."

The basic plot is straightforward. Two aged parents, Dan Jefferson (Dean Jagger), an archetypal Irishman full of booze, militant Catholicism, and patriotic rage, and Lucille Jefferson (Helen Hayes), an overweening mom right out of Philip Wylie, riding on the emotional rollercoaster of menopause yet stoically refusing to take the medicine her doctor prescribes, have two young sons, who proudly march off to Korea straight from the football field, and one older boy, John (Robert Walker), who has drifted away into a weird, intellectual universe, full of strange professors, drugs, and nefarious allegiances. When FBI agent Steadman (Van Heflin) visits their prototypical suburban home, their worst fears are realized, and they turn to their priest (Frank McHugh) to seek help in confronting their son's latent Communism and his obvious sexual corruption. (It's unclear in sexual terms whether his affair with a Communist agent or his homosexual gestures are the danger. McCarey seems to hint, as Stefan Kanfer points out, that corruption is "all one bag." In that case, it's both his sexual liaison with a beautiful female spy and his namby pamby style that are so unsettling to Mom and Dad. Vito Russo in his *Celluloid Closet: Homosexuality in the Movies* notes that "The parents' reaction on learning of their sons' Communist activities is exactly the same as if they had discovered their child's homosexuality.") Mom and Dad hit John with Bibles, rosaries, World War I songs, novenas, nervous breakdowns, and evening prayers; and eventually John responds to his family's fervent pieties and nocturnal prayer meetings and repents, only to be killed by his Communist colleagues. This last twist may have been necessitated by actor Walker's untimely death, but it is consistent with the melodramatic pattern of the film and does provide McCarey with a compensating punishment for all John's dope, sex, treason, blasphemy, and disrespect for parents.

James Baldwin in his *The Devil Finds Work* writes at length about *My Son John,* and his biggest surprise, he notes, came in the freedom McCarey gave Robert Walker to mock Church,

family, and country. Baldwin, who admits his first reaction to
My Son John was that "Nothing can possibly redeem so grisly
a species of sentimental dishonesty," seems to cherish Walker's
"gleefully vicious parody of the wayward American son." As
Baldwin says, "The moment he [Robert Walker as John Jeffer-
son] enters the family house, he makes the reasons for his
leaving it very clear: his American Legion father, his adoring
mother, his football-playing brother, bore him shitless, and he
simply does not want to be like them." Stefan Kanfer, who
demolishes the prejudices of the film at great length in his *A
Journal of the Plague Years*, finally admits that he too finds a
perverse delight in McCarey's ode to the FBI, to informing on
your friends, and to monitoring your children's ideas and allegiances. In its right-wing hysteria, Kanfer notes, the film is
"in its own strange way" the truest American film of this period
in isolating the "deep traditional appeal of the left." John's
conversion to Communism came not in college, Kanfer protests, but long before, because of "his father's booming facti-
tious ideology . . . his mother's neurotic fear of the new . . .
[and] his brothers' grinning incurious acceptance of obscene
circumstance." Kanfer's argument is, of course, disingenuous,
and Baldwin's analysis, delightfully idiosyncratic (he dreams
of Walker finally falling to his knees and singing "Mammy"),
but they do suggest the problem in films as unbalanced as Leo
McCarey's *My Son John*. Pulling all the stops out, linking the
Catholic Church and the FBI, aligning intellectual curiosity with
Communism and homosexuality, pitting Mom and Dad against
professors and perversion, finally faces the peril of unconscious
parody and high camp. For many years, *My Son John* made a
late night circuit of college campuses, where young people came
not to celebrate but to mock. *My Son John* unwittingly became
a rallying point for the opposition. A sad footnote to the whole
controversy is George Morris's confessional article "McCarey
and McCarthy," which appeared in the January 1976 issue of
Film Comment. After an intriguing shot-by-shot analysis, Morris
lapses into the kind of emotional personal reverie that McCarey
obviously wanted to exploit, and after a few tearful lines
wherein he confesses that *My Son John*, "in its harrowing,

inarticulate confrontations between parent and son, strikes a deeply personal chord within me, related to similar experiences with my own parents," Morris leaps to a new aesthetic faith: "The flaws of this final reel notwithstanding, *My Son John* is still a masterpiece of the highest order." Morris's hyperbolic excesses reveal the emotional, irrational level McCarey exploits in the film. *My Son John* exists in a curious Freudian universe of Oedipal displacements, with images of religion, patriotism, and potency sadly scrambled. Mom's breakdown, Pop's drunken fits, and son's narcotic haze and sexual confusion really do uncover a nexus of serious problems in Cold War America. As Glen Johnson observes in his article "Sharper than an Irish Serpent's Tooth: Leo McCarey's *My Son John*," McCarey's message proves clear enough "to satisfy the most exacting patriot or to affront the mildest liberal intellectual."

Simplistic political and moral exaggerations also mar John Brahm's *The Miracle of Our Lady of Fatima* (1952), his Cold War rendition of a spiritual apparition accepted as valid by the Roman Catholic Church, the 1917 appearance of the Blessed Virgin Mary to three Portuguese children near Fatima. Brahm's film begins with a doctrinaire reprise of Portuguese history, which heavy-handedly derides a "socialist minority" for establishing a police state after deposing a popular king. These Marxist thugs haughtily run roughshod over peasants and villagers, taking special delight in humiliating nuns and debasing priests. Brahm lingers on scenes of long lines of priests and monks forced to queue up for humiliating mug shots and other such public indignities. These atheistic revolutionaries gleefully proclaim that they will destroy the Church, as Hollywood's solemn narrator intones the portentous question, "How often have we heard the same words since then?" Brahm's cinematic interpretation of the events at the Loca de Cabeco near Aljustrel is, as Leslie Halliwell indicates in his *Film Guide*, obviously less pro-Catholic than anti-Communist, and Halliwell speculates that the whole project might be Jack Warner's "means of atoning" for *Mission to Moscow* (1943) and other films that raised the hackles of right wingers.

Brahm constantly emphasizes Mary's pronouncements as

184

political statements and subordinates visions of spiritual peace to visions of a converted Russia. The villains in his film are brutish government officials who warn the peasants that "under the laws of the Republic, reports of miracles are a crime." The overwhelming impression is of a country occupied by socialist tyrants, a country where the moon is down. These Marxist functionaries seem to have learned their political manners from the Gestapo; when they're not browbeating and interrogating peasants, they're kidnapping and torturing the poor visionary children. One of the longest sequences of the film involves the revolutionary government's fetid schemes to make Lucia, Francesco, and Giacinto renounce their vision. First the children are roughed up a bit, then they're threatened with long prison terms far from their parents, and finally they're separated and told they will be tortured and killed. With the screams of the two younger children echoing outside, Lucia is warned she must renounce the miracle or hear the others die. When she still refuses, the government official leers and assures her, "I'm going to give you the full treatment."

Eventually even these dumb, sadistic lackeys realize that martyring innocents is bad for national morale, so they change their tactics and mock the children's religion. With bitter scorn, they deliver the children to the grotto and demand a sign, an instant miracle. Mary's intervention, the famed "miracle of Fatima," during which 70,000 saw the sun dance in the sky and plunge toward earth, thus seems in Brahm's film more a repudiation of atheistic Communism than a call to Catholic renewal. Brahm's film constantly emphasizes the part of the Lourdes secret aimed at the Soviet Union. Brahm repeatedly shows the Blessed Mother surrounded by an aureole, making wondrous prophesies for Cold War enthusiasts: "In Russia, there is an evil scheme to destroy the peace of the earth. To prevent this, I ask that she be consecrated to the Virgin Mary. If this is done, she will be converted."

John Brahm's belabored Cold War histrionics and shallow political bombast provide a stunning contrast to the more traditional treatments of spiritual marvels. The much better-known Catholic feature, Henry King's *The Song of Bernadette*, for example, though it was released in 1943, during American involvement in World War II, and though it was based on Jewish emigré Franz Werfel's novel—which he wrote in thanksgiving for having been delivered from the Nazis—still it focuses almost entirely on the divine graces that accrue to individuals as a result of the Virgin Mary's visitation at Lourdes. King's long, reverential retelling of the spiritual agonies of Bernadette Soubirous (an Oscar-winning performance by Jennifer Jones) suppresses any political themes, any mention of the conversion of nations or global peace, in favor of an emphasis on personal salvation. Catholic Henry King studiously avoids manifestos, as he discreetly manages to show the miracle through the eyes and in the face of his peasant mystic. Bernadette's illumination and awakening provide the focus for the whole narrative; her divine visitation centers on spiritual realities, not earthly combats. Cinematographer Arthur Miller, who received an Oscar for his work on the film, explains in great detail in his interview for Charles Higham's *Hollywood Cameramen: Sources of Light* how he employed a spotlight on Jennifer Jones, beginning as a little glow and growing in intensity to suggest Bernadette's aura of sanctity. In his interview, Miller chides Henry King, a devout mystic, for confusing Hollywood lighting with a spiritual nimbus. As Miller recalls the production, King was unaware of the special spotlight and quite excited at the rushes to see a halo surrounding Jennifer Jones. Miller was reluctant to tell the director about the special light because he thought King envisioned this nimbus around his star as "something spiritual that had crept into the picture from heaven."

No special graces may have poured from heaven, but there were no political messages from the sidelines either. King's *The Song of Bernadette* eschews partisan politics and pro-war messages as it details the spiritual transformation Bernadette causes in her eventual champion, the Dean of Lourdes (Charles Bickford), and her even more reluctant admirer Sister Marie Theresa Vauzous (Gladys Cooper). *The Song of Bernadette* proved immensely popular for war-weary audiences seeking mystical uplift and clear indications that God and the saints still existed, but intellectual critics like James Agee recognized that "the cruel, ridiculous, and unfathomable concentrics which spread from her [Bernadette's] naive ecstasy composed one of the most appalling and instructive events of our time," and only an "almost unimaginably brilliant film" could capture them. King's film was, Agee felt, not up to the task; it was, he wrote (Agee 1966), "tamed and pretty image, highly varnished, sensitively lighted, and exhibited behind immaculate glass, the window at once of a shrine and a box office." Most later critics and historians have seconded Agee's judgment; and the reputation of this film, so celebrated in its day, has declined precipitously, though few would probably embrace Joel Greenburg and Charles Higham's verdict in *Hollywood in the Forties* (1968) that *The Song of Bernadette* was "one of the ugliest and most vulgar quasi-religious pictures that has ever disgraced the screen, inexcusably inept in every department." Higham and Greenburg's words would seem more appropriate as a description of John Brahm's *The Miracle of Our Lady of Fatima*, though Leslie Halliwell's dismissal of the film as "a real cold war piece" might be more to the point.

Cold war rhetoric and Hollywood had a very difficult time coping with Korea. The issues were so confusing, the objectives so unclear, and the revelations about Americans cracking under brainwashing so unsettling that Korea became a favorite subject not of rabid anti-Communists but of opponents to war in general and to Asian wars in particular. No more dramatic reversal of fortunes in Hollywood history exists than Ring Lardner, Jr., and the Oscar he received for his screenplay for Robert Altman's *M*A*S*H* (1970). Lardner was the second blacklisted writer in a row to win the best screenplay Oscar, but his victory was especially ironic since *M*A*S*H*, as William Froug notes in his volume of interviews, *The Screenwriter Looks at the Screenwriter*, helped save Twentieth Century Fox from bankruptcy; twenty-five years earlier, Fox had dismissed the politically controversial Lardner for refusing to testify before the House Committee on Un-American Activities and explaining that "I could answer it [the Committee's infamous question about affiliation in the Communist Party], but if I did, I would hate myself in the morning." Lardner's Oscar was doubly sweet, too, because his script settled many of the old accounts by lacerating the "god-damn army," debunking super patriots, and exposing the hypocrisy and insanity of the war happy religious. *M*A*S*H* was, in the words of *New York Times* reviewer Roger Greenspun, "the first major American movie openly to ridicule belief in God—not phony belief; real belief." Catholic director Altman's *M*A*S*H* was especially hard on Catholics; it pictured their chaplains as totally ineffectual and bumbling, mocked their sacraments as silly charades, and transformed the miracle of the Last Supper into a prolonged smutty joke.

Altman's belabored, often hilarious, equation of the Holy Eucharist and sexual potency reveals the central transposition in *M*A*S*H*; the phallus has become the only source of meaning in the film, replacing family, nation, and God. As Daniel Spoto notes in *Camerado: Hollywood and the American Man*, older war films always placed their trust in authority, in social standing, in nationalism, or ultimately in religion. In *M*A*S*H*, war is such a horror that it denies any possible ultimate meaning to man's life, negates any conceivable rationale for patriotism, and obliterates any belief in the efficacy or existence of a God. In the absurd universe of this mobile surgical hospital, as Spoto writes, "there is only the possibility of humorous sex and sexual humor."

Catholicism in *M*A*S*H* is clearly subordinated to the sexual dynamic. Parker Tyler's allegation in *Screening the Sexes* that *M*A*S*H* "morally . . . is a pure cock and cunt tract" comes very close to the central metaphor of the film, the substitution of sexual conquests for religious victories. The saints in *M*A*S*H* are the devil-may-care playboys, and the demons are the repressed hypocritical incompetents who say their prayers at night and satisfy their sexual urges with impassioned exclamations that "God meant us to find each other" and choruses of "His will be done." One of the most stunningly inventive and effective shots in the film shows the pious Major Burns (note the pun) being carted off in a straight jacket (a physical symbol for his sexual repression) with the camera placed in such a way that the flame in a trash can (a meaphor for the waste of men and materials Korea involves) surround his tortured face. Altman holds the shot long enough for everyone to realize that this hapless Bible-whacker can never escape his morbid Inferno. What makes this scene so overwhelmingly effective is Altman's clear desire that Robert Duvall play Major Burns as a typical hard-nosed hero right out of World War II movies. In laughing at Duvall, the audience is repudiating once and for all, all the nonsense about a Christian war.

Altman builds slowly to this scene. Major Burns is introduced teaching a Korean how to read by having him recite the twenty-third Psalm, probably the most frequently cited prayer in war movies. The new doctors on the scene suggest that the boy find something a little more interesting to read and slip him a copy of a pornographic magazine. This is, of course, the typical substitution in the film: the comfort of naked bodies replaces the solace of the Good Shepherd.

Moments later, Major Burns kneels in his tent and recites the "Our Father," another prayer much intoned in war movies; as he prays, the new doctors come in and again repudiate his earnest efforts. Hawkeye (Donald Sutherland) asks Duke (Tom Skerritt), "Have you ever seen this syndrome before?" and gets the quick reply, "Not with anyone beyond eight years old." Obviously flustered by their banter, Major Burns prays even more fervently, "Dear God, protect our young men on the field that they may return to their loved ones, and dead God, protect our supreme commander in the field and our commander in chief." His prayer, which might well have been a heart-warmingly inspirational moment in dozens of other war movies, quickly becomes the object of savage satire similar to the debunking the whole film gives to its opening citations from General MacArthur and President Eisenhower. Hawkeye sardonically asks, "Frank, were you on this religious kick at home, or did you crack up over here?" and Duke complains in an exasperated tone, "How long does this show go on?" To cement the sympathy for the protagonists' charges that all religion is a juvenile, insane pretense, Altman has them rise to an exaggerated rendition of "Onward Christian Soldiers," with each chorus drenched in the bitterest of ironies. Hearing this anthem, virtually everyone at the hospital joins the parade and repudiates Major Burns. It's worth noting that the humor is so black here that even Ring Lardner, Jr., objected to it, telling William Froug it was "the only really clumsy piece of direction in the whole picture . . . for some strange reason, Bob [Altman] added a contrived, unrealistic bit in which other members of the unit outside the tent join in the singing, practically making a musical number out of it."

Major Burns's next major scene comes the night the boys put a microphone under the cot he and Major Margaret "Hot Lips" O'Houlihan (Sally Kellerman) use for lovemaking; their antics, interspersed with religious metaphors, are broadcast to the whole camp. Major Burns breaks down the next day when Hawkeye tries to force him to describe his lovemaking; the public display of his sexuality is more than he can stand. Hot Lips will also be further exposed to public scrutiny and mockery as a seeming penalty for her prudishness when the boys drop the tent during her shower. The lesson seems to be that the sacraments of sex must also be publicly performed.

This is surely the case when the venerated saint of the phallus, the Painless Pole (a typical pun in a film featuring Spearchucker and a Lieutenant Dish), suffers a momentary bout of impotency and plans his suicide. The boys turn an army tent into the cenacle and merrily prepare a bacchanal for the well-endowed dentist, which includes a quick blessing from Dago Red, the last rites, and a mock resurrection when Lieutenant Dish inspires an erection of gargantuan proportions. Dago Red's ceremonial role in this elaborate production number is indicative of the priest's ineffective bumbling through the film. When Hawkeye asks Dago Red to supply the last rites for the dentist's suicide, the flabbergasted chaplain mumbles a few clerical reservations about checking with the Military Vicar's Office and about the mortal sin involved in giving absolution to a man about to commit suicide, but a few mild rationalizations from Hawkeye are enough to befuddle Dago Red and he follows his natural inclinations to do whatever his army buddies want. In return, they give him a fainthearted, "Okay, Padre," and a "Good going, Father Dago." In M*A*S*H, the priest suffers the ultimate insult: he's so incompetent and irrelevant that the soldiers have to humor him and show him what to do. They work on the assumption that he's too stupid to understand anything and too inconsequential to be an irritation, let alone an obstacle. It is Dago Red, for example, who constantly wanders through the operating room with little to do except ask if he can help. The one time he tries to act like a priest and administer last rites, the doctors shout at him to ignore the corpse and come hold a clamp for the living. When he drifts in on the broadcast of Major Burns's lovemaking, he mistakes it for his favorite radio show, "The Battling Bickersons"; and even when he finally understands what's happening, he merely gets flustered and asks to be excused, so he can float around outside some more. Dago Red's religion gives him no sense of purpose whatsoever and no resolve; Altman has Rene Auberjonois constantly look befuddled, stare vacantly, wander aimlessly, and lose himself in prayers or a well-thumbed Bible. When everyone else is saving lives and patching up the wounded, Altman's priest is off blessing jeeps or inventorying the tons of missals the pious folks in America keep sending to an outpost that needs plasma and bandages.

Altman's evisceration of religion in general and Catholicism in particular does little to detract from his aesthetic achievement in *M*A*S*H*. His attitude may be profane and his tone sacrilegious, but his film coheres as high art must. His is a daring new vision of war; a landmark film like *M*A*S*H* is a rare phenomenon and must be evaluated on its own terms. Theologian James M. Wall makes a critical comment about *M*A*S*H* in his *Church and Cinema: A Way of Viewing Film* (1971). Wall, one of the first religious leaders to respond to Altman's daring iconoclasm, intuits the central truth; Altman's film, he argues, "deliberately offends the myths by which we live in order to expose their inadequacy." Viewed in that light, Altman is an important critic, whose vision may contravene what cult director Samuel Fuller called Hollywood's "War That's Fit to Shoot" in an *American Film* interview in November 1976, a war stereotype which, Fuller charges, "glorified, romanticized, musicalized, propagandized, tomfoolerized, and canonized" in the "reel" world the lunacy of war in the real world. Altman's powerful images may also help to foster more attention from American Catholics to the reality of modern war and their Church's place in the war effort.

Some Catholics in the seventies and eighties have, of course, already begun to question nuclear war, and the pastoral statement from American bishops on the subject has given great comfort to the many anti-war activists. Hollywood has been slow to respond to this unexpected religious crusade, but a number of small, independent productions do suggest some of the revisions which the Hollywood catechism on war and Catholicism may undergo.

Sometimes, these films suggested that that Church's best role was outside the war, helping victims. A good example of this is director Peter Werner's *Don't Cry, It's Only Thunder* (1982), an underrated project of Sanrio Communications, featuring Dennis Christopher as corpsman Brian Anderson, a terrible soldier but a charitable man whose love for kids and two Catholic nuns is a beacon of hope in an otherwise insane combat zone in Viet Nam. Like *M*A*S*H*, this film reeks of blood, gore, and cynicism; assigned to the morgue where the endless parade of massacred Americans are autopsied, Anderson is surrounded by bloated corpses, inept administrators, black market racketeers, bureaucratic red-tape, neatly bagged carnage in antiseptic refrigerators, and other less tidy evidence of real human suffering. Life for him is a jumble of venereal diseases, mangled bodies, and moral equivocations, which he escapes through drugs, wry humor, and total disengagement. Then one day he meets Sister Marie (Lisa Lu) and Sister Hoa (Thu Thuy), and their innocent charges, orphans adrift in this world of booby traps, terrorist massacres, and rowdy but sad whorehouses. The nuns give Anderson the one piece of advice he needs to change his life: "Trust God, not your army." His one moral imperative becomes those hungry kids, and the overwhelming message of this often bleak and frequently scary film echoes the famed motto of Mothers Against the War, "War is not healthy for children and other living things."

Lynne Littman brings a similar message, "We must deserve our children," to bear on the war ethos in her quite accomplished drama, *Testament,* which was produced for National Educational Television's American Playhouse, but first released to movie theaters by Paramount Films. This harrowing vision of the slow death that follows a nuclear attack was based on the story "The Last Testament" by Carol Amen, published in the *St. Anthony Messenger* in September 1980, and it affords Jane Alexander an opportunity for a tour de force performance as a mother who must comfort her dying children when the community around them slowly and agonizingly disintegrates in the aftermath of the bombing. The infants go first, then the old folks, and then the children; the parents live longest and see most clearly the moral lesson. It is the parents watching the doomed children's production of the *Pied Piper of Hamelin,* who understand that the rats of that play and the blindness of the play's townspeople are the perfect metaphor for America, its armies, and its apathetic populace. Everyone must learn the play's hard lesson: "Your children are not dead, just gone until the world deserves them." Interestingly, the screenplay holds out little hope for an effective reaction from contemporary Catholic clergy. The priest in the film is shell-shocked and has little consolation to offer. When the townspeople meet at the church after the bombings, there is little talk of God and much more focus on the vain hope that "we can make this community work." When the real horrors come—the bleeding that will not stop, the silent pain that cannot be allayed, the unendurable deaths that plague every household—the priest wanders as distractedly as Dago Red, mumbling ironically charged lines about "Whosoever believeth in me shall never die," but Jane Alexander knows better and pushes him out of the way, screaming that no one is going to bury her child until she finds his teddy bear, a consolation much more tangible and real than any the Church has offered. By the end of the film, even the priest has repudiated the divine and finds his release in a passionate erotic kiss and a curse for "whoever did this."

Other anti-war productions of the Viet Nam era hold out more hope for the power of the Catholic clergy. In Jaylo International Films' production of *Cowards* (1970), for example, Father Reis (Philip B. Hall) leads his "cowards" in an attack on a draft board office. The most dramatic attack on the Selective Service comes, however, on May 17, 1968, when a ragtag army of priests—missionaries, nuns, ex-Peace Corps members, and other morally indignant pacifists—burns the records of Local Board 33 in Catonsville, Maryland, using homemade napalm. Daniel Berrigan wrote a famous play about the aftermath of this event, *The Trial of the Catonsville Nine,* and actor Gregory Peck devoted his own personal fortune to seeing it filmed by director Gordon Davidson. The film, distributed by Cinema V, was a labor of love for all involved, and the principals all worked for union scale (most put their earnings right back in the production or contributed them to anti-war movements). No more literate and thoughtful indictment of American involvement in Viet Nam exists. Daniel Berrigan dramatically repudiates the whole tradition of Cardinal Spellman and Church blessings for modern wars, proclaiming the necessity to say no to such a Catholic Church. Berrigan wants everyone to know he is Catholic, but a new kind of committed Catholic willing to embrace civil disobedience in pursuit of faith. In his testimony, he tells the world: "May I say if my religious belief is not accepted as a substantial part of my action then the action is eviscerated of all meaning and I should be committed for insanity."

Daniel Berrrigan is quite cognizant of how far he has traveled from the world of Cardinal Spellman, whom he charges thought "the highest expression of Christian faith" was "to bless our military by his Christmas visits to our foreign legions." Berrigan laughingly identifies New York and Saint Patrick's Cathedral as "not an auspicious place to be a peaceable American priest"; yet Berrigan knows, and Hollywood is learning, that the same Catholic cathedral that serves as a focal point for Catholic immigrant families who made their rites of passage in World War II, and who now boldly display their American flags and their ethnicity in Pulaski Day parades, Columbus Day parades, and Saint Patrick Day parades, the same cathedral that saw military guards of honor lay the assassinated Kennedy brothers to rest, also serves as a rallying point for nuns and priests in candle-lit vigils, marching silently for Daniel Berrigan's dream, a time when "truth has birth" and "all former truth must die."

FIVE

The Horror Movie:
priests, rituals, and demons

"I've covered all of this in my classes, the psychology of religion, folk tales, legends, the idea of some Supreme Universal Force endlessly at war against devils and demons, for something as intangible as a human soul. I never believed any of it. I made cocktail party jokes about it. I can't believe I'm worth all this."

Richard Crenna as Professor C.J.,
the protagonist in *The Evil* (1977)

The blustery Christmas holidays of 1973 saw throngs of adolescent New Yorkers defy frostbite to line up outside Donald Rugoff's tiny arthouse cinemas, waiting patiently (sometimes for hours) to gain admission to a film about two dedicated though flawed Catholic priests ministering arcane Latin rites to a twelve-year-old atheist who masturbated herself with a crucifix. Mr. Rugoff's employees had never seen anything like this furor. Normally the staid purveyors of sensitive foreign fare to educated and refined East Side audiences, his managers, ushers, and ticket takers were working with uniformed security guards and other burly reinforcements to avoid panic and rioting. When the theater operators finally crammed every soul possible into their small auditoriums, they knew mass hysteria was to follow; patrons would scream themselves hoarse, vomit their popcorn and sodas into the aisles, charge blindly toward exits in terror, and collapse in paroxysms of fear in the lobby. Nurses were on hand to soothe the most distraught, while a triage system directed others to comfort stations and sofas. The feature film which precipitated all these around-the-clock calamities was intended, its author William Peter Blatty suggested, as an "apostolic work," an inspirational tale about the existence of a transcendent spiritual reality who commands man's attention. And in a bizarre way, William Friedkin's *The Exorcist* was, in the words of critic Pauline Kael, "the biggest recruiting poster the Catholic Church has had since the sunnier days of *Going My Way* and *The Bells of St. Mary's*" (Kael 1976, p. 249).

For an America soaked in "God is Dead" promulgations, *The Exorcist* was a startling revelation, an everlasting no to secular humanism, a homage to the demonic and the angelic, an epic poem of Catholicism. The film proved a cultural phenomenon of the very first magnitude, a runaway "must-see" hit that garnered headlines everywhere, provoked riots, prompted television specials, monopolized talk shows, and created a new movie genre—the horror film about demonic possession—a whole new spinoff film cycle. Everyone everywhere was boning up on demonology, citing the Book of Revelations, and dusting off Ouija boards. Sociologists and psychoanalysts had a new metaphor: the "demons" that possess us individually and collectively, the demons of violence, the demons of sex, the demons of doubt, the demons . . . *ad nauseam. Time, Newsweek,* even the Jesuit weekly *America* had cover stories on exorcism. Meanwhile, chanceries and rectories were besieged by families seeking exorcism rites for their "generation gap" adolescents.

At first glance, everything appeared symbiotic in this

196

interaction between Roman Catholic ritual and popular film. Author Blatty was lionized as he drifted from one adulatory interview to another, solemnly recalling the fateful day in 1949 when he first encountered *Washington Post* accounts of the possession of Douglas Deen, a fourteen-year-old living in the Mount Rainier section of Maryland. Blatty, then a junior at Georgetown University, marvelled at the horrendous ordeal this adolescent scion of a Lutheran family with Ku Klux Klan sympathies endured. The impressionable Blatty considered the eventual exorcism and cure of Douglas at the Alexian Hospital of Saint Louis under the direction of a Jesuit priest on the "Black Fast" exactly the miraculous confirmation of the efficacy of Catholic faith he needed. Where scientist Dr. J. B. Rhine of Duke University saw the finest evidence of poltergeist ever recorded, fledgling artist and wavering Catholic Blatty found, he reveals in his memoir *I'll Tell Them I Remember You*, just the "corroboration—though not proof—of the life of the spirit" he always hoped for. Just as Christ's suffering led the centurion who crucified him to salvation, Blatty felt that the agonies of this contemporary energumen, who spoke with ten demonic names, were calling him back to the cross. Encouraged by Father Thomas V. Bermingham, S.J., the Vice Provincial for Formation of the New York Province of the Society of Jesus (who plays the president of Georgetown University in the film), Blatty used Douglas Deen as an inspiration for his Regan MacNeil; and he earnestly offered his own tale of spiritual warfare as a cautionary tale aimed at Doubting Thomases across America.

By the time his novel was filmed and released, Blatty was no longer a practicing Catholic, and he identified himself as a Christian, not an ex-Catholic. In his anthology *Exorcism: Fact Not Fiction*, Martin Ebon quotes Blatty as arguing that there is no such thing as an ex-Catholic, for the Catholic Church is, Blatty proclaims, "like a woman you've had children by; she's always in your blood." This curious simile unlocks many of the problems film critics and Catholic theologians have isolated in *The Exorcist*. It is well worth noting how Blatty's Catholic Church is physical, indeed carnal; how his Church is feminine, indeed maternal; and how he focuses on progeny and family, not the traditional doxology. *The Exorcist* and the dozen or so similar possession films it spawned over the next decade constitute a very problematic chapter in the Hollywood catechism. These features are but pseudo-religious; their crypto-spirituality conceals baser elements of warped sexuality, misogyny and misogamy, crass exploitation, and unsettling nihilism. Behind the flamboyant recruiting poster, as Pauline Kael wisely observed, there was little substance, no transcendence, and much sensationalism. No wonder her review of *The Exorcist* for *The New Yorker* on January 7, 1974, sounded such a clarion call for a concerted Catholic reaction to Hollywood's insult: "Others can laugh it off as garbage, but are American Catholics willing to see their faith turned into a horror show?. . . Aren't those who accept this picture getting their heads screwed on backward?"

Most teenage thrill seekers flocking to late night screenings of *The Exorcist* didn't intellectualize the experience at all; for them it was a "head" movie, a psychedelic tour of the underworld, best savored with some mild hallucinogens. Director Friedkin, a taskmaster of cinematic illusion, had transformed the detective antics of *The French Connection* (1971) into the most vertiginous chase of all time. When he turned to Lucifer, his minions and the inferno, Friedkin, who said he wasn't a card-carrying anything when it came to religion, ensnared his audience in a narrative rollercoaster, plummeting deeper and faster than any rational being could stand—an intolerable and interminable free-fall of the imagination in a land of perversion and deception. *The Exorcist* combined metaphysical horror, sexual grotesquerie, unrelenting blasphemy, and physical suffering to create a dark night of the soul almost beyond comprehension. The whole project generated such demonic narrative energy and such stylish verve that thought and theological speculation seemed beside the point. Everything polarized into black and white, good and evil, heavenly and hellish. The demon Pazuzu was warring with Father Lankester Merrin (Max von Sydow), another Hollywood caricature of an agonizingly mortal Teilhard de Chardin plagued by heart disease and human frailty, and with Father Damien Karras (Jason Miller), a Jesuit psychotherapist with a Harvard and Johns Hopkins education, religious doubts, and a crushing sense of guilt. At stake is the troubled soul and maturing body of Regan MacNeil (Linda Blair), a seemingly passive victim of her mother's ambition, her father's indifference, and her own awkward transition from child to woman.

The main action in *The Exorcist* follows the six classic stages of exorcism which Malachi Martin isolates in his analytical survey of well-documented possessions, *Hostage to the Devil*. In nine out of ten cases, Martin maintains, several clear plateaus of activity are involved. At first, there is the "presence," a vague and foreboding air of the unnatural, parallel to the noises in the MacNeil home, the so-called rats in the attic. Then comes the "pretense" when the demon disguises its intentions; in *The Exorcist*, Regan talks of a friend called Captain Howdy (who resembles the contemporary television puppet Howdy Doody, undoubtedly a childhood fixation of hers) and his antics at a Ouija board. Then comes the "breakpoint" when everyone, including skeptical physicians enamoured of their own technology and rationalism, realizes the presence of a demon. In Regan's case there are the poltergeist phenomena: the levitations, the wild curses and obscene imprecations, the throaty foreign voices, the penetrating chill in her room, the eerie light, and the bold sexual horrors—all hell has clearly broken loose. Next comes the "Voice" when the more powerful and clearly more pronounced demon personality speaks of its mighty legions, names itself, and screams out for Father Merrin, warning the aged scholar-scientist-theologian that desolation is at hand. Once the clear identification of the principals is made, with demons on one side and exorcists on the other, then comes the "Clash," a monumental war of the wills, with the power of Christ constantly invoked to contravene the devil's legendary force and seductive energy. The resolution comes in the "expulsion" when the demon finally leaves its victim. Blatty's clash and expulsion are uncommonly complex, as a triangle of interests interact. The devil is actually confronting the spiritual strength, the intellectual pride, and the physical weakness of

Father Merrin as well as the human compassion, medical knowledge, and spiritual doubt of Father Karras. Paradoxically, Merrin's body fails him; he dies of a heart attack. His physical death confirms the fears of his superiors, but it also leaves open the validity of the claim of the demon Pazuzu that in this encounter he will defeat Merrin. Merrin's salvation is clearly in question—his pride may have been his downfall or his resolve may have been his moral salvation. The question becomes the jumping off point for the eventual film sequel, *The Heretic* (1977).

Merrin's death and the demon's awesome powers (which Blatty says he intended as a perverse mirror and stunning confirmation of God's strength) strengthen Karras's resolve, and he calls out to the devil to leave the childish Regan and possess him, a more adult and accomplished foe. This act of defiance also has several ambiguities. Stung by blistering criticisms of his film and novel, author-producer Blatty wrote *America* magazine in February of 1974 to argue that there was "goodness" in *The Exorcist*, that Father Karras acts out of *love*, and that through this love he defeats the devil, sacrificing his life for Regan, her family, and the world. Other sage critics, like Colin Westerbeck who reviewed the film for *Commonweal*, find the action not Christian love but Karras's "desperate escape from the maddening dis-ease of apostasy." Incapable of human love, incapable of spiritual belief, Westerbeck argues, Karras actively "chooses damnation" in the devil he can feel: "In the end he hasn't found anything he can sacrifice himself for, but only something he can sacrifice himself to. The vanquishing hero of this movie, then, is the Devil."

What is clear in the film, thanks to special effects Dr. Jekyll and Mr. Hyde would be proud of, is that the demon Pazuzu, a figure from Babylonian mythology, the personification of the southwest wind whose domain is sickness and disease, does dominate Father Karras's body after leaving Regan's tortured flesh. When Karras feels the horrible power of the demon in him, urging him to strangle Regan, he runs to the window, flings himself out in a bold *felo-de-se*, destroying the demon and himself in this defenestration. Then, in a scene added after prerelease screenings, his friend Father Dyer (played by Jesuit priest Father William O'Malley, one of Blatty's ecclesiastical mentors) hears his confession and offers him absolution for "all his sins."

One critical point in this narrative, which author William Peter Blatty truly belabors in his novel, and which director William Friedkin inexplicably obscures in his film, is the absolute linkage, the clear relationship, between the earthly power of Pazuzu and the heavenly energy of God. Blatty, the aspiring Catholic intellectual steeped in Jesuit lore, knew quite well that Regan's exemplary exorcism, if it is to have a theological dimension, must be related to her salvation, the destinies of Father Merrin and Father Karras, and to the problem of evil in the contemporary world. Blatty became so entangled in the complexities of this theme that he frequently risks tendentiousness in his novel to allow Father Merrin to coach the more practically oriented healer, Father Karras, on the fine points of metaphysics. In a key speech in the novel, Father Merrin carefully explains that the battle is not for Regan's immortal soul at all. Because she is possessed and incapable of acting freely, Regan cannot sin, and therefore cannot be eternally damned. Her possession is really a battle for the two priests' souls and for the souls of everyone she knows: ". . . the point is to make us despair; to reject our own humanity, Damien: to see ourselves as ultimately bestial; as ultimately vile and putrescent; without dignity; ugly; unworthy. And there lies the heart of it, perhaps: in unworthiness." Merrin's constant message involves this sense of human worth. God has not made trash, he avers, and every soul is worth fighting for; every soul has resplendent cosmic import. The belief in God, he argues, is not a rational act at all; it is instead an openness to love, a willingness to accept "the possibility that God could love us."

Merrin's ideas here echo much of the thinking of Rudolf Otto in his classic *The Idea of the Holy: An Inquiry into the Non-rational Factor in the Idea of the Divine and Its Relation to the Rational* (1923). Otto was quite intent on the "numinous" aspect of God, an incalculable energy and power, which he felt also explained the ferocity of God's fallen angel, Lucifer. For Otto, God's goodness posited its opposite, a demon who is "fury, the *orgē*, hypostatized, the *mysterium tremendum* cut loose from the other elements and intensified to *mysterium horrendum* . . . the negatively numinous." Otto called on his confreres to do a "special inquiry" on the horrors and depths of Satan, "an analysis of fundamental feelings, and something very different from a mere record of 'the evolution of the idea of the devil'." Blatty's novel, while no theological plumbing of the demon's negative numinousness, does reverse Otto's reasoning process to see evil in its most blatant physical manifestation as an overwhelming proof of God's existence. Blatty's exorcists in their confrontations with Regan's devilish tortures are releasing their own demons of intellectual pride and solipsistic despair. Their minds and hearts are opening to God's love as they exorcise not just that Babylonian demon Pazuzu, but their own contemporary devils; the healers are being healed.

Father Karras, for example, who begins the novel with the despairing admission of his own loss of faith and a plea to be released from his pastoral duties to other struggling priests, feels so fortified in faith by his experience of spiritual evil that he challenges the terrifying demon to a duel of wills, imploring his adversary to spare childish opponents and turn to more adult foes: "Come on! Come on, loser! Try me! Leave the girl and take me! Take me! Come into . . ." When the demon accepts his invitation, Karras makes a dramatic leap (symbolic of his newfound faith in God's love) which saves Regan and seemingly himself: "No! I won't let you hurt them! You're not going to hurt them! You're coming with . . ." After his sacrifice, Father Karras in the novel *The Exorcist* apparently has found peace (only in the companion novel *Legion*, written a decade later, does an alternate ending emerge). In the original novel, his confidant and mentor Father Dyer sees *shantih*, the peace that surpasses understanding, in the middle-aged (seemingly dead) exorcist's eyes. As Dyer gazes at the transfigured Karras, he witnesses the birth of a saint: "his eyes filled with peace; and with something else: something mysteriously like joy at the end of heart's longing. The eyes were still staring. But at nothing in this world. Nothing here." Pazuzu has inadvertently brought Karras to Christ, the original novel clearly suggests;

evil has given way to Rudolf Otto's "the Holy." This link between seemingly motiveless malignity and the divine plan stands in the novel as the main theme, Father Merrin's principal message to the younger, despairing Karras, who eventually takes up the mantle of the older exorcist. Father Merrin assures Karras that from evil "will come good" in a way that the devil can never understand: "Perhaps evil is the crucible of goodness. And perhaps even Satan—Satan, in spite of himself—somehow serves to work out the will of God."

None of this, not one word of explanation, not one mention of Merrin's discovery and of his theological justification of evil appears in the release print of *The Exorcist*. The scenes were shot, author Blatty urged they be in the film, but director Friedkin (who admitted they were the central thematic scenes in the novel) refused to put them in the film. Friedkin even alters Karras's last words to make his fate truly ambiguous. Blatty's original screenplay (reprinted in the fascinating study of the film's evolution, *William Peter Blatty on The Exorcist*) featured a virtual transcript of the novel's dialogue with Karras pleading, "Come on loser! Try me! Leave the girl and take me! Come into me! Take me! Come into me! Come into—" In the original screenplay, the possessed Karras continues his act of love when he regains some control: "Good! Yes, you're stupid! Stupid, loser!" And to the demon's promptings to kill Regan and others, he answers, "No! No, you're not going to harm them! No! Over here! Over—!" and hurls himself and the demon out the window. The final script, and the scene as shot, leave Karras's fate clearly in doubt. The audience hears a much more satanic challenge, "You son of a bitch! Take me! Come into me! Goddamn you, take me! Take me!" sees the demon possess Karras, and hears him say only "No" before he throws himself out the window. The transcript of the film that Blatty prepared describes Karras winning the fight "for control of his body" and "compelling it" toward the window; theater audiences saw only death and had to choose their own victor.

Most critics recognized what a cosmic shift in the narrative these omitted scenes and altered dialogue represented; stripping the explanations away and obscuring the outcome made the film of *The Exorcist* a real horror show devoid of both God and humanity. Here was physical evil up against godless girls and infirm priests weakened by intellectual pride and a hardening of the heart. Merrin knew the answers, but he was so locked up in intellectual pride that he never shared them; Karras had only questions, vomit on his face, guilt, a dead mentor, a fiendishly besmirched and bedeviled young girl crying out for solace, desecrated churches, wayward priests, seemingly damned mothers, angry relatives, and the void. No wonder, then, that Andrew Sarris assailed the film in *The Village Voice* with unmitigated venom. Recalling the lost scenes, the displaced moral, and the added horrors, Sarris reminded his readers that in the novel, the devil is after "the intellectually vain Father Merrin and the emotionally self-deceiving Father Karras." On screen, Sarris intimates, different devils are after the very souls of the movie's spectators: Sarris opines that Blatty and Friedkin withhold all the theology because such knowledge has "insidious implications in terms of the supposedly ethical relationship between film-maker and viewer." Like Pazuzu, Sarris suggests, *The Exorcist* wants modern audiences to see themselves as vile, ugly, putrescent, and unworthy of God's love. Sarris's jeremiad about *The Exorcist* finally explodes in a charge that is both perceptive and persuasive: "*The Exorcist* succeeds on one level as an effectively excruciating entertainment, but on another, deeper level it is a thoroughly evil film."

Sarris makes an extraordinarily useful distinction in separating the box-office appeal, the so-called "entertainment" values of *The Exorcist* from its moral import and tone. Warner Brothers had the biggest hit of the Christmas season not by celebrating an infant God of love, but by offering a horror masterpiece that wallowed in curses, blasphemies, desecrations, spirit-rappings, levitations, sexual perversion, hysteria, evil spirits, frustration, doubt, and despair. Audiences were coming not to be uplifted, but to be "grossed out." The film presented a Catholic Church with primitive rituals, anachronistic liturgies, and a fixation on spiritual icons, on miraculous medals, holy water, and plaster of paris statues. By deleting the theological context, the film fixed its focus even more intently on ceremony; incantation replaced faith and chant replaced charity. Catholicism appeared a creed of forms without substance, of vestments without commitments, of sacramentals without sanctity. A minor demon emerged as at least God's equal and more than a match for God's minions. *The Exorcist* begins the most Jansenistic chapter in the Hollywood catechism, a disgusting procession of demonic interventions in human life, where at best, God, through the clumsy agency of very ignorant and incompetent priests, painstakingly crawls his way back to a standoff with a devil who makes his task look easy and fun. *The Exorcist* provides for a whole generation of cash-happy filmmakers and artists the perfect financial rationale to proclaim their "sympathy for the devil."

Producer Blatty was all too cognizant of the stunning deletions in *The Exorcist* as film: after all, research in possession had been the focus of his apostolate for many years, and the novel was his fitful contribution to Catholic apologetics. In his lengthy account of the evolution of the film's production, he admits that he would very much have preferred (and still desires) the inclusion of a key scene in which Merrin explains teleology and Divine Providence to Karras, a scene which Max von Sydow, who plays Merrin, evidently played with true artistry, but which ended on the cutting room floor. Blatty blames director Friedkin for the exclusion: "Billy said it was a 'showstopper' not in the usual sense but in that it stopped the action dead in its tracks by pausing for a 'theological commercial'." Confirmation of Blatty's assertion can be found in an interview Friedkin gave Peter Travers and Stephanie Reiff for their detailed presentation of *The Story Behind "The Exorcist"* (1974). Friedkin obviously did not want his horror show pausing for any interruption and clearly not for a "theological commercial." Friedkin told Travers and Reiff that "There will be no theological messages up front." Developing his rationale, Friedkin proclaimed his whole film "theological" and displayed his populist, egalitarian, liberal piety by refusing most sanctimoniously to preach to this teenage audience: "I take the intelligence of the audience for granted. I'm not going to suggest that the audience will not get the message of the picture, unless they are told overtly, unless it is spelled out for them."

Friedkin's argument seems disingenuous in the extreme. One afternoon in any theater showing the film, or an hour's chat with any of Donald Rugoff's employees could convince even Friedkin that it wasn't a sweet "Amen" audiences were yelling at the screen and it wasn't the rapturous acceptance of Divine Love which transported them. Director Friedkin terrified and terrorized audiences and never put the evil in a clear context. Father Karras was dead, Father Merrin was dead, and Pazuzu seemed merely transported back to his home in Nineveh, waiting for another vainglorious old priest to dare disturb him. Even Regan and her mother, Chris, weren't moved to the life of faith in this film. The MacNeils (fallen away Irish Catholics?) gave the sacred medal back to Father Dyer, kissed his Roman collar, wished him well, and took off to Europe to forget the whole unsavory episode. Jonathan Rosenbaum makes the fine point in his charming memoir *Moving Places: A Life at the Movies* that "stories alone were not what one came away from the movies with, that atmosphere and impressions were more enduring." Audiences leaving *The Exorcist* weren't fragrant with the odor of sanctity, they reeked of the ordure of Pazuzu; they weren't blinded by celestial light, they were stupefied by Stygian darkness; they weren't tranquil in their acceptance of providence, they were catatonic after an unendurable assault on their senses. John Simon, normally the master of overkill, was right on target in *Esquire* when he offered a most odorous and scatalogical figure of speech to characterize the experience of Friedkin's film. Reminding his readers that Church fathers had seen birth taking place *"inter faeces et urinas,"* Simon opined that the spiritual life of this film occurs "between the urine of Regan and the excrement of William Peter Blatty."

In place of theology, viewers of *The Exorcist* could find a good deal of pop science torn right from the pages of *Psychology Today* and *Transaction;* simplified Freud, Jung, Laing, and Adler replaced the thornier musings of Maritain, Bloy, von Balthazar, and Schillebeeckx. As so often happens in the Hollywood catechism, complex theological concepts and involved moral tangles were transmuted into simpler, more straightforward genre formulas. The Gordian knot of metaphysics was cut by the Occam's razor of contemporary fads; the mysteries of faith displaced by the problems that kept women's magazines afloat; the quandries that kept soap operas topical; and the perplexities that made such books as *I'm O.K., You're O.K.; Open Marriage; Transcendental Meditation; Tuning In, Turning On, Dropping Out; The Greening of America; The Pursuit of Loneliness;* and *The Culture of Narcissism* the mainstay of publishing houses everywhere.

The Exorcist contains a grab-bag of half-digested theories, buzz-words, and pseudo-insights; recast the script as a table of contents and one could easily generate an issue of *Cosmopolitan* or *Seventeen*. Consider, for example, a litany of such burning issues as how to cope with menstruation, what to do when Mom's a famous actress, or how to deal with the absentee father. Add to this such questions as why do bad things happen to good girls, how do you face the demon you cannot suppress, and is God really running with you, and you're well on your way to a holiday double issue. The movie has all of these and more, featuring everything except that "theological commercial" which would insult its audience's intelligence.

The sexual issues loom particularly large. In his research on possession, Blatty discovered that over 90 percent of the reported cases of demonic possession were frauds or delusions; only very few cases demanded further investigation or merited serious attention. In over 80 percent of the modern cases, the victim of demons was a woman. The ratio is, Blatty asserts, "so disproportionate as to suggest, as opposed to possession, a common disorder once alluded to as *furor uterinus,* an expression that speaks, I would think, for itself." By transforming Douglas Deen to Regan MacNeil, Blatty made his product more typical and more marketable, since misogynistic Hollywood always seeks female victims, preferably voluptuous virgins, powerful screamers with scant or no clothing, to chase down Freudian dark alleys, up symbolic staircases, and into dark closets, caverns, and tombs. Friedkin's emphasis on the possibility that menses and demons are linked (a connection Brian

De Palma uses time and time again, notably in *Carrie*, a misogynistic nightmare) can be seen in his first few interludes with Regan and Chris. Sex and physical maturity dominate Chris's conversations with her daughter. When Regan rhapsodizes about seeing a man on a beautiful gray horse in the park, Chris uses the occasion to quiz the twelve-year-old on sexual identity, asking the inexplicable question, 'Was it a mare, a gelding, or what?" Regan answers, "I think it was a gelding," and Chris murmurs, "Um-hum." Later that night, Chris discovers Regan reading an issue of *Photoplay* with their picture on the cover. Aside from suggesting the social status of this pair and paying homage to the magazine from which the film borrows its narrative flair and intellectual substance, this visual allusion also generates another conversation about bodies, sexual identity, and physical maturity. Chris teases Regan about the cover photo, admonishing that "It's not even a good picture of you. You look so mature." The camera obviously doesn't lie; Chris is just unable to see Regan's developing sexuality. Regan responds rather cattily to her mother, "I wouldn't talk." Chris tries to dismiss the slight with a hug, but adds, "I didn't have my makeup man there." Even the slowest soap opera aficianado would recognize the clear generation gap here, the refusal of a mother to let her daughter grow up, and the green-eyed monster of sexual jealousy threatening to possess the girl. Commentator Stephen E. Bowles reports in his "Damnation and Purgation: *The Exorcist* and *Jaws*" (*Literature/Film Quarterly*, Summer 1976) that "Many adolescent girls, afflicted with the social-physical changes of puberty, tended to identify their own *apparently* inexplicable and abnormal malady with that of Regan's symptoms of possession."

This sexual dimension also de-mystifies the desecration of the statue of the Blessed Virgin Mary. Someone had transformed the madonna into a whore, glueing an erect penis to its loins and fashioning immense breasts for the demure maiden. Pazuzu, it should be remembered, was a demon notable for his ragged wings, his taloned feet, his feral grin, and his threatening, always erect, penis. The possessed Regan drives her doctors away with her shocking screams, "Fuck me!

Fuck me!" After she lacerates her vagina with the crucifix, she forces her mother's face into her pelvis, screams "Lick me," and calls out in the voice of her first victim, Burke Dennings. "Do you know what she did, your cunting daughter?" It is clear why critic M. [Madonna] Kolbenschlag finds Regan MacNeil one of her most important examples of the pubertal girl as a grotesque in her article "The Female Grotesque: Gargoyles in the Cathedrals of Cinema" (*Journal of Popular Film*, Winter 1978).

Another exaggerated theme, a gargoyle if you will, in Friedkin's secular cathedral is the problem of divorce and the potentially wicked stepfather. Regan obviously loved her daddy very much and is quite disturbed that only ten months after the divorce, Burke Dennings (Jack MacGowran), a rather foulmouthed, vulgar, nasty drunk, has mesmerized her mother. Chris tries to assure Regan that the relationship isn't serious, just a casual intimacy with a lonely man, but Regan persists, "Well, I heard—differently." Burke Dennings dies soon thereafter on the steps behind Chris's house, seemingly hurled from Regan's window (a disturbing foreshadowing of Father Karras's self-willed plunge). Compound Regan's animosity for Burke with her stoic lack of reaction to her natural father's total indifference (he even forgets her birthday), and one has the perfect environment for a poltergeist, devoid of any theological import. Psychoanalyst Harvey R. Greenberg makes this line of inquiry the major focus in his professional dissection of *The Exorcist* in *The Movies on Your Mind* (1975). In Greenberg's medical opinion, Regan's maturation demands that she achieve a "healthy psychological separation from Chris," a more mature relationship with her father, and "a gradual consolidation of identity." Her father's neglect, Greenberg feels, "casts a shadow over the growth process, and the desire for closeness with the mother may escalate out of proportion, impeding or permanently compromising individuation."

This focus on momism as a debilitating and disorienting malaise finds its parallel in Father Karras's problems with Mother Church. Karras neglected his natural mother to serve his spiritual one; his vocation meant isolation and material deprivation for his immigrant mother, who finds herself alone, hiding in a world of foreign radio broadcasts seemingly oblivious to her squalid apartment and the urban ghetto around her. Her legs give out first, and Karras's attempts to bandage them cannot alleviate her pain. Then her mind cracks, and her son, the shrink with the vow of poverty, must watch her languish in the psycho-ward at Bellevue Hospital. Her agonies are so intense here that the normally stoic woman calls out, "Why have you done this to me, Dimmy?" Mrs. Karras dies alone, and her corpse rots for days before anyone finds her; around this time, Damien begins to doubt the efficacy of his spiritual mother. Filmmakers Blatty and Friedkin obviously wanted the images of mother to be central in the film. Blatty admits that his affection for the abrasive director came in part from their common dedication to their mothers: "I felt a special kinship to Friedkin. He had been very devoted to his mother and had taken her death three years before very hard . . . the woman he cast to play the role of Karras's mother looked a blend of his mother and mine." Surprisingly, however, this composite mother speaks through Regan's demonic visage; the clear suggestion is that Father Karras's neglect of her led to her damnation. His mother lost her faith because of him, and he is losing faith in Mother Church. In healing Regan, he restores her to Chris, the mother who may be impeding her psychic development, the mother who chases her to a psychiatrist in *Exorcist Two—the Heretic* although she is the guardian Regan feels she must hide the truth from, at any cost. If, as Blatty intimates in *I'll Tell Them I Remember You,* his mother was the critical influence in his artistic life, it is dreadfully clear that he has some real ambivalences about mother love, ambivalences he also stirred up in his audiences.

It's Mother Church, however, that takes the worst beating in *The Exorcist.* All the *au courant* subtexts in the film undercut any relevance of theology to the issue at hand. Theology is more than ignored; it's hidden beneath the superstructure of adolescent sexual fears, fragmented family structures, and a destructive matriarchy. Author James Baldwin expands on this idea of the misplaced focus of *The Exorcist* in his exciting essay *The Devil Finds Work.* Like many other critics, Baldwin thinks the devil in *The Exorcist* is too banal to be interesting, too straightforward, too obvious; Baldwin chides that Satan "was never like that when he crossed my path." But Baldwin then digs a little deeper to uncover a darker secret in the film. *The Exorcist*, he shrewdly notes, is not "the least concerned with damnation." Its real focus is capitalism, not sanctity. Regan matters because this is Georgetown, Chris is a superstar, and money talks. Father Karras ignores many equally possessed souls in Bellevue's charity ward; he avoids beggars who mumble about their days as altar boys and beg for a dime; yet he gives his life for a society matron with a big brownstone and a spoiled, would-be debutante. Father Karras is living out the fantasy of Father Dyer, who struggles so hard to be glib at upper echelon cocktail parties, mocking himself with a most revealing patter as he belts out some Bing Crosby style ditties on the piano: "I don't need any encouragement. My idea of heaven is a solid white nightclub, with me as a headliner for all eternity, and they love me." His sad version of "Home Sweet Home" (a Blatty irony) brings Regan down to reward him with a torrent of urine.

The order being disturbed in *The Exorcist* is the social order, not the moral one. Regan's defilement threatens, Baldwin wisely observes, America's most sacred cows, "property . . . tax shelters, stocks and bonds, rising and falling markets, the continued invulnerability of a certain class of people, and the continued sanctification of a certain history." Such threats deserve the big guns of the Church to quiet them: Father Merrin comes scurrying from his studies, and Father Karras, "the best the Church has," leaves doubting priests at bay to protect moneyed children. His mother may suffer and die poor, but the rich MacNeils must never be threatened by demons. One can almost hear the redoubtable Mother Jones railing again that "these sisters of God are owned lock, stock, and barrel by the Rockefellers."

Because *The Exorcist* so strongly concerns itself with the physical side of things, it becomes difficult, if not impossible, to accept any pretense of moral purpose. Producer Blatty was surely floundering about for a justification when he tried to convince interviewers that "I think the audiences are making the unconscious connection between the repulsive monstrosity on the screen and the moral evil in their lives, like stealing from their brother and calling it business." It's a huge metaphorical leap from bloody crucifixes, profane language, green slimy vomit, a serpent's forked tongue, heads that turn full circle, beds that levitate, and messages carved on abdomens to any moral sensitivity at all. Critic Jon Landau, who reviewed *The Exorcist* for *Rolling Stone* seems considerably closer to the truth when he argues that the very physical horrors of this prolonged sideshow vitiated any possibility of including Merrin's theological overview: "The inclusion of a statement of what the movie should have been about would have surely exposed the crassness of its [actual] intentions." As Landau sees it, *The Exorcist* is a "religious porn film, the gaudiest piece of big budget schlock this side of Cecil B. DeMille." Blatty was not unaware of how Friedkin was confusing the supernatural with the impossible, the demonic with the obscene, and suggested, for example, modifications in the famed rotation of Regan's head. His pleas were largely unheeded, however, and he eventually had to admit that, while it seemed excessive and unreal to him, "audiences loved it, proving me an idiot once again." One wonders if Blatty would change everything in the film if audiences loved it—is idiocy really a refusal to go along with mass taste? Director William Friedkin is obviously of two minds on the subject. He wants to pack them in for *The Exorcist*, but he also wants to force them to look away. In place of a theology of evil, he advocates a plentitude of visceral thrills to suggest the nature of the demon's power: "You can't make the devil into Donald Duck. You have to make people nauseous, create the inability to look at the screen, to cover your eyes, to turn away." Friedkin achieves his goal in many sections of the film. He makes the exorcism too disturbing to watch; he creates a film that screams out not to watch it. One wonders at the splendor of such an achievement. Stephen Bowles seems so correct in his assertion that "The film transforms Blatty's moral inquiry into an unrelieved image of abuse." All the agonies become, in the words of Dr. Harvey Greenberg, "grisly routines to be ticked off with sadomasochistic relish." In the place of morality, theology, and sanctity, *The Exorcist* offered special effects, shocks, and solipsistic half-truths. One wonders if Father Patrick Sullivan of the Department of Film and Broadcasting of the United States Catholic Conference didn't have the right reaction when, in Blatty's words, "he went straight up through the ceiling" as he read the script of the film. Blatty mentions Father Sullivan in an interview reprinted in *The Story Behind the Exorcist* because this noted Jesuit theologian (a Blatty aside jokes, "Would you believe, a Jesuit!") wouldn't allow Holy Trinity Roman Catholic Church to be used as a locale for the film, despite the urgings of Father Thomas Bermingham, the Jesuit provincial of New York (a player in the film). Sullivan's interdict stood, and the so-called Catholic church scenes were shot in an Episcopal cathedral.

However, Father Sullivan's moral ire couldn't stop the juggernaut of sensationalism that became *The Exorcist*, just as the serious aesthetic reservations of William Peter Blatty and William Friedkin couldn't stop Warner Brothers from commissioning a sequel, *Exorcist Two: the Heretic*, which suffered a terrible death at the box office. The Seventies was an era of sequels; *The Godfather* gave us *Godfather Two*, *Jaws* begat *Jaws II*, *Airport* begat *The Concorde*, *The Planet of the Apes* spun off galaxies, and James Bond disproved the thesis that *You Only Live Once*. *The Heretic*, however, afforded a most potent warning that one success doesn't insure another. For a few days, the widely advertised feature drew the hard core fans of Pazuzu, but even they soon punctuated their laughter with hisses and boos. When this trade disappeared, there was only silence, theaters as desolate as the plains of Nineveh.

Planning a sequel to *The Exorcist* was, everyone admitted, a problem; the obvious question was where do you go from here? Quizzed about this in public, William Friedkin deadpanned that he was already working on *Regan Goes to College*. Author Blatty was a trifle more serious, detailing a plot for *The Son of the Exorcist*, an apocalyptic novel about "a nuclear sub whose commander has an abcessed tooth and migraine headache, is apparently possessed by Attila the Hun and in the midst of a painful divorce . . . the sub [is] lurking hidden off Asbury Park." In other articles, Blatty wondered aloud about the real nature of the devil. Thus in 1974 he wrote a piece speculating that the devil may not be a single personal intelligence, but Legion, a horde of different evil personages. Ten years later this idea would percolate to the surface in Blatty's novelistic sequel to *The Exorcist, Legion*, which features a resurrected Father Karras locked in a padded cell, describing gruesome murders happening all around him. *Legion* de-emphasizes Pazuzu in its focus on "the evil in the fabric of creation": "the songs of the whales were haunting and lovely, but the lion ripped open the stomach of the wildebeest and the tiny ichneumonids fed in the living bodies of caterpillars underneath the pretty lilacs and the lawns." Everywhere Blatty's protagonist Detective Kinderman (a Blatty name) looks, he discovers the flaw in God's fabric.

Director John Boorman, a surprising choice on Warner Brothers' part to direct *The Heretic*, tried very hard to film just the opposite kind of sequel. Boorman labored mightily to see the good that overwhelms the darkness of Pazuzu, and while his film proved poison at the box office, it does contain some powerful thrusts at a philosophy of creative evolution, a Teilhard de Chardin-like movement towards the good. As Todd McCarthy convincingly argues in his article "The Exorcism of *The Heretic*" in *Film Comment*, September 1977, (one of the finest portraits of the reworking of a film ever written and a model of film scholarship) Boorman may well have molded a film too challenging for its audiences—a theological film working at the very borders of Catholic thinking. In his generally negative assessment of the impact of the new Catholic theology, *The New Church: Essays in Catholic Reform* (1966), Daniel Callahan had warned that while "the new realm of Catholic thought—of I-thou encounters, salvation history, omega points, Lonergan-like insight, *sein* and *dasein, kerygma*—is a delightful place to live," it was also a lonely place, since Catholics are "the only ones who live there, along with a few scattered Protestants." Callahan was so discouraged because he feared that the recent progress in Catholic thought which had been nothing less than spectacular enjoyed little popular acceptance; it languished in the theological institutes and meant no more to the man on the street than "the old scholastic panoply of clear and certain ideas." Callahan's fears may well have been justified in *The Heretic*. The ordinary moviegoer wasn't interested or intrigued by Boorman's metaphysics in *The Heretic*, and Friedkin's thrills clearly weren't there. The film was, paradoxically, too bright and too dull to be a success. It was all Catholic theological commercial and its British director forgot to stop for the physical horrors American audiences craved.

Boorman's film has been so drastically reshaped for its various abortive incarnations that one almost needs Todd McCarthy's article just to follow the narrative. The central theme and critical idea of the film, though frequently obscured in re-editings, concerns the ongoing war between emerging good and the negativism of evil. Both forces seem capable of shaping the world around them into plagues of locusts or bountiful harvests; both can inspire human adulation, leading souls to celebration or immolation; and both can shape the planet's destiny in a choice between apocalypse and parousia. Powerful spiritual presences like Father Merrin, whose mind is a beacon for others to follow, draw equally powerful demons to tempt them; in his case, subtle devils of pride, intellectual arrogance, and heretical respect for Satan. Regan, a gifted psychic healer in this film, stands ready to lead man on the next evolutionary step, the next leap toward the Christ who is to be; her demons are horrible physical afflictions, the concupiscence of Pazuzu, and the whirlwinds of adversity. Father Lamont, the new exorcist, courageously seeks to protect the truth wherever he finds it, but his faith is easily shaken by the tremendous seductive power of Satan, and there are naked women waiting everywhere to call him to perdition. The black saint in the film, Kokumo, has both the talisman and science on his side, and he represents the hope that science and theology will unite to control evil, but he, too, has had his brush with Pazuzu's locusts and seems as drawn to their headdress as he does to the laboratory.

Boorman's focus on theological truth emerges quite early

in the film. Father Lamont (Richard Burton) receives orders from his cardinal to investigate the death of Father Merrin. Powerful elements in the Church have attacked the exorcist for his alleged "Satanism," his adulation of the powers of darkness. Lamont, the cardinal, and Merrin were old friends, and the cardinal wants Father Lamont to divine the truth of what happened in Georgetown. Father Lamont, aware of his growing lust and faltering faith, asks to be excused from the quest, but the Cardinal insists he make himself "worthy" as a "soldier of Christ." The focus in the film clearly revolves around Lamont's destiny, his ability to discern and to act on the truth. Boorman is back to Blatty's original conception: the exorcist is the one being exorcised, the investigator is the person under investigation. Lamont is "the heretic" who must rediscover orthodoxy and join the Church's progress to salvation.

Father Lamont's earliest encounters involve an apostle of rationalism and psychology, Dr. Gene Tuskin, who ardently hopes to avoid taking Regan back to the reality of Georgetown, and who plans to solve Regan's problems with the gadgetry of medical science, a hypnotic device that allows two persons to experience the same psychic reality. Dr. Tuskin's rationalism, her focus on adolescence, divorce, and social adjustment, embodies, of course, the fads so prominent in *The Exorcist*; as played by Louise Fletcher, she come very close to being a parody, a Dr. Feelgood. When Lamont warns her, "You realize what you're up against? Evil!" she drifts off into a superficial anodyne about "mental illness, or, if you like, the casualties of a diseased society." Such claptrap may have been good enough for *The Exorcist*, but Father Lamont insists that this apostle of modernity confront a more ancient truth: "Evil is a spiritual being . . . alive and living . . . perverted and perverting . . . weaving its way insidiously into the very fabric of life." By the end of the film, Dr. Tuskin the scientist will accept the axioms of Lamont's theology; like Kokumo, she too will be ready to use science and technology to speed a new order shaped by the power and example of the good.

The hero in *The Heretic*, Kokumo (James Earl Jones), has survived an exorcism more harrowing than Regan's; it was that first exorcism in Africa by Father Merrin, referred to in *The Exorcist* and shown here. Kokumo, a powerful healer, can quiet the frenzied locusts, spit leopards at Pazuzu, and plan to eliminate world hunger. He also has seen Merrin's great truth: that evil comes to test the good, and as it is vanquished, evil takes its proper subordinate place in God's beneficent plan. Kokumo, whose psychic powers are immense, already knows of Regan, "the girl in the dreams," who holds great powers and hope for all mankind; and he warns Father Lamont to embrace her goodness, though Lamont has "been brushed by the wings of Pazuzu" and has lost faith in God.

From this point on, the question in *The Heretic* becomes whether Lamont can embrace Regan's goodness, reject Pazuzu's powers, and facilitate mankind's leap to a new spiritual plane. Father Lamont can educate Regan about the teachings of Teilhard de Chardin, "a French priest who thought we'd all come together in some sort of mental telepathy, a world mind in which everyone would share," but to help her reach that new spiritual consciousness, he must overcome his own very human weaknesses. When Dr. Tuskin asks a rather leading question of the handsome priest, "Don't you ever need a woman, Father?" his answer is a disarmingly truthful, "Yes." Originally director Boorman hoped to cast Jon Voight or Christopher Walken opposite Linda Blair and George Segal was to be the doctor; the sexual complications intrinsic in such characterizations were to be a focus of the film, with Linda more tempted by *eros* and thus less driven to *caritas*. As the film stands, this erotic dynamic seems muted, and the request Regan makes to Lamont when he's mesmerized by the thrill of Pazuzu's supernatural energy, seems much more to do with faith and humanity than sexual ecstasy: "Father, please don't be lost to me." Lamont doesn't lose his soul, and Regan manages to calm the locusts and other evil spirits in that Georgetown brownstone. In the original ending, Lamont makes their victory a clear statement of a new theological age: "The time has come, now we are saved and made strong. An enemy of the human race is subdued," and he and Regan walk off, holding hands, "toward the city, a future." In the print now in release, the explanation is excised, and one sees Regan standing victorious in the rubble, with subdued locusts around her as the screen fades to white.

John Boorman's desperate attempt to make *The Heretic*, a disaster in America, successful in its European version, provides an unintentional insight into how it was theology that turned audiences away in the United States. Boorman, a consummate craftsman whose films *Point Blank* (1968), *Deliverance* (1972), and *Zardoz* (1973) reveal a filmmaker of considerable intellectual substance and cinematic sense, sat through many theatrical screenings of *The Heretic* to try to isolate what had the audiences giggling or booing; he then made over a hundred alterations in his work, which Todd McCarthy summarizes in his *Film Comment* analysis of the film. A perusal of the major shifts suggests a generalization McCarthy hints at but avoids exploring; it was Boorman's daring attempts at theology and philosophy which brought the scorn. For its European release, Boorman made *The Heretic* the same sort of spiritual eunuch *The Exorcist* was. To cite but a few changes of the many he made, all dialogue about Merrin, his heresy, and his adulation of evil are gone; Tuskin's question to Lamont about needing a woman is cut; Lamont's summary of Teilhard de Chardin disappears; Kokumo's explanation of the locusts and their brushing wings is eliminated; and the ending is truncated even further. What audiences could conceivably make of this butchered film is unclear. All that remains is weird rituals, unconnected subplots, and accomplished special effects.

Unfortunately, most of the progeny of *The Exorcist* make similarly frustrating and incomprehensible contributions to film history. Bizarre transpositions take place in these visions of demonic possession, but evil always seems quite powerful (and very frequently triumphant); Catholic priests seem an enervated bunch suffering male menopause and spiritual anorexia; and Catholic laity seem preoccupied with sexual hangups and an all-encompassing guilt. One sees the stubby penis of Pazuzu, his taloned feet, and his feral grin everywhere in the decade; omega points and evolutionary leaps seem far away and long ago. The nihilism of this chapter in the Hollywood catechism rankles as much as the mindless exploitation, the sideshow atmosphere, and the perverted sex. These films depict an "unworthy" universe, controlled by an unfathomable force; Kafka and the Marquis de Sade are much more at home in this penal colony than Teilhard de Chardin or Pope John XXIII.

Undoubtedly the best-known imitation of *The Exorcist* is *Amityville II: the Possession* (1982). The bizarre numbering is really immaterial; horror buffs don't worry about which is sequel and which is prequel, and besides, *Amityville II* shares only one element with *The Amityville Horror* (1979), that fabled house at 112 Ocean Avenue, Amityville, Long Island, where on the morning of November 13, 1974, at 3:15 A.M., Ronald De Feo, acting under the instruction of "voices," shot and killed his entire family: his father, his mother, his teenage sister, his two younger brothers, and another younger sister. This mass murder dominated the headlines in New York City for months, and there were bizarre tales of demonic possessions, heretical priests, poltergeists, and incest. The irrepressible Hans Holzer turned his eye on all these carrying-ons and the result was *Murder in Amityville*, the putative basis for Tommy Lee Wallace's screenplay. A comparison of Holzer's relatively restrained reconstruction of the events leading up to that horrible November night and Wallace's all-stops-out melodrama affirms the Hollywood catechism's drive for sensationalism. Holzer is no shrinking violet when it comes to speculation on the events, but the screenplay and the film play out his every card in trumps.

Holzer's hints of an unhappy home life in Amityville are magnified in the film into a demonic family circle lorded over by a brutish Italian lout who finds pleasure in reminding his adolescent son that "the peach fuzz" on his face doesn't mean his old man can't spank him whenever he likes; this same crude tyrant uses his belt freely on his younger children and manhandles his wife, repeatedly denouncing her as a "fucking cunt" who is ruining his new home. Mom, a devout Catholic scared stiff of sex, swears to kill him as soon as possible, while his children denounce him as a "creep." The oldest son, the eventual murderer, even holds a gun to his father's head to end his reign of terror. Little wonder, then, that the demon pig of the film (pictured several times) mocks the Fourth Commandment in his grafitti: "Dishonor thy parents."

These explosive antics form a minor prelude to the baring of the darker secrets of this Catholic family. Dad is a non-Catholic, and he demands that his frigid Catholic wife fulfill his sexual fantasies. Mom protests loudly, Dad has his way amidst further uproar, and all the while the children listen to the arguments, the grunts, the screams. The teenage daughter, Patricia, suffers special agonies about this sexual contretemps, so when the obviously disturbed Sonny saunters about her room and praises her beautiful body, she revels in his attention. His startling request that she strip for him prompts her to pose naked in postures gleaned from *Playboy* magazine. Sonny is agitated by all this bare skin and sexual exuberance and gives her the panties he's stolen from her drawer. She protests not at all then when he joins her in bed and they consummate their incestuous lust. As always, Hollywood focuses on the wanton hidden under the Catholic uniform; this high school innocent with the face of a cherub need only be asked and she'll submit gleefully. No clearer association exists in Hollywood's image of Catholic women than the link between piety and repression, sanctity and sexual appetite. Patricia here joins the long line of Catholic girls that Hollywood suggests are just waiting to be set free. Her sisters include the Catholic schoolteacher in *Looking for Mr. Goodbar,* the Catholic factory worker in *An Office and a Gentleman,* and the Catholic welder in *Flashdance.*

Like so many of her Catholic sisters in Hollywood films, Patricia has the sexual sophistication of a harlot, and the guilty conscience of a soiled Madonna. She is like a Mary Magdalene yet to be saved by the Redeemer. The morning after is her hell, and she dashes off to confession with Father Adamski. Hollywood keeps its Catholic maidens in the confessional a lot, and the dialogue there is often much worse than the devastatingly sad transcripts that Norberto Valentini and Clara di Meglio scandalized Catholics with in *Sex and the Confessional* (1974); Valentini and de Meglio at least admitted their text had as its focus "the advice given by celibates" which they thought so distorted, perverted, and repressed "instinctive sexuality" that the sacrament constitutes "a crime against humanity." Hollywood merely dramatizes unsatisfactory confessional scenes and leaves the summary judgment up to the audience.

At her confession, the guilt-ridden Patricia lies, hesitating a bit, then identifying her big sin as going "all the way" with ". . . a *friend*!" The soothing rejoinder from Father Adamski contains no spiritual admonition worth mentioning; he talks instead of being chaste so she can bring her innocence to husband and family: "You must resist this temptation. Perhaps someday, you'll meet somebody, marry, and raise a family. Even if you love your friend very much you must resist." Patricia isn't calmed and presses on, "We do not love each other." The priest is angry and incredulous, "You mean this is only a sexual matter?" (His scorn for purely "sexual" matters is a reinforcement of Hollywood's image of a puritanical church.) Patricia continues her efforts to bring everything into focus by explaining that her lover acts "to hurt God." The priest flounders a bit, warns her, "Child, you shouldn't say that," and implores the sobbing girl to "Tell me everything from the beginning." Her tortured "No" ends the confession, and she dashes from the forbidding church back to her troubled home and an unshriven death.

It takes Father Adamski (James Olson) an inordinately long time to piece together the many evidences he has of a deeply disturbed family and a strange household. Many bizarre things occur when he tries to bless the Ocean Avenue house: an obviously demented father torments him with anti-Catholic tirades, various poltergeists shake the house, move the crosses, and cry out at the asperges; he hallucinates about blood-filled rooms and his prayer book is shredded. Then there are the constant telephone calls from the mother, whose cadaverous body does little to conceal the physical and mental abuse that has been visited upon her. One look at her would send the normal family counsellor off in search of a sheriff. Then, there's Sonny, who lurks around the house, hisses, and in every other way suggests he's a candidate for long-term institutionalization. And there's Patricia, whose breakdown in the confessional surely requires more than the gentle reminder that "You'll feel better when you confess it." Add to this Father Adamski's second sense that the phone call that November night is from the Montellis, and his decision to ignore the phone and go off on a hunting trip becomes rather shocking. The Jewish psychiatrist in *Ordinary People* would never desert his battered Christian patients like that. Miles away, in his sleeping bag, Father Adamski participates vicariously in Ronald's bloody rampage, as do audiences, who all through the film are transported to the demon's point of view to savor all the gore. Father Adamski then races back to bless the corpses as they are hauled out in body bags by the coroner. At the strangely subdued funeral, his confession that "I am responsible" has a sad ring of truth to it. This "possession" needed an exorcist a long time ago, or at least a priest with enough savvy to understand the real problems of his parishioners. All of Father Adamski's later heroics, including the taking of the devil to himself as Father Karras did, must be seen as an exculpation of his pastoral lapses. Much of the real horror in the film version comes from Adamski's blindness to the needs of humanity and his reliance on the forms of benediction, mass, and confession. These forms no longer seem efficacious in *The Possession*. Even Father Adamski's solemn recitations of the rites of exorcism don't work. Like Karras, he must lay down his life for his brother. The liturgy is not enough, the Hollywood catechism declares; demons need heroes, not priests.

If Father Adamski seems dense in *Amityville II*, his religious superiors are pictured as prudent and cautious to a fault. When he finally asks to be allowed to exorcise Sonny's demon, the older priests opine that "The worst thing is to rush into anything. We will take our time." These clerical angels fear treading anywhere near 112 Ocean Avenue and do everything they can to deter Father Adamski. A monsignor comes to warn him that the bishop has ordered him to take a leave of absence and sternly rebukes him for "forgetting obedience and humility." His clerical mandate is to "go home and do nothing on your initiative." This separation between hierarchy and cleric makes for interesting ambiguities in the Hollywood catechism. For those who might protest that the Devil wins in the film, since Father Adamski ends up possessed and moaning for the "Lord of my life" not to forsake him, the filmmakers could say it wasn't the Church that failed, but one minister. For those who might protest that Adamski's cure of Sonny is unrealistic, there is the careful psychological explanation that Sonny's demon really was Patricia, and his schizoid charge in the assumed personality of his sister that the priest "thought about making love to me" during the sacrament of reconciliation, may have snapped Sonny back to reality; this psychological approach would justify the consolation another priest offers Sonny at the end, "It's all right, Sonny; we'll make them understand it wasn't your fault." The one thing that is clear, however, is that the demon has it right in his last test of Adamski: "You've decided to do this on your own without the support of the Church. You disobeyed the Church. Now you are alone, Adamski." The film ends on a shot of the solitary Adamski stranded in the house of horrors, with the demon welling up in his blood. The Church has afforded him no more protection than he offered the dead family. If the demon left Sonny, it has taken hold of Adamski, and one wonders about that confessional and all that sex.

The Catholic Church and its priests both lose to demons in *The Amityville Horror* (1979), Stuart Rosenberg's evocative version of Jay Anson's non-fiction best seller. George Lutz, a Methodist, and his Catholic family (note how dangerous mixed marriages are to all concerned) buy the haunted house on Long Island, ignoring tales of the Shinnecock Indians who penned their infirm up there to die, the ghosts of John Ketchum, a warlock exiled from Salem who lived in the neighborhood, and, of course, the distressing chronicle of the recent misadventures and eventual bloody deaths of the De Feo family. Very quickly, the Lutzes regret their taste in real estate and their haughty rejection of the spirit world. Poltergeists are everywhere: black sludge fills the plumbing, the heat never dispels the chill on the house, and a psychic friend of theirs tells them they've purchased "The Gate of Hell"—which any real horror fan knew from *The Sentinel* (1977) was really in downtown Brooklyn and well protected by a blind nun who held back hordes of naked deformed devils. The sign outside their house, "High Hopes," becomes grimly ironic, and when George starts menacing his brood with an axe, they wisely leave for a less hostile environ. The film ends with the disquieting note that "George and Kathleen Lutz and their family never reclaimed their house or their personal belongings."

The big losers, however, in Rosenberg's film are the priests foolish enough to confront the devil. Rod Steiger, the most well-known and established star in the film, a talent who looks a little out of place in such sensational antics, plays the courageous Father Delaney (modelled in part on Father Mancuso, the family counselor in the Amityville diocese who worked with the Lutzes and eventually converted George Lutz to Catholicism). The devil has it in for Father Delaney from the first minute the cleric enters the house. Doors slam shut, windows lock, and hordes of Beelzebub's flies gather. These pesky demons overpower the priest; he perspires profusely, suffers a crushing headache, and seems on the verge of a heart attack. He barely manages to stagger from the house and collapse into his car. Round One and every round to follow goes to the minions of Satan, the evil flies of human frailty, the all-conquering temptors. Even back in his rectory, Father Delaney is incapacitated by strange maladies, burns that will not heal, and boils that seem to fester forever. His initial physical defeat resembles the thrashing the demons give the Lutzes' Aunt Helena, a pious nun who cannot make it over the threshold, and flees, vomiting uncontrollably as she goes. These good souls obviously summon evil spirits; it's just that there's no contest once the devils take center stage.

Even in his chapel, surrounded by statues and confessionals, altars and holy water font, and before the Eucharist, Father Delaney is no match for Satan. In his mass, he prays for the Lutz family, only to see the church statues disintegrate and himself blinded. When last we see Father Delaney, he's sitting catatonically in a park, looked after by a young priest, Father Bolen (Don Stroud), who endured the horrors of Viet Nam as a chaplain only to come home and see his spiritual mentor blinded by the devil and locked in the darkness of despair. If

Father Adamski, the Polish priest in *Amityville II*, was damned for neglecting his parishioners, Father Delaney, the Irish cleric, seems equally lost for having immersed himself in their care. Hollywood's catechism suggests no way to beat the devil without losing your life and more.

Father Delaney also resembles Father Adamski in his contempt for his superiors, prelates who would hide from the supernatural and deny evil. In an extended and thorny theological debate in *The Amityville Horror*, two important clerics try everything to move Father Delaney from his resolve to exorcise the demons in the house; when reason fails, they also speak of obedience to the bishop's wishes and of long leaves of absence. Interestingly, Father Delaney is identified in the debate as "a modernist who thought that Vatican II didn't go far enough"; given this political posture, the other priests argue, his focus on demons seems "a little medieval." His spiritual fathers reject Father Delaney's impassioned argument that "To me the Church, it's my home. The Church is my strength. And I need her now—and that family needs her—now!" The remedy the hierarchy suggests in this case is not exorcism, but a "long vacation" for Father Delaney with his own family and a "shave and a haircut" for his friend, Father Bolen. Tom Figenshu dismisses these clerical scenes in *The Amityville Horror* as "gaga . . .destructive . . . [and] totally unnecessary" in his insightful article "Screams of a Summer Night" (*Film Comment*, Sept. 1979), but they do suggest a sinister segment of Hollywood's treatment of Catholics in the sixties and seventies. The combination of massive change in the Church and massive turmoil in the country set the stage for old demons which the new Church seemingly couldn't control. The Age of Kennedy and the tragic aftermath of Camelot shifted the focus to the evil assassin's magically accurate bullet and the devil's dark powers. At home, the troops had seized the Special Prosecutor Archibald Cox's files, surrounding his offices with tanks, while a distraught president wavered between protestations that he was "no crook" and tearful annunciations that his mother was "a saint." Abroad, America was destroying villages to save them, bringing apocalypse now to Viet Nam.

President Kennedy, miraculously resurrected in good health after his assassination, plays a critical role in one of the earliest and best treatments of demonic possession, Roman Polanski's eerie realization of Ira Levin's best-selling novel, *Rosemary's Baby* (1968), a work Renata Adler shrewdly labels "a highly serious lapsed-Catholic fable." Rosemary (Mia Farrow), an innocent adrift in New York City, clearly symbolizes many young ex-Catholic girls fearful about their marriage, their abilities as lovers, and their potential as mothers. Rosemary, like so many characters in recent Hollywood films, has outgrown her Catholicism; it seems so quaint and small town and repressive. Yet Catholic images fill her dreams; her most vivid nightmare features a repressive high school where overbearing nuns stifle minds and brick over windows.

Because Rosemary still bears all this Catholic guilt and repressive dream imagery with little of God's peace and solace, the idea of Satan impregnating her at a black Mass becomes the focus of Satanists cavorting around the halls of the "Black Banford," a Gothic apartment house with a history of cannibalism, infanticide, suicide, and demonology. Catholic girls, especially lapsed, demure, shy ones with alluring bodies, the Hollywood catechism suggests, make exceptional mates for demons; this idea of the willowy virginal ingenue ready for despoiling so permeates American popular culture, and Mia Farrow from *Peyton Place* was so clearly such an icon, that Ira Levin admits he had her in mind when he wrote his novel. The strange fixation with ethereal Catholic girls, so straightforwardly explained in Billy Joel's song on the topic, has wide-ranging implications about the spiritualism associated with the Church's medieval cathedrals (the setting for numerous Harlequin romances), about the mystery surrounding the Church's dogma on sexuality, and about the widespread preconception that Catholic girls either accept frigidity or embrace promiscuity—they, more than any other group of women, are divided into two groups, madonnas and whores.

This Irish ex-Catholic pixie, Rosemary, loses her modesty and all her clothes on a yacht party with the Kennedy clan during a bizarre, quite realistic dream she has after eating the wicked witch's chocolate mousse (a pun on mousse-mouse plays a critical role in Rosemary's dream). Even the stupified Rosemary notices that only Catholics are on this luxurious modern ark, but John Kennedy soothes her fears with the rather incomplete explanation, "Catholics only—I wish we weren't bound by these prejudices, but unfortunately. . . " Soon thereafter the nude Rosemary is paraded through a crowded room, and the radiantly beautiful, constantly smiling Jackie Kennedy spreads Rosemary's bare legs and straps her to the altar-bed. Others in the coven paint her, and a demon—first resembling her husband Guy, but then shifting shapes—possesses her. As soon as Rosemary sees Lucifer's eyes, she understands everything and screams out, "This is no dream, this is really happening!" This time her comfort comes from the pope himself, who sympathizes in a surrealistic comment: "They tell me you've been bitten by a mouse." Rosemary accepts this strange balm, explaining, "Yes, that's why I couldn't come to see you." The scene ends with the pope forgiving her "absolutely" and Rosemary kissing his ring. When critic Joseph Gelmis asked Roman Polanski why all the dream figures during Rosemary's impregnation by the Devil were Catholic, Roman Polanski explained that it was due to Rosemary's Catholic background, arguing that dreams always combine the mythic, the well known, and the recognizable. Polanski explained further that "The girl is Catholic. All her associations are necessarily in such circumstances the people who represent married Catholicism for her."

Artistically acceptable and successful as this rationale may be, the choice of Catholics as the participants in prolonged bizarre sexual rites, nude black masses, and ritual impregnations of innocent women, does make the kind of association Jonathan Rosenbaum was so sensitive to in *Moving Places*. You don't have to say Catholicism is a perverse, superstitious, archaic religion, full of demons and warlocks. All you need do is throw Catholic icons everywhere in your film, parade familiar Catholic faces in front of cowering naked women, and have the pope absolve mouse bites, and even the dream takes on an unfortunate cinematic reality. To continue this narrative with a chilling defeat of virtue, a perverse exploitation of maternal love worthy of De Sade's *Justine,* and to conclude with the shaken protagonist blissfully suckling the devil as a revitalized coven chants "Hail, Adrian. Hail Satan. Welcome the Year One" all make *Rosemary's Baby* a powerfully blasphemous celebration of the *Time* cover featured so prominently in the film, the fabled *"God is Dead!"* issue. Polanski's film, while skillfully executed, finally seems sophomorically perverse and rather juvenile in its blasphemies—like a black mass at a fraternity party. *Rosemary's Baby* in its jolly celebration of Lucifer's victory foreshadows the salutes to Satan in *The Exorcist* and *The Amityville Horror.* Polanski's surrealistic sideshow heralds the "season of the witch" in American film.

Among the most popular films in Hollywood's celebration of the tiumph of evil were the features in the *Omen* trilogy, produced by Harvey Bernhard, and offering a cartoon strip reworking of the theme of the "Antichrist" from the Book of Revelations. The films, whose narrative infelicities are frequently obscured by the fine pseudo-Carl Orff threnodies of Jerry Goldsmith (an Oscar winner for these compositions), highlight decapitation, impalements, disembowelments, and demonically inspired animals. They are, unfortunately, extremely short on character motivation, logical coherence, and plausibility. The filmmakers obviously envision an audience restless for popcorn, sallies to the restrooms, and teenage conversations, so the "good parts" are trumpeted by eerie music and separated by dreary stretches of unimaginative exposition. The aesthetic norm at work features carefully orchestrated shocks; long, lulling interludes; then even greater gore and horrors. The program is as predictable as any sequence in a behavior modification drill.

Roman Catholic clerics and rituals play central roles in all these antics; if anything, they are the comic relief, the inept buffoons striving to do good but always tripping over their feet or their cassocks and plunging into the abyss. Most of the time their heroic plots to thwart the Anti-Christ have the sophistication of the Three Stooges and the grace of the Keystone Cops. With tonsured enemies like this, hidebound in medieval lore and trusting in seven magic knives (like silver bullets and stakes in the heart, Satan's only fear on earth), Satan doesn't need his legions; a few intelligent lackeys will do. These inept priests and their feverish rantings make Satanism appear a model of rationality and corporate efficiency. In the *Omen* trilogy, the Catholic Church and its agents play Don Quixote to some very gigantic windmills. Audience sympathies may be with the "impossible dream," but the foe definitely looks unbeatable. A measure of the demon's modern powers can be gleaned from the fact that "the desolate one" wins Round One, *The Omen* (1976), quite convincingly; annihilates his opponents in Round Two, *Damien—Omen II* (1978); and declares Round Three, which includes incidentally a melodramatic "Second Coming" of Christ, *The Final Conflict—Omen III* (1981), a pyrrhic victory for his opponent, remind the Nazarene he has "won nothing."

Part one of this juvenile caper—*The Omen*—which defames the Bible by even alluding to it, was directed by the reasonably competent British auteur, Richard Donner, and profits from the estimable services of Gregory Peck as Robert Thorn, the demon's earthly foster father, and Lee Remick as Katherine Thorn, his foster mother. The project was an adaptation of David Seltzer's best selling Gothic novel, a work which had as its avowed purpose to chronicle an age when "democracy was fading, mind-impairing drugs had become a way of life . . . God was dead" and where "from Laos to Lebanon brother had turned against brother, father against children; school buses and marketplaces exploded daily in the growing din of preparatory lust." The time and place awaited its Anti-Christ. Donner's film remains true to this apocalyptic vision; it is, as Robin Wood notes in his scintillating article "Return of the Repressed" (*Film Comment*, July 1978), a horror epic which envisions the end of "the bourgeois capitalist patriarchal establishment," a film where the young demon is the "implicit hero," and a film that makes no sense except to a society "prepared to enjoy and surreptitiously condone the working out of its own destruction." As Wood indicates, the annihilation in the film is complete and inevitable; in his words, "humanity is now completely powerless, there is nothing anyone can do to arrest the process."

One surely cannot trust in the Catholic Church of *The Omen*. Rome, after all, emerges as the center of superstition which engenders this son of a jackal and a whore, and the priests and nuns of the Oespedale Generale are all cloistered satanists anxious to find a home in American social circles for their infant Anti-Christ. They chose the Thorns, both fallen away Catholics, because of their wealth, their symbolic infertility, and their position in politics. Even when one of their number, Father Brennan, repents of his crime and tries to warn the Thorns, his new-found Catholic faith has the look of fanaticism and mental imbalance. His feverish lamentations and wild admonitions, "Take Holy Communion—Drink the Blood of Christ and Eat His Flesh—Only through Christ can you fight the Demon," prompt Ambassador Thorn to summon armed guards; the graphic metaphors of drinking blood and eating flesh make his faith sound as bizarre as the clandestine infanticide in the basement of a Catholic monastery and the other clerical horrors acted out in the Cimitero di Sant' Angelo. Even the punishment for Father Spiletto, an exile in a Catholic monastery, combines with numerology, some hocus pocus about archaeological digs, and some half-digested Jansenism ("for everything holy, there is something unholy . . . this is the essence of temptation") to make all religion seem redolent of charms, amulets, and incantations. As frequently happens in the Hollywood catechism, Roman Catholicism falls somewhere between voodoo and shamanism in its rationality and efficacy. When the spiritually enlightened Ambassador Thorn tries to eradicate the demon and sacrifice his son on an altar, the forces of American law and order massacre the demented father in a flurry of police bullets, and the charitable father of the country, the president himself, takes the prince of evil to his bosom, adopts him, and ensconces him in the White House.

Damien, Omen II (1978) has a new, less inspired director, Don Taylor, a few lesser luminaries in its feature roles (William Holden and Lee Grant), and even more superstition and anti-clericalism in its narrative. The Anti-Christ is now an adolescent in an all-boys military school, so there's much more emphasis on sexuality and "the whore of Babylon." The murders are even bloodier, the clergy even more inane, and the defeat of Catholicism even more inevitable. By the time of *The Final Conflict, Omen III* (1981), Damien is even mocking a statue of Christ, mounted backwards on the cross and continually sodomized by the barbs of this demonic presence. For most of the film, the unholy terror of the Thorn empire holds sway. One inept clergyman after another, Brother Matthew, then Brother Paulo, then Brother Benito, thn Brothers Simeon, Martin, and Antonio, bite the dust, usually the victim of their own blindness, stupidity, or weakness. Their seven knives seem rather puny and silly; fortunately, an impassioned mother anxious to defend her progeny, the infant Christ, is there to crush the serpent's head. She defends what Thorn calls "the two thousand years of His grubby mundane creed," vanquishes Thorn and his kingdom of melancholy, loneliness, and pain, and ushers in the film's rather mundane recreation of the parousia. The shallowness of conception here almost beggars belief. After hours of Satan's horrors, endless defilements, murders, perverse wonders, sexual conquests, and untold wealth and power for Damien, God's Reincarnation comes in a poorly realized "happy ending," the same kind of filtered light and organ music finale that has greeted every cinematic martyr since cameras reached the Pacific.

God and Catholicism don't even win a token victory in *Evilspeak* (1982), director Eric Weston's homage to Father Lorenzo Esteban, a fictional Satanist banished by the Spanish Inquisition, and reincarnated centuries later at the West Andover Military Academy by computer maven Cadet Coopersmith (Clint Howard), an overweight wallflower mercilessly persecuted by his Catholic friends on the soccer team. Out of his frustration and anger at their locker-room humiliations, Coopersmith unleashes an army of demons who devour everything in sight, including the soccer team, the Catholic chaplain, and a buxom secretary cavorting naked in a Hitchcockian shower. Coopersmith gets the recipe for his black mass from a computer (a concoction replete with blood, toads, and consecrated hosts), but his energy is clearly Freudian. Coopersmith epitomizes Walter Evans's sexual theory of "Monster Movies" outlined in

231

the Fall 1983 issue of *The Journal of Popular Film:* Evans theorizes, and *Evilspeak* confirms, that the key appeal of monster films for teenage audiences is the theme of "horrible and mysterious physical and psychological change" of adolescence that horror films sublimate and translate into monsters and violence, voyeurism and misogyny.

Evilspeak also features a sop to youthful iconoclasm and sophomoric anti-clericalism in its climactic scene, during which the literal pigs of hell squeal in a Catholic chapel, rampage freely, and desecrate statues, confessionals, and the tabernacle. Clearly the omnipotent God of old no longer rules his own churches; a minor Spanish heretic, fond of naked ladies and bloody decapitations, defies God's power even on consecrated ground. The iconoclasm reeks of youthful absolutism: nothing is holy any more, Daddy's God is dead, and young heroes had better beware of other bandersnatches. To reinforce this theme of the irrelevancy of religion, screenwriter Joseph Garofalo has Father Jameson (Joseph Cortese) deliver an inspirational homily, a sermon so full of hackneyed images and tired metaphors that it could win a parody prize from *Mad* magazine or *National Lampoon.* Father Jameson's peroration develops the least adept sports and sanctity metaphor possible; warning his "little soldiers" about the "game of life" and its stern rules, he cautions them, "I know a lot of you soccer jocks think it's okay to go out there and try to pull one over on the referee when he's not watching . . . [but] nobody pulls anything over on the head referee . . . in the big game." Father Jameson continues his conceit, talking about Satan as a losing coach, behind in the standings and plagued with a losing record. The devil, the priest warns, has no influence with the big scorekeeper in the sky, a bookkeeper god who gives you "hell to pay" if you're not on the winning side. His sermon also warns about the pigs men become when they gorge at the trough of sin; just then, the demons burst in and make these Catholics their fodder. For anyone concerned that the authorities outside the college may reverse the demon's victory, there is a giant conflagration, and a news report in the conclusion talking of the "tragic accident" at West Andover Academy. Then Coopersmith's computer printout takes over, and outlines its own black litany: "By the four beasts before the throne, by the fire which is about the throne, by the most holy and glorious Satan, I, Stanley Coopersmith, will return. *I will return!*"

By the early eighties, however, a dramatically viable return for a literal Satan was becoming less and less feasible. Theology had moved away from its focus on Lucifer, and American film audiences had seen the possession motif too frequently parodied. William Blatty's *The Exorcist* had inspired *The Blues Brothers*, John Belushi and Dan Aykroyd, on their 1980 "mission from God." Their Mother Superior, "the Penguin," lived in a world of red lights, levitations, demons, and guffaws. Possession was also central to Chevy Chase's *Modern Problems* (1981), a mélange of air-traffic controllers, broken appliances, and other secular ills. The best parody, however, was Robert Mulligan's *Kiss Me Goodbye* (1982) with a defrocked priest who assures his friend that he still has his ecclesiastical powers, "the touch," because "you always have it"—a comic riff built on a doctrine sacred to Catholics, *'Tu es sacerdos in aeternum."* This "touch," the ex-priest continues, is like a good fast ball; it can go on you: "One season you've got it good and the next season it's gone." As the film evolves, it's clear that the devil and the ex-cleric's touch are both gone; all that remains is fine slapstick comedy full of holy water, Latin, exploding heaters, mean dogs, and mistaken identities. *Kiss Me Goodbye* was a fond accomplished farewell to Pazuzu. The Hollywood catechism clearly envisioned a long hiatus before doubters would find faith in supernatural confrontations between demons and exorcists. It wasn't so much that audiences had returned to Ben Hecht's fabled Production Code American dreamland, where "the most potent and brilliant of villains are powerless before little children, parish priests, or young virgins with large boobies." It was more that America had come to James Baldwin's realization that evil was far more subtle and provided no clear confirmation of God's power at all. After Viet Nam and "Watergate," Americans and Hollywood knew you needed more than a Ouija board to find heaven.

The Romance:
catholics, sex, and guilt

Aunt Josephine [to her young
nephew]: "You are as handsome
as my favorite saint was, Saint
Carmine, when he first met Saint
Ramona, and he gazed upon her
beauty and had bad thoughts—
that you don't know about yet. So
to prove his saintliness before
her, he plucked out his eyes,
washed them in his blood,
crushed them on the ground, and
bestowed them upon her. And
that's what love is."

Made for Each Other (1971)

Peter Nichols's *The Pope's Legions*, a well-researched
and illuminating analysis of contemporary Roman Catholicism
rarely lapses into judgmental rhetoric. By and large, Nichols
allows his data to speak for itself. At most, he suggests a framework, an intellectual structure, for his provocative statistics and
discoveries—that is, until he turns to his chapter "The Failure
with Sex." In this section, Nichols proves both harsh and persuasive. In his opinion, if there is one issue that "Christianity
as a whole, and Catholicism in particular, has failed to handle

successfully, it is sex." Nichols can find no rational explanation for Catholicism's terrible perplexities in dealing with sexuality, and he concludes that there is no excuse whatsoever for this botched opportunity other than "a kind of urge to be gloriously wrong at any cost, like the handling of the Light Brigade." In post-Production Code films, the Hollywood catechism confirms Nichols's assertion; the valley of death for seven hundred million Catholics worldwide, recent films suggest, lies near the mons veneris, the cannons to the left, right, and center are phallic, and the psychic wounds far from unfading glories.

Consider, for example, director John Badham's *Saturday Night Fever* (1977), one of the decade's most popular musicals and one of its most revealing sociological documents. Starting with Nik Cohen's dazzling article in *New York* about the bar scene in Bay Ridge, Brooklyn, screenwriter Norman Wexler develops a powerful script detailing the conflict between two value systems and two generations, an older immigrant, family-oriented, churchgoing, puritanical tradition, and a secular, mobile, iconoclastic, hedonistic, Americanized life-style. Teen idol, superstar, and sex object John Travolta as Tony Manero dances on the edge of each of these universes—the Roman collar of Italian Catholicism threatens to strangle him, yet the bridge to the modernity of Manhattan also seems slippery and perilous.

Dichotomies abound in *Saturday Night Fever:* there are two brothers, two neighborhoods, and two girls. The Manero family has two sons: Frank, an introspective priest, and Tony, an exhibitionist stud; the one, a quiet man of the cloth and the other, a flashy man given to contemporary threads; one, the socially concerned, puritanical, level-headed intellectual, and the other, the narcissistic, hedonistic, flamboyant illiterate. In place of the law-and-order polarization of the two Powers boys in *The Public Enemy*, the issues in *Saturday Night Fever* involve wine, women, and song. Denial and indulgence, restraint and license, guilt and joy, are balanced in John Badham's choreography of sexual mores and traditional morals. The fabled disco, the *2001 Odyssey*, operates in the "City of Churches"; its topless dancers swing their pendulous breasts just a few blocks from the cathedral of Our Lady of Perpetual Help.

Disco king Tony Manero, who saves pennies all week to squander big bucks on weekends, must embark on his own odyssey; this overgrown adolescent, whose heroes range from Al Pacino to Bruce Lee, must choose an adult domain, a grownup world spacious enough to contain his dancing feet and his restless soul. If Tony admires the stability of perfect architecture and rhapsodizes over the mastery and perfection of the Verrazano Bridge, he also loves to go with the flow as he glides through a kaleidoscopic night of pliant women, graceful dance, and sexual bliss.

The Manero family estate, a modest house in a working class section of Brooklyn, proves too small and restrictive for its many troubled inhabitants. Dad, an unemployed construction worker, berates his dumpy wife and his preening son out of feelings of impotence and rage. Dad symbolizes the displaced Catholic immigrant, a hardworking manual laborer, who broke his back building a new country only to see his beloved industrial America shutting down, crushed by foreign competition, and a new American service economy emerging under the direction of educated white collar WASPs who live in Scarsdale. Dad has lost his self-respect and now recognizes his wife's diminishing deference; the lord of the manor has fallen on very dark days. Most of all, this insecure middle-aged padrone fears his sons' pity; he is terrorized by the prospect of the inevitable totem feast. To forestall any further castrations, this aging Romeo still ogles Farrah Fawcett Majors's breasts and goads Tony in a sadly Oedipal duel designed to prolong his macho feeling about his status as breadwinner and father. Dad is so insecure that he forbids Tony to aid in clearing dinner dishes; some things, he reminds his less chauvinistic son, are "woman's work."

Tony's mother tuned out reality long ago, using religion's other world as a haven from her constrained life and second-class status. Mom typifies the Italian Catholic wife who recognizes the injustice of her situation, but feels powerless to rebel. Mom is atypical, however, in that she can't even cook well; her spaghetti sauce "don't taste and it don't drip." She's Michael Novak's "unmeltable ethnic," but she also lacks Italian passion and flair. She wastes her religious energies, frequenting the local Catholic chapel, imploring God to remind her angelic firstborn, Frank the priest, to call home; Tony recognizes her frivolity in church, reminding her that she has turned Christ into "a long distance operator." Mom's lot is truly pathetic; her hell, a Sartrean inferno, absurdly full of trifling plagues. Mom suffers stoically, but she is eternally buffeted by the overcrowding and litter in Bay Ridge, annoyed by her bellicose and impotent spouse, and fatigued by Tony's constant mindless lies and evasions. She, in turn, hounds her errant child, working her own psychological terror by admonishing him that he should have been a priest like his brother.

Tony has actually made the odious comparison with his sainted brother, "Father Frank," a major pole in his universe; Frank's perfection highlights and excuses Tony's imperfections—Frank's vocation affords compensating graces that balance the Manero family accounts. Greg Keeler develops this idea quite perceptively in his 1979 *Journal of Popular Film and Television* article "*Saturday Night Fever:* Crossing the Verrazano Bridge." Keeler explains the Italian parents' chiding tolerance of Tony as the direct result of Frank's sanctification: "Tony can deck his room out with posters of sex symbols, spend hours styling himself into a sex symbol, and fight openly with his parents because they expect all of this from him, just as they expect celibacy from Frank." A revealing confirmation for Keeler's analysis comes in Sylvester Stallone's popular sequel to *Saturday Night Fever, Staying Alive* (1983), a film which ignores thematic complexities in favor of uninspired choreography. In one of the few quiet moments in Stallone's noisy, vacuous imitation of *Flashdance* (1983) and MTV, Tony and his mother reminisce about the old days in the old neighborhoods. She confesses that she and his father didn't come down heavily on him back then because they accepted him as a black sheep in a family that had already given its holy lamb to the Church. Tony summarizes the situation in language which keeps his mother laughing: "What you're saying is that I've always been this bastard, but it's all right, because it comes natural to me." Mom gladly assents to this vision of his childhood.

238

In *Saturday Night Fever*, when Father Frank leaves the Church and renounces his vocation, Tony's status as Prodigal Son is challenged. The first night Frank sleeps at home, Tony intuits a truth which will alter his whole life. As he probes his brother's religious despair, Tony finds new hope for himself; Tony disarms Frank with his buoyant recognition that "Maybe if you're not so good, I ain't so bad. You know. Yea!" Frank understands Tony all too well. His renunciation of Roman Catholicism is less a matter of apostasy or indifference and more a question of discovering his own autonomy: "Momma, Poppa, their dreams of pious glory, they turn you into what they wish. . . . You can't defend yourself against their fantasies. All I ever really had was their image of me as a priest. That's all."

Autonomy proves hard to come by in Bay Ridge, especially for Italian Catholic women. Tony has trouble functioning as the cock of the roost, but he's much better off in his plumage than the besequinned "chicks" who crowd around him, groping for love. The Catholic women in this film fall over themselves to do what the boys want; these love-hungry young females spend a lot of time wiping their heroes' brows, stroking male egos, parading their bodies in tawdry bars, and providing sexual favors in the backseats of jalopies. Tony explains the harsh reality of Brooklyn's love life to his doughty admirer, Annette, reiterating the classic double standard of sexual morality she has internalized all her life. In Italian Catholic culture, every man worth his salt must try to seduce every girl he meets, yet each woman must choose either the virgin life of the "nice girl" or the whorish existence of a "cunt"; no middle ground exists in this absolutist universe of religious virtue or carnal excess, of Madonnas and Magdalenas. As Tony warns Annette, "You can't be both. That's the thing girls gotta decide early on. You gotta decide whether you're gonna be a nice girl or a cunt." The choices are abstinence or promiscuity, frigidity or nymphomania. Annette tries to win Tony as a "nice" girl; on their only date, she spends the whole evening describing her married sisters and the joys of married life. All this domesticity bores Tony, however, and he tolerates Annette only when he needs her as a dance partner. When Tony finds a new beauty who dances more elegantly, the spurned Annette despairs, and tries to win her champion with sexual favors. Nice girls aren't good lovers, however; her interlude with Tony goes awry, and the devastated Annette achieves "cunt" status not by enthralling Tony but by taking on all his friends. For her, the rest is not silence, but hysterically loud sex.

Bobby C., one of Tony's friends, loses even more in the perverse sexual rituals of Bay Ridge, and he is destroyed by the strictures of his poorly understood Catholicism. Bobby, the gentlest soul in the film, needs counselling, but his hesitant, tongue-tied, inarticulate pleas for help fall on deaf ears. Frank Manero, lost in the shadowy world between ministry and friendship, begs Bobby to stop fantasizing about Papal Indulgences for an abortion and instructs Bobby to see a priest. Bobby, however, feels too overburdened by the pregnant Pauline, her parents, and "the priest on the corner," all of whom tell him that abortion is impossible. For them and for Bobby, sex seems a cruel game, and if "you play, you pay." Yet Bobby does not want to marry the despoiled Pauline; in his eyes, his radiant virginal lover has become a "fucking cunt." Unable to have his nice girl any more, and trapped by other people's expectations, Bobby feels "paralyzed" and "out of control." His release comes in a fatal tumble from the Verrazano Bridge.

Tony knows that he, too, must end his old life; his fate lies across a different bridge. As ex-priest Frank Manero warns his younger brother, "The only way you're gonna survive is to do what you think is right, not what they want you to." To reinforce this point, Frank leaves Tony a souvenir, his "uniform" as a priest. Tony tries it on for size and quickly turns the Roman collar into a hangman's noose. In a daring image, the most striking anti-Catholic metaphor in the whole Hollywood catechism, Tony imagines himself strangled by the vestments of the old creed. The scene, a pantomime, details the central idea about Catholicism and sexuality in contemporary film—Catholicism is a "hangup" that kills. Catholicism, this image asserts, strangles the young with outworn ideas, stifles desires, and makes growth, happiness, and autonomy impossible. In cinema's new cosmology of sexuality, Roman Catholicism is the dark star, the death principle, a somber creed steeped in thanatos and crippling guilt.

Tony's first substitute religion is his "strut," boldly assertive, self-centered, iconoclastic disco dancing, which, as his brother Frank marvels, has a truly miraculous effect on everyone who beholds it. Dance becomes Tony's magic staff to part the Red Sea, to succor him in his exodus from Bay Ridge, and to lead him into Manhattan's promised land of independence and maturity. Disco dancing is Tony's sacrament, his Holy Grail, and he will not see it profaned. The *2001 Odyssey* may seem a rather gaudy temple: the Italian bully boys there get their kicks joking about "a piece of the pope's ass"—"He ain't got no ass; that's why he's the pope"—as they brandish their ostentatious gold crosses, but for acolyte Tony, the multicolored dance floor is a shrine to graceful movement and kinesthetic perfection. When the greedy local promoters sully this chapel with a rigged dance contest that favors Italian contestants and slights two Puerto Rican apostles of disco dancing, the self-righteous Tony refuses tainted benedictions, and he gives the coveted trophy and lavish prize money to their rightful Latin winners. Tony's repudiation of the fix marks his traumatic discovery of a harsh truth of American life. For the first time, Tony understands that Roman Catholicism and its cult of charity have been displaced by a new, avaricious and exploitive secularism, in which "everyone is dumping on someone," "a fucking rat race," which pits men against women, Italians against Puerto Ricans, and the educated upper classes against the unlettered working class.

Tony's vision of the upper class comes largely through an inept social climber, Stephanie, a girl who loves "snobs," not "slobs." Stephanie tries almost too hard to learn the newest dance steps, to wear the latest fashions, to see the trendiest movies, to chat about tomorrow's best sellers, and to appreciate the classics; her "stairway to the stars" involves New York's famed New School extension courses, half-digested book reviews, and unadulterated hero worship. Tony identifies quite closely with Stephanie's rites of passage; he also agonizes about his own metamorphosis from working class caterpillar to cultured butterfly. So when Tony discovers that Stephanie has been sleeping around as a means of breaking into Manhattan society, that she has been living as the young mistress of an older, more sophisticated record producer, Tony consoles her rather than rebukes her. Instead of treating Stephanie like a "cunt," Tony opens his soul to her, shares his private places and his visions of beauty, and soothes her with some very humane advice not to cry about her prostitution and not to "worry about nothing." Tony's ability to transcend "nice girl-cunt" dichotomies frees him once and for all of the chains of Bay Ridge; like Tom Sawyer and Huck Finn, he can head out to the frontier. At the end of the film, Tony takes New York's famed "RR" subway into Manhattan, and he comes to Stephanie's apartment, not to "promote pussy" but to be friends. Stephanie recognizes what a tremendous metamorphosis this is for her superstud dance partner—after all, only a few hours before he tried to rape her—and the film ends on her most revealing question: "Could you stand being friends with a girl?" Travolta whispers meekly, "I could try, I could try," and they embrace gently in the most emotionally satisfying boy-girl contact of the whole film, a warm hug that stands outside the endless cycle of gender stereotypes and exploitative sex games.

Many Italian men in contemporary Hollywood films could never be good friends with a woman, and Hollywood draws a powerful equation between their guilt-laden hangups, their inflexible gender stereotypes, their peculiar fixations on sexual dominance, and their Roman Catholicism. The Hollywood catechism seems quite fixated on the schism between Italian sensuousness and Irish puritanism in the American Catholic Church, making powerful films about the distinction between the chaste ideal of religious dogma and the carnal actuality of the Catholic laity's sexual behàvior. The contradictions and complexities of the disjunction between creed and life-style form the core of Hollywood's recent forays into the Catholic milieu.

The Irish-Italian split is relatively easy to understand. Irish immigrants, who used the Church as a ladder to climb in society, brought a particularly austere, puritanical, legalistic, somewhat Jansenist creed to America; their hierarchy and clergy preached self-denial, abstinence, vigorous purity, and very cold showers, a sermon described exquisitely in James Joyce's *Portrait of the Artist as a Young Man*. Italian Catholics, on the other hand, distrusted a formal church and an inflexible theology, and clustered around family, pious sacramentals, and glorious, fun-filled holydays. Their religion was given to festivals, carnivals, processions, and bountiful meals—an ethnic Eucharist. As a result, as Stephen S. Hall writes in his long discussion of "Italian Americans: Coming Into Their Own" (*New York Times Magazine*, 15 May 1983): "To Italians, Irish Catholicism seemed to be severe, doctrinaire, unemotional, and conservative; to the Irish, Italian Catholics were excessively superstitious, overly influenced by folk customs, fatalistic, almost pagan." Normally, Italian Catholics in Hollywood films seem torn between their national heritage and the formal church teachings of an Irish clergy. As Pauline Kael notes in her accomplished analysis of Martin Scorsese's *Mean Streets*, these Italians born to paganism but bred in puritanism take on a fatalistic air which fascinates American filmgoers torn between hedonism and traditional morality. The fatal flaw of living in an Irish Catholic church which condemns them gives Italian males, Kael opines, a "warm, almost tactile glow," and their "voluptuous vacant-eyed smiles tell us that they want to get the best out of this life; they know they're going to burn in eternity, so why should they think about things that are depressing?"

As Pauline Kael well knows, however, many of the finest films about the Italian Catholic experience in America focus on these "depressing" demons, the perplexing split between Italian culture's sensuous pleasures, its rapturous carnality, and the Irish Catholic church's nagging insistence on purity and the temperate life. A good case in point is Martin Scorsese's *Who's That Knocking at My Door?* (1968), an autobiographical work in which this one-time seminarian film director attempts again to reconcile the strictures of his eternal church and the erotic energy of city streets. J. R., Scorsese's protagonist, well-played by the brooding Harvey Keitel, loves "the girl" (Zina

Bethune) until that fateful afternoon she confesses that she is no virgin; years ago, a boy drove her into the country, turned the radio on very loud, and raped her. Ever since this episode, she tells J. R., she has felt degraded and dirty, so she's never told anyone else about it. Now, however, she trusts that their love will make her whole, and their honeymoon will be "the first time" for both of them. J.R. explodes at her with atavistic fury; he is so caught up in the Italian world of "girls" and "broads" (his version of Tony Manero's "nice girls" and "cunts") and so convinced that rape only happens to girls who flaunt their sexuality, that he pushes her away with almost demonic energy and aversion. All his agonies of conscience only make things worse; his would-be bride can never wear the white of innocence, and she can never fulfill his Catholic dream of an unbroken vessel, a hymen *intacto*. When J.R. finally decides to put his scruples aside and swallow his pride by proposing to this "broad," his sullied lover, he only makes things worse with his unconscious condescension. His offer, "I'll marry you anyway," raises the girl's consciousness, and she refuses to accept him on that basis. The more she reminds J.R. of her value, her personal worth, the louder he bellows about her tarnished virtue: "You ought to be glad I'm willing to marry you." The climax comes when she decides his proposal isn't loving enough, and he explodes, "Who do you think you are, the Virgin Mary? Who else is going to marry you, you whore?" Their fiery encounter ends with recriminations, no handshakes, no breakthroughs, no hugs, and no illuminations. J.R. is more psychologically devastated and more morally confused than ever; he'll never calm all those demons possessing him. All he can do is wander off to an unsatisfactory Confession, during which sensuous images of statues, rape, bloody crucifixes, and nude lovers are juxtaposed in intense dichotomies; the frenzied editing suggests J.R.'s inner turmoil, for he is truly one of the damned now, doomed to wander aimlessly around an urban ghetto. It's clear he'll never escape Little Italy despite all his hegiras on the Staten Island Ferry.

One curious footnote to the saga of *Who's That Knocking at My Door?* (also released under the titles *Bring on the Dancing*

Girls, I Call First, and *J.R.*) involves its production history and eventual distribution. This early work by a fledgling Catholic artist was largely financed by friends, including New York University film professor Haig Manoogian and his wife Mitzi. When the film failed commercially, all the principals agreed that mainstream America wasn't interested in films about Italian Americans, their religion, and their guilt trips, so Martin Scorsese shelved his script for a companion piece, *Mean Streets,* for several years. Distributors, on the other hand, saw potential in the sex angles of the story, and a small company which specialized in promoting and distributing sexploitation films agreed to distribute Scorsese's vision of Catholic guilt and moral blindness if he added a lengthy, provocative sequence with a naked model making love to J.R. Desperate for any kind of exposure, director Scorsese flew with Harvey Keitel to Amsterdam, hired a starlet willing to strip and fornicate on camera, and shot a lot of torrid footage—much of which is in the release print. The young Scorsese, not too many years away from seminary training, was so worried about his raw footage being seized by United States Customs officials when he reentered America that he smuggled the steamy sequences into the country himself, hidden in the pocket of his raincoat. Eventually *Who's That Knocking at My Door?* played the Eighth Avenue circuit of theaters where most of the patrons also wore raincoats.

East Side theater patrons got their own sordid glimpse of Italian Catholic sexual hangups in Francis Ford Coppola's most personal venture, *The Conversation* (1974), a Kafkaesque parable about a professional voyeur, Harry Caul (Gene Hackman), whose almost God-like electronic eavesdropping has become so legendary that it has obliterated even his own privacy and personal life. Harry's self-effacing guilt over the bloody murders, gruesome decapitations, ugly divorces, and other psychic agonies his work has generated, has driven Harry into a nihilistic form of eudaemonism; he has stripped his apartment bare, crushed his religious statues in his quest to rid himself of electronic bugs, and isolated himself from any human contacts; yet he's still haunted by toilets which back up in torrents of blood and carnage. Harry has given up on the idea of joy and salvation; now he seeks only the Buddhist state of ahimsa, fearing not his death but further bloodshed and murder indirectly caused by his discoveries. Harry has no room in his life for real women, for meaningful human relationships, but he still marches to his local Catholic church for regular confessions. In a church symbolically populated by old women, infirm matrons, and remorseful young boys, the middle-aged Harry confesses the petty offenses of his last three months, including occasional blasphemies, some stolen newspapers, and a few guilty pleasures "deliberately taken from impure thoughts." When Harry turns to his real concerns, the harms that may come to two young people from his work, he constantly denies any real responsibility and gets no response from his priest. David Thomson in his provocative study of *Overexposures* makes much of this clerical silence; for him, the priest's head is "an enigma" as seen through the grille, "a luscious riddle," and the whole confession sequence is shot with such "exquisite stylistic ambition" that "there is no way the soul can stay naked in that baroque visual atmosphere." The setting and mood, Thomson argues, "has diminished the possibility of the people," and the result is a film he labels "the most despairing and horrified film Coppola has made," a bleaker film even than *Apolcalypse Now* with its literary "heart of darkness" and horror.

The horror of moral quandary, sexual incapacity, and overwhelming unquenchable guilt suffuses director Joseph Ellison's *Don't Go in the House* (1980), a Gothic tragedy with an abusive mother, an ineffectual Irish priest, and plenty of hell fire. The Italian protagonist, Donny (Dan Grimaldi) epitomizes Catholic misogyny and irrepressible lust. His mother, a devout woman who never recovered emotionally from her husband's abandoning her for more erotic lovers, decides that his darling son Donny must have these sexual demons burned out of his young flesh, so she regularly holds his arms over the gas burners of her old-fashioned kitchen stove. Donny's dramatic physical scars, which he hides under long sleeved shirts and sweaters, are the outward physical manifestations of his warped mind. When his mother dies, Danny props her up in a rocking chair, and begins his revenge on all the women who fired his lust. Donny's *modus operandi* is laden with religious and Freudian symbolism. When he lures a woman into his house, he overpowers her, strips her, and hangs her naked body in his own metal-lined libidinal shrine. Donny then douses his victims with gasoline, and clad in a prophylactic asbestos suit, sprays them with a flaming ejaculate from his phallic blowtorch. His lust demands that his conquests be punished by the fires of hell, that his mother's morality be perpetuated.

The thematic weight of Donny's sado-masochistic behavior comes into focus in his one visit to a church. Startled by a priest as he tries to steal large quantities of holy water from an ornate font, Donny asks the priest if holy water really "puts out the flames." When the priest tries to understand the seemingly demented boy, Donny blathers on about the devil and visions of evil. The priest tries to assure Donny that demons are only symbols and that evil lives only "if we let it," but the possessed Donny knows better; he shows the startled pastor his scars, explaining, "I was burned just like in hell." The priest recoils from Donny's talk of evil, punishment, and retribution, and tries to convince Donny to "forgive his mother." Disillusioned, Donny leaves, muttering about "other problems" and "other people," but the rather obtuse priest takes no further action other than to remind Donny to "put these ideas out of your mind, resist, and you'll find peace" and to urge Donny to come back to see him. The next time the priest and Donny meet, Donny has his flame thrower, and he turns it on this minister from a Church that seemingly cannot solve his problems, cannot quiet the voices that haunt him, and cannot quench his inner fires.

A nightmare aura also surrounds Catholic sexuality in director Philip Kauffman's haunting vision of mainstream Italian life, *The Wanderers* (1979). In his world of teenage gangs, where Chinese, black, and Italian collide, a world lorded over by the Fordham baldies, the tongs, and other ethnic cliques, sex is the biggest worry and the problem *numero uno*. One gang terrorizes another by marching them to a park, tying rocks to their penises, and throwing the stones off the bridge—a rather straightforward metaphor for the castration and mutilation games these boys play all the time. Another Italian lad, when he accepts his own homosexual urges, loiters outside a mysteriously alien Irish Catholic church in a distant, forbidding Irish parish, until a smiling Ducky Boy emerges from Communion, invites his caress, and then stabs him; as the wounded Italian staggers away, the other Irish Ducky Boys surround him and kill him in a surrealistic vision of moralistic avenging devils. Still other Italians play macho games with their philandering fathers and cheat their girlfriends at sniggering games of strip poker. Everywhere sex is stunted, perverse, dirty, leering, and unfulfilling. Its one sure consequence is the unwanted pregnancy. Richie (Ken Wahl) must forget his dreams of escape to Bleecker Street, willowy lasses, and the new music of Bob Dylan, when he impregnates the Don's giggly daughter; his universe is Little Italy, a land inhabited by overweight gangsters in garish Miami Beach sport shirts, pock-marked with bowling alleys and noisy taverns, and governed by old country morality and guilt. His new father-in-law, who always smiles whether he's crippling a hustler or giving his brainless daughter away, cannot see the contradiction in his proud boast that he was quite a sexual athlete in his day, but "never did it with nobody's daughter." Richie will spend the rest of his life paying for those few intimate moments with the Don's daughter, moments, Kauffman suggests, which may have been enacted in the dark recesses of an ornate subterranean Catholic shrine. These two lovers seemingly spend a lot of time in the candle-lit recesses of these strange catacombs. The confusing aisles and narrow passages of the shrine provide a fitting visual counterpoint to their medieval version of love, a vision of a woman "standing by her lover in thick and thin" and craving "the baby of the man she loves" and of a man desperate for that lover to "have his baby." The girl's father translates all this adolescent poetry into an ironclad rule of Italian sexuality: "The thing is, you knocked her up and now you gotta pay the price—the sportsman's way." Pop assures them that they haven't lost everything: "You can live in our basement—we got wood panelling." Eventually Richie sees the wisdom of all this, puts on the proud silks of the homebound "Wanderers," and banishes those troubling thoughts that "the times they are a changing." In the movies, Italian sexual life is as immutable as the granite Irish Catholic Church that contains it.

That's not to say there aren't some winners in the game of love. The million-in-one shots do come through, like Rocky Balboa, whose exploits as lover and boxer made Sylvester Stallone one of the richest, most celebrated, and proudest sons of Italy. Rocky, an ethnic superstud if ever there was one, knocks blacks silly whether they're as handsome and jive as Apollo Creed or as mean and ugly as Clubber Lang. This hero of a seemingly endless film cycle (three have been released and there is persistent talk of many more) resurrects a great white hope, a lovable Rocky Marciano-like hulk, to exorcise such real-life heavyweight nightmares as Mohammed Ali.

But Rocky wins more than the heavyweight crown; he also seduces Adrian and lets her share his Cinderella story. If his journey from an uninspiring Thanksgiving fight in Philadelphia's Resurrection Athletic Club, a dull contest fought in front of a saccharine image of an effete Christ holding the Eucharist, to center ring slugfest at Madison Square Garden, an arena festooned by American flags and advertising logos, seems miraculous, Adrian's transformation is even more mindboggling. Adrian begins as a mousey, repressed waif pining away in a pet store, only to emerge as a glamorous, fashionable liberated woman and a radiant, dynamic, warm mother who inspires her fearful husband to go out there and "win, win, win," not for her, not for his family, but for himself.

The sexual dynamic in *Rocky I*, *Rocky II*, and *Rocky III* is a lot more interesting than the bone-rattling, highly predictable boxing exhibitions; audiences cheer Rocky so loud largely because he has seduced them, too, with his mumbling mixture of populism, sanctity, and common sense; with his tender eyes and his clear vulnerability. Rocky's the gangland enforcer who can't bring himself to break legs, the superstar who can't hype shampoo, the racist with hundreds of black friends, the Catholic who can cry at Jewish funerals and chant of Israel, the club fighter who still applauds class and style, the Philadelphian who gives mediocre statues to bedeck the fabled steps of its celebrated art museum. He's the boxing champ still pious enough to ask the parish priest to bless him, the Italian husband still religious enough to ignore training and the heavyweight title when a vigil in a Catholic shrine might turn God's attention to his comatose wife. He's an engaging combination of beautiful loser and fabulous winner. He mirrors every ethnic prejudice, yet transcends them all.

Rocky's such a lovable lummox that he almost makes the old "nice girl-broad" categories sound like an arcane piece of folk wisdom. One night, as Rocky the nobody prowls his neighborhood, he runs into teenagers on a corner and hears one girl, Marie, tell a friend to "Stuff it, man." Rocky calls Marie aside and walks her home, lecturing her all the way about the realities of a woman's role in Italian culture. Rocky's moralism extends to smoking, since it yellows teeth, and to wine, since booze erases inhibitions, but he saves his sternest remarks for a homily on the importance of both being pure and seeming pure. Rocky warns Marie that Italian men laugh when girls talk dirty, encourage girls to act cute, but after a while, the same men withhold their all-important respect for girls with a bad reputation. Talk or act like a "whore," Rocky warns, and "boom! that's it; you got a bad reputation and everyone will treat you like that little whore who hung out down the corner." Marie does not heed Rocky's lesson, however, and the whole sequence ends on a comic note when she escapes his ministrations and tells him, "Screw you, Rocky, Creepo." Audiences rarely miss the complexity of the message here. Rocky's stereotypes are sad but true elements in Italian culture; Marie's bold iconoclastic curses are directed at a chauvinistic double standard, yet they do make her seem vulgar and common and silly. Rocky's morality may be poorly framed and sadly misguided, but his Church still seems more sacred than Marie's profanities.

Rocky's intrinsic humanity and his wholehearted love for marriage, his wife, and his kids afford a moving witness to Roman Catholicism's emphasis on the sanctity of the family. Rocky's no macho philanderer; he courts Adrian in *Rocky I*, weds her in *Rocky II*, and renews his vows in *Rocky III*. Theirs is a storybook romance, where fidelity is a given and love abounds; in every crisis, they reaffirm their commitment and think only of their partner—they're living examples of the efficacy of a real marriage encounter. Adrian, it might be remembered, was in her own brother's eyes "a frigging loser" before she met Rocky Balboa, a woman approaching thirty years old and about to "dry up." Rocky hammers at her door, urging her to come out and "maybe laugh a little bit," a line that seems stolen from Paddy Chayevsky's *Marty* (1955), an earlier Academy Award winner about Catholic sexual repression. Together, Rocky and Adrian fill the gaps in each other's lives; she's the girl with no body, told to develop her brain; and he's the boy with no brain, told to develop his body—together they make a resplendent new person. When Rocky first kisses Adrian, he tells her she needn't kiss back if she doesn't want to. She hesitates at first, but everything is so warm, so tender, so perfect, that they swoon together in love, and all her repressions evaporate in one most dramatic sigh.

Adrian's older brother and substitute father Paulie has obviously been more crippled by sexual repression than the gregarious Rocky. He seems never quite able to accept the fact that he's an overage bachelor, a sad fate he blames on Adrian: "What am I, a pig, a fucking loser? I didn't get married because of you—you couldn't live by yourself—you owe me!" When Rocky and Adrian hit it off so well, Paulie wants some tangible reward, a share in Rocky's victories as a boxer, and reminds his pal, "I gave you my sister." Adrian, who hears all this, lashes out at Paulie, reminding him that she cooks, cleans, and looks after his home despite the fact he makes her feel like a loser. In the passion of this argument, Paulie reveals the darkest secret of all: he hates Adrian and Rocky because they have had sexual intercourse. Paulie vanquishes the unmarried Adrian with the pathetic charge that "You're busted, you're not a virgin!" Paulie's reminder of her "broad"status prompts Adrian's hysterics, and Rocky's acceptance of her as a permanent roommate. By the end of *Rocky I*, they're calling their love across the arena; the last victorious words of the film are "Adrian, I love you" and "I love you, Rocky," a victory sweeter than going all the way in a fight with Apollo Creed, "the most dangerous fighter in the world."

Rocky II, the most overtly religious segment of the trilogy, begins with the Catholic wedding of Adrian and Rocky. After the nuptials, even the flustered priest clamors for Rocky's touch, and he snaps a quick Polaroid of the retired fighter. Rocky has promised Adrian never to fight again, and he stoically endures Apollo Creed's slings and arrows. Finally, however, the need for money and the desire to retain his pride as an Italian man combine to force Rocky into a title bout; just then, Adrian delivers their baby prematurely and lapses into a coma. Nothing will move Rocky from her side, not even his trainer Mickey's impassioned sermon about "the biggest title in the world" and reminiscence about Rocky's "most beautiful moment on earth," his first fight with the aptly named Apollo Creed. Mickey apologizes for getting mad in "a biblical place," the hospital's Catholic chapel, and he promises to kneel with Rocky before the tabernacle if that's what the champ wants. The two men, Catholic and Jew, do stay and pray until Adrian finally awakens, calls for her child, and implores her husband to do just one thing: "Win this time." Girded with the mantle of Adrian's love, Rocky seems invincible; even Mickey tells him "Tonight's our night" before the match. The battle is grueling, but the outcome is never in doubt; Rocky picks himself up from the mat, tells the defeated Creed he's a great fighter, gives thanks to God, and tells all the world that "Tonight's the greatest night of my life." His final words, as always, are for Adrian: "Yo, Adrian, I did it!" *Rocky III* rehashes many of these themes as the champ wrestles with his fears of failure and disgrace. Mickey warns his protégé that "the worst thing that can happen to any fighter" has happened to him: "You got civilized." Rocky's opponent this time is Clubber Lang, an evil monolith who clearly recognizes the iconography in their battle, warning the Italian Catholic father figure that this lean, mean black dude is going to "torture" him, to "punish" him, to "crucify" him "real bad." Clubber Lang underestimates, of course, the power of Rocky's secret weapon, Adrian, and her impassioned pep talk inspires Rocky to knock the black devil senseless, pulverizing him at his own game in a stunning victory for Italian pride, Catholic marriage, and the family circle.

Few contemporary film portraits of Catholics celebrate such stirring accomplishments. Usually, the outcome is much more tangled and unsatisfactory. In the Hollywood catechism, Catholics have more capacity for suffering than for joy. Most contemporary portraits of ethnic Catholicism are dark portraits of stunted lives, compulsive guilt, and abiding despair. Consider, for example, the Irish Catholic friends in Sydney Pollack's *Absence of Malice* (1981). Divorced Michael Gallagher (Paul Newman) can never escape his family's history of rum-running and mob activity; the Justice Department slanders him in the hopes of catching bigger fish. For him, the ensuing publicity means the death of his dearest friend, the end of his business, and a total loss of hard-earned respectability. His friend, Teresa (Melinda Dillon), suffers even more cruelly. In an attempt to provide him an alibi for his whereabouts on May 25, 1980, Teresa tells Megan (Sally Field), an unscrupulous cub reporter, that she and Gallagher were in Atlanta, where she was having an abortion to rid herself of the child of another man she barely knew and never loved. Megan makes the story front-page news, and when Teresa sees she cannot collect all the newspapers from everyone's lawns, that she cannot hide her sexual misconduct from her infirm father, and that the scandal of her sexual dalliance and subsequent abortion will make it impossible for her to continue as the assistant to the principal at Saint Ignatio's School, the repressed Catholic spinster commits suicide. Michael Gallagher makes sure that Megan, a reporter who tried to sleep with him to get a story, understands the horror of Teresa's death, emphasizing all its physical details: "They found her naked in a tub, she was such a good girl she didn't want to make a mess . . . just her naked in a tub. Can you imagine how she felt?" The aftermath of her death, he reminds Megan, will be equally revolting: "You know something I didn't know? Suicides are homicides, so they do autopsies, and will split her wide open. When they get up here [pointing to Megan's chest], they use shears—shears, for Christ's sake!" Gallagher's elaborate revenge destroys the overzealous prosecutors, the ambitious district attorneys, and the sensation-hungry journalists, but it can't restore Teresa and it does not afford him spiritual peace. He has to take to the sea for that, and perhaps visit his long-lost daughter; he needs more than the sex Megan offers and the retribution his intellect works upon his enemies.

Paul Newman's finest portrait of a spiritually lost Irish Catholic comes, however, in Sidney Lumet's deeply satisfying realization of a complex David Mamet screenplay, *The Verdict* (1982), a film about a drunken Irish attorney who takes on the most celebrated lawyer in Boston, Ed Concannon (James Mason), "the Prince of Fucking Darkness," the renowned doctors at St. Catherine's Hospital, a prejudiced Irish Catholic judge, and the whole Archdiocese of Boston. Armed only with the truth, an old black doctor, and a Catholic nurse who rediscovers her conscience, Frank Galvin (Paul Newman) wins a huge cash settlement for his Irish clients, but along the way, he loses what might be his last change for personal happiness when the lover who enters his life (Charlotte Rampling) turns out to be a well-paid employee of Ed Concannon, sent to spy on the opposition.

There's no denying the courtroom victory in *The Verdict;* the jury comes in and asks if they can award Newman's working class clients more than the huge sum they sued for, and the judge tells the foreman, "You are not bound by anything other than your good judgment." But the mood of *The Verdict* as a whole is anything but victorious: its clergymen are modern day Machiavellis shunting down corridors of power and sequestered in limousines; its doctors are overworked, arrogant demigods who tyrannize nurses and patients and lie about their abilities and their mistakes; its lawyers are corporate hit men eager to find the loophole that absolves their clients of any legal responsibility. The Irish Catholic laborer who sees all this calls the shots exactly right when he laments that no one gives a damn about him. Kaitlin Costello Price (Lindsay Crouse), with her heartrending confession that all she ever wanted to do was "be a nurse" until she fell victim to some unscrupulous doctor's lies, suggests the sense of loss that anchors the film in reality and defuses the elation over the minor justice the jury is able to do. Like attorney Galvin, the good people in the film seem rather isolated, and the phone is always ringing with new temptations.

Lumet's vision of the Catholic hierarchy in *The Verdict* offers a stern corrective to the pluperfect cheerfulness and laughable impracticality of the Irish priests in *Going My Way*. Lumet's modern prelate, Bishop Brophy (Edward Binns), is a post-Watergate authority figure, coolly efficient, enchanted with his power, yet pragmatic to a fault. He wants answers before he acts; he wants to know he can win the case before he even tries to negotiate. If anything, Bishop Brophy is more unscrupulous than his legendary lawyer, Ed Concannon. Bishop Brophy pays little attention to the human side of the case; the girl obviously does not matter to him, and his patter about her suffering lacks conviction and sincerity. He's just trying to garner Galvin's signature on a check for $210,000, an amount his insurance company assured the bishop would make a rather straightforward appeal to a lawyer looking to take $70,000 home, an even third. In their conversations, Bishop Brophy keeps talking of "generous offers" and admits that "Nothing we can begin to do will make that woman well, but we can at least try to compensate, make a gesture." Galvin, however, isn't swayed by the bishop's ring, his obsequious cleric, or the pragmatic figure the insurance company suggested. Unlike the Roman Catholic bishop, Galvin, a caring man, has visited the young victim and he empathizes with her tragic plight; to settle without a public trial, Galvin asserts, would obscure an important truth about this woman's misplaced faith in Catholic doctors, Catholic hospitals, and Catholic clergy: "That poor girl put her trust into the hands of two men who took her life . . . the people who should care for her—her doctors and you and me—have been bought off to look the other way." Galvin refuses the blood money, explaining that if he took it, he would be "lost," just "another rich ambulance chaser," another professional living well by exploiting the working class. Bishop Brophy clearly has fewer qualms about his vocation and the Catholic Church's enormous wealth; his fears concern the publicity attendant on this lawsuit. Later in the film, when an aide comes to tell the bishop that "legally" the suit is all but over—given some favorable rulings from a partial judge—the prelate senses that more fundamental human questions will sway the jury. When Bishop Brophy asks whether his aide believed Miss Costello's disturbing charges about altered hospital records, one glance reveals that the aide and the world at large know the truth. The bishop looks away mournfully, aware that St. Catherine's Hospital will be disgraced, that the suit is lost, and that he has been on the side of the devils, the vain deceivers now vanquished by Galvin's appeal to a transcendent reality. In *The Verdict*, attorney Galvin speaks of laws as "prayers . . . fervent and frightened prayers," and reminds the jury that "If you act in faith, faith will be given to you . . . if we are to have faith in justice, we have only to believe in ourselves and act with justice." Galvin seeks Catholic justice "in our hearts"; there obviously is little justice in the Catholic chancellory.

Galvin's internalized sense of just behavior has broken his own heart, however, more than once. His well-planned career, his education at Boston College, his years on the Law Review, his apprenticeship at a powerful law firm, and his marriage with the boss's daughter went up in smoke the day he decided to report a senior partner's attempt to bribe jurors. In the real world of Boston courtrooms, such scruples got Galvin arrested and almost disbarred: his law firm could frame him more easily than it could live with the scandal of a compromised partner. When Galvin capitulated and withdrew his accusation, the charges evaporated, but so did his marriage. What followed were years of dirty jokes about cheap whores in Irish bars, infamous bastions of male camaraderie and besotten chauvinism. When an old friend, his one-time law school professor and mentor, brings Galvin the plum of a clearly negotiable negligence suit against St. Catherine's Hospital, Galvin knows this civil case is his last chance at wealth and security. Just then, his last chance for love walks into his local bar, in the person of a mournful, beautiful, mysterious woman who seems interested in Galvin's life, sexually pliant, and quite supportive. When it turns out she's a whore too, a well-paid minion of Ed Concannon, Galvin's romanticism is crushed forever. In one of

256

Sidney Lumet's most startling and controversial images, a harsh scene in an otherwise subdued and coldly civilized film, attorney Galvin confronts his female betrayer, then smashes her face with a brutal punch. Spectators in the cocktail lounge can barely believe what's happened, but theater audiences actually feel relief to see this woman get what's coming to her.

Most celluloid images of impassioned, disillusioned, frustrated, self-righteous Catholic men brutalizing beautiful women are a lot less justifiable and satisfying. An important corollary of the Roman Catholic emphasis on "nice girls" and the spiritual deification of purity, chastity, and virginity in word and action, the Hollywood catechism suggests, is a pathological hatred for female sexuality, a cosmic fear of bare breasts and naked pudenda, and a terrifying disgust with temptation and arousal. Catholic men in Hollywood films don't pluck out their eyes if visions offend them or cut off their aroused sex organs—they destroy instead the object of their lust, raping and mutilating the females who attract them. For their part, Catholic women are the perennial victims: virgins waiting to be savaged and unspeakably defiled.

Lamont Johnson's *Lipstick* (1976), a feminist tract on rape and the inadequacy of laws and courts in dealing with this crime, makes its kinky rapist, Gordon Stuart (Perry King), a music teacher at an old fashioned, very restrictive all girls Catholic high school. Sister Margaret and Sister Monica stand by Gordon throughout his trial; no one can believe that this gentle Catholic intellectual could do those dark evil things that a sexually liberated high fashion model, Chris McCormick (Margaux Hemingway), accuses him of. She lost her credibility when she lost her virginity; the nude pictures of her in glamorous magazines totally undermine her case. Only when Gordon tries again—chasing Chris's school girl sister who still wears her Catholic uniform—can anyone see that something's amiss. Even then, Chris has little faith in courts, so she castrates the rapist herself, firing round after round into his dead body. Kathleen Sullivan, the Irish Catholic schoolteacher in Tay Garnett's *Deep in the Heart* (1984), finds a subtler way to revenge her rape by a Texan lawyer, but her anguish mirrors Chris's torment. Everyone believes Kathleen was raped, but no one wants to help her. Her rapist actually tells the psychologically devastated beauty that it was her own fault for being so "irresistible" and that her attempts to resist intercourse with him were a result of "something in your psyche that's slightly maladjusted." The police remind her that she was no virgin, so any courtroom confrontation with a rich young lawyer would be self-destructive at best; her sexual proclivities will be maligned, not his. Even her priest cautions that forgiveness is the most prudent course of action; after all, she must have been somewhat attracted to the man who raped her since she was on a date with him the night the attack occurred. Catholic girls, school teachers or not, praised by their parents for being "good" or not, obviously have nothing to fall back on once they've surrendered their virginity, whether the surrender is voluntary or not. As Rocky noted, the appearance of unsullied virtue is at least as important as morality itself.

The most memorable contemporary Hollywood image of the sexual dilemmas of Catholic women, Richard Brooks' *Looking for Mr. Goodbar* (1977), is an amalgam of fiction and fact; Brooks synthesizes the tawdry details of the brutal murder of Katherine Cleary, an Irish Catholic school teacher who worked with deaf children and who was dismembered by Joe Willie Simpson, a married drifter she met in a singles' bar, on New Year's Day, 1973 (a lurid incident skillfully chronicled and well-analyzed by Lacey Fosburgh in her non-fiction best-seller, *Closing Time: The True Story of the "Goodbar" Murder*) with the powerful, often surrealistic fictions of Judith Rossner's immensely popular novel, *Looking for Mr. Goodbar*, a Freudian narrative about a dedicated Irish Catholic teacher, Theresa Dunn, who uses promiscuity and drugs as a refuge from the horrors of modern life and the stifling restrictions of her Roman Catholic heritage, only to die at the hands of a drifter she picks up in a singles' bar on New Year's Day. The mere fact that the Cleary murder took such a hold on the American psyche, generating television specials, magazine articles, paperback best sellers, and a major film, suggests that its amalgam of Catholic guilt and sexual license, of loving school teacher and spaced out sybarite, of suffering Irish parents and slaughtered flesh still mesmerized the popular imagination. All America, it seemed, yearned to see the Catholic maiden school teacher stripped bare, to experience the flesh beneath the gold crucifix. Richard Brooks's avowedly moral film about women's issues, about subjugation and oppression, about the feminist revolution and the "Decade of the Dames," also features nudity, mayhem, and misogynistic violence as part of its popular appeal; one of Brooks's casting coups had been to sign Diane Keaton to play Theresa Dunn, a role which required this well-known star to show a lot of her previously well-concealed flesh. Audiences in 1977 had two Diane Keatons to choose from, the frumpy, funny Annie Hall and the neurotic, guilt-ridden Theresa Dunn. On the one hand, a WASP queen with a demented brother and on the other, a Catholic commoner who can never erase the taint, the cursed blood and twisted genes, she feels are her Irish Catholic father's legacy.

Feminists, by and large, hated Brooks's film, yet they also sensed how important its stereotypes and prejudices were to the American psyche. When E. Ann Kaplan selected the modern film most worthy of extended analysis in her volume *Women and Film*, she chose *Looking for Mr. Goodbar*, a film she detests. Kaplan convincingly demonstrates that the whole project is a nightmarish realization of all the old dichotomies in a patriarchal, chauvinistic society: nice girl/whore, daughter/defiant nymph, dutiful child/bold tart, faithful wife and nurturing mother/fickle lover and sterile strumpet. The dichotomies in Brooks's film, Kaplan suggests, all mirror divisions in Theresa's pesonality as it is presented in the film—splits between her daytime madonna-like ministrations to her school children and her nighttime sexual services to men who enrapture her. In Kaplan's view, all the women play sadly limited and symbolic roles: "Teresa's [Kaplan's spelling] two sisters are, on the one hand, Brigid, the mother (and unattractive), and, on the other, Kathleen, the 'whore' (and sexually exciting). Mrs. Dunn, the mother of all three girls, is totally subdued, beaten, and unattractive." As Kaplan sees it, Theresa's promiscuity is her response to her failure to win her Irish father's love and admiration: "Teresa is seen as desperately needing her father's love and approval, but, unable to obtain it, she becomes what he most hates."

Kaplan's analysis comes very close to the psychological heart of the film, and given the length at which she analyzes the film, it is rather surprising that she doesn't discuss director Richard Brooks's many public statements on *Looking for Mr. Goodbar*, remarks in which he tries unsuccessfully to negate analyses like hers. In an important interview, for example, in *American Film* (October 1977), Brooks defines the key difference between Rossner's novel and his film in terms of Theresa's sexual identity; Rossner, he argues, made Theresa too much a victim of guilt and depression. His film, Brooks argues, takes more cognizance that she is "a very joyous woman, full of the joy of life." Developing his thesis, director Brooks details for his patient interviewers his recent discoveries in Catholic literature that modern surveys by "a group of Catholics" have told Church fathers that there is "a massive drift among United States Catholics away from the Church ban on contraception and toward a greater tolerance of extra-marital intercourse." Catholic theologians, Brooks summarizes, are now talking of measuring sexual conduct on a scale weighing whether it is "self-liberating, other-enriching, honest, faithful, socially responsible, life-serving, and joyous." All this sounds rational enough, and rather trite, but then comes one of those mental leaps so difficult to follow that the mind boggles. These new liberated Catholic sexual tenets were, Brooks unexpectedly concludes, "what I was talking about and thinking about two years ago [when he began work on *Looking for Mr. Goodbar*] and that's what our story is about." In Brooks's view, Theresa's frequent orgasms show her at "the apex of lovemaking." Her tragedy isn't retribution for rejecting her assigned place in male society (as Kaplan argues), but pure chance. Director Brooks is especially explicit on this point: "The point of the story—what happens to the girl—is that it could have happened on any day, at any hour, and to any of a number of other people."

Although Kaplan does identify Catholicism as part of the

patriarchy that crushes Theresa and Brooks intimates his abiding interest in the changes sweeping the American church, neither really suggests how critical Theresa's Irish Catholic heritage is to an audience's perception of *Looking for Mr. Goodbar*. The very first words in the film detail Theresa's "Last Confession," a revealing essay she submits to Professor Engle, the English teacher who initiates her into the world of sex (in this case, adulterous, subservient sex—this older man, a clear father figure, even tells her he hates to be around girls after he has "fucked them"). Theresa's last interlude in the confessional at fifteen-years-of-age provides a coda for the whole film, detailing the inferiority she feels and her inability to fit her burgeoning sexuality in the constrictive "hot booth" of the Irish Catholic sacrament of Penance: "I felt afraid to confess and afraid not to. I felt no contrition, not even shame. I still felt the same lust. Was it in my mind or in my body?"

Theresa goes to her last Confession largely to purge her "envy and lust." Her teenage envy centers on her sister Katherine, the beautiful daughter with a straight back, straight teeth, and voluptuous figure; Theresa's adolescent lust touches all of Katherine's boy friends, male admirers she covets with all her heart. Katherine plays the same role in *Looking for Mr. Goodbar* that Father Frank plays in *Saturday Night Fever*, only Katherine is the evil force Theresa must counterbalance for the Dunn family. Several clear equations are established between Katherine, her beauty, and her earthly bliss; and Theresa's dedication, her sacrifices, and her heavenly rewards. To teach deaf children, Theresa is assured, is "to touch heaven." Katherine may celebrate lovers, garner husbands, even have abortions and divorces; and it doesn't matter a great deal. Theresa, however, must stay at home, meet curfews, live by her father's stern precepts, and be contented with television on New Year's Eve. When Theresa finally leaves home, she obviously throws the scale out of balance. Only retribution, guilt, and recriminations can result. Not even the evil Katherine can, the film suggests, ever really escape her Catholic puritanism. One day she must and does awaken in "a room full of naked asses" only to realize that hers is one of them. Katherine draws her own self-portrait when she laments, "I guess that's all I've ever been, just another naked ass."

None of the Catholics in *Looking for Mr. Goodbar* ever make peace with their family, their Church, or their bodies. Perhaps the most pathetic character of all, social worker James Morrissey (William Atherton) suits the Dunn family perfectly as Theresa's potential spouse; he relishes tired jokes, Notre Dame football, noisy households, overcooked meals, beer straight from the can, and sexual abstinence. James Morrissey, like so many Irish Catholics in contemporary Hollywood films, is a terrible lover— never assertive enough at the right time, inept at foreplay, shy to a fault, and quite clumsy with his outmoded prophylactics. This minor revision in the Hollywood catechism, an emendation since the era of Cagney, echoes Andrew Greeley's sad "impression" in *That Most Distressful Nation: The Taming of the American Irish* that second generation Irish-Americans got "rather little enjoyment out of sex and are not very skillful in the art of lovemaking." His experience of life in the Irish ghetto convinced the celibate Father Greeley that "the Irish male, particularly in his cups, may spin out romantic poetry extolling the beauty of his true love, but he becomes awkward and tongue-tied in her presence and clumsy, if not rough, in his attempts at intimacy."

James Morrissey in *Looking for Mr. Goodbar* leaves his women laughing in scorn and totally unsatisfied; he's an abysmal failure as a man, crippled by self-loathing and impotent with rage at his own tortured legacy. All his liberal philanthropy can never erase the guilt he felt over a trauma he experienced as a boy. James tells Theresa some horrible secrets about his mother and father before he tries to sleep with her. After his abysmal failure in bed, obviously crushed by Theresa's uncontrollable laughter, James screams back that all his sad revelations were lies. True or false, however, his words, be they confession or pathetic seduction ploy, create a frightening vision of warped sexuality, inadequate parents, and real pain. James describes an unforgettable dark night, the night his father abandoned him and his mother, in images of a Freudian nightmare. James, a twelve-year-old frightened by the dark, wanders into the bedroom where his naked, alcoholic mother, sprawled on her marriage bed, taunts his father, "What's the matter, big boy, can't you get it up?" and she provokes a savage beating: "My father hit her, but my mother just kept on laughing and he kept on hitting her and she kept laughing and laughing. There was blood all over the bed and blood all over my mother." James Morrissey, just a few seconds later, will hear similar goading laughter from Theresa: there seems no escaping sexual inadequacy, inherited or not. And his eerie image of a blood-spattered bed foreshadows Theresa's own fate. Sex obviously is no laughing matter for Irish-American Catholics; the sins of the father can never be erased.

Theresa's relationship with her father and the value system he represents forms, as critic Kaplan notes, the major concern in Brooks's movie, a focus much more clearly drawn on screen than it is in Judith Rossner's novel. In Brooks's realization, Mr. Dunn embodies all the worst features of Irish Catholic life in film: the drinking, the rowdiness, the brutality, the insensitivity, and the hysteria. Dad's an ogre who manhandles Theresa and feeds his ego by belittling her. Theresa, he shouts, will never be beautiful like Katherine; her childhood disease, the unsuccessful operation, and the incomplete recovery have scarred her body for all eternity. Theresa, he rants on, has also chosen a freedom which pollutes her soul: "Freedom this, freedom that—free to leave your family, free to quit the Church, free love—free to abort your own kids, free to go to hell." Theresa, he asserts in his last and nastiest attack, is the only imperfect child in the Dunn family tree, a misshapen daughter whose scoliosis uniquely symbolizes God's judgment, her guilt, and her inevitable perdition. This insult is the one abuse Theresa will not tolerate, the lie she cannot stomach, and she finally slays her tormentor with the truth she can't hide anymore, the reality her father can no longer conceal about his whole family: Theresa's obsessive attempts to understand her malady have revealed that her scoliosis is congenital. In a heart-wrenching confrontation, central to any understanding of the film, Theresa screams at her distraught father that the fault, the disease, is "in your blood, Father." This painful medical and psychological truth prompts her father's stammering admission that his mother did have all perfect sons, but one imperfect daughter, "little Maureen," whose "poor twisted body" was an abomination to her brothers. Their outrage destroyed the afflicted girl. Mr. Dunn sadly recalls how these chauvinistic Irish bullies attacked, cursed, damned, and abused Maureen until she took her own life. "Freedom," he sighs, "how do you get free of the awful truth?" Mr. Dunn remains blind, of course, to the fact he has never escaped his evil misogynistic attitude; unchanged by the horror he and his brothers committed, he is now driving his own scoliotic daughter to her death.

Finally, of course, a diagnosis of congenital scoliosis provides no more satisfactory key to *Looking for Mr. Goodbar* than the "Rosebud" sled provides to *Citizen Kane*; at best it's a limited metaphor for more complex concerns. Theresa's quandary will never be resolved. She begins the film admitting that her disease baffled her: "I never did understand what terrible thing I did to make God so angry." Patrons leaving the theater had to face a similarly perplexing question: What did Theresa Dunn ever do to deserve her horrible death? Is it retribution for challenging woman's role in society? Is it God's judgment on her promiscuity? Is it Camus's Sisyphean rock at the bottom of the hill?

The priest who eulogized the real life victim, Katherine Cleary, told the family and friends gathered at St. Mary's Catholic Church in Queens that the girl's death had a lesson for all humanity: "She was a sincere girl who tried to open our lives and the lives of others. And now, in her death, she tells us how to be open and to try to understand His plan, even when it seems to be so contradictory that the innocent must suffer." Brooks's film with its dark apocalyptic ending—a death mask fixed in time by a strobe light—posed its own sinister version of the problem of evil.

Treatments of Catholic sexuality in Hollywood films frequently raise fundamental questions about why bad things happen to basically good people and where joy fits in the world. Sometimes these questions take a sociological cast like John

Cassavetes's *A Woman Under the Influence* (1974), a severe tale of Mabel Longhetti (Gena Rowlands), a Los Angeles housewife with three kids, whose mind is reduced to pulp by six months of shock therapy, itself a seeming consequence of life with her brutal, retarded, almost sub-human Italian Catholic husband and his stone age blue collar friends. Other times, the evil seems more cosmic, inescapable, and relentless, as in Alan Pakula's *Sophie's Choice* (1982), a fine interpretation of William Styron's justly lauded novel. Pakula emphasizes the allegorical schema in Styron by simplifying his narrative and focusing entirely on the unlikely triangle of lovers, the Catholic Sophie (Meryl Streep), the Jewish Nathan (Kevin Kline), and the Protestant Stingo (Peter MacNicol). Faced with the Holocaust and six million dead innocents, Nathan seeks answers in science, only to have his mind destroyed by drugs and madness. Sophie tries to deny her father's anti-semitism by her love for her own children, but a tragic moment in a concentration camp shatters her ideals and destroys her family. As she explains later, the barbarous choice given her by a sadistic warder, a choice which he tells her is given to Catholic "Pollacks" and not to God's chosen people, has shattered her faith: "I knew that Christ had turned his face away from me and that only a Jesus who no longer cared for me could kill the people I love and leave me alive with my shame." To assuage her guilt, Sophie embraces the "Angel of Death," Nathan, and welcomes his abuse of her mind and body; his sexual torments and physical beatings keep her deeper psychic problems at bay. Eventually his neurotic love helps her in her quest for death; these lovers consummate their relationship not with sex, for that they have all the time to remind them of their tortured bodies, but with death. Their truest fidelity expresses itself in thanatos, not eros; they die in each other's arms. The remaining friend, Stingo, who has one glorious night of sex with Sophie before she dies, has only his art and the poetry of Emily Dickinson as answers to the holocaust and the recurring death of beauty and innocence.

The most popular portrait of a Roman Catholic in love ever filmed actually begins with a now immortal re-phrasing of the theological problem of evil: "What can you say about a twenty-five-year-old girl who died?" Erich Segal's *Love Story* (1970), which made Harvard Yard the "in" place for romantic adolescents, actually conceals some important sociological insights in its tear-jerking melodrama. Step back from the story for a second, and it's "Cinderella" for adolescent lovers: a pretty young Italian pauper on the road to assimilation meets a young, athletic, wealthy WASP, and only a wicked king, that is, an industrial robber baron, opposes the match. They marry, are disinherited, struggle their way back to the top, and poof, the coach turns back into a pumpkin when a mysterious fatal illness (a malignant curse) fells the beautiful princess. In *Love Story*, the warm-hearted Italian Catholic Cavalleris, proprietors of a cookie shop in Cranston, Rhode Island, are poor but happy; the aristocratic Barretts have buildings but no soul. Their interaction, an update of *Abie's Irish Rose*, mingles ethnics and preppies, interdenominational, "do-it-yourself" weddings and traditional Catholic funerals, Harvard intellectualism and Italian folk philosophy, in a bittersweet potion that enchanted a whole generation. Even the hardest hearts seemingly wanted to believe that love could lift a Catholic girl up where she belonged. Positive images of Catholic women all emphasized the social mobility that sex and then marriage offered. In *An Officer and a Gentleman*, Paula Pokrifki (Debra Winger) spends many hours in cheap motels, but eventually her man wins his aviator's wings and they leave her factory behind. Watching this chauvinistic anachronism in an age of women's liberation, audiences still cheered and wept to see Prince Charming rescue the beleaguered maiden. Their courtship might be a little rockier and more given to explicit sex than older, pre-Ratings Board films, but marriage still solved any questions about guilt and sex, especially marriage with an aviator. A serious relationship with a factory owner could also alleviate guilt, it seems. Catholic welder and dancer Alex (Jennifer Beals) in *Flashdance* (1983) is merely the most recent incarnation of girls who tell their confessors, "I think of sex all the time," and "I want so much"; her romance with her boss gives her the break she needs to escape her cultural ghetto.

In a priceless anecdote he labels "Don Juan in Hollywood,"

Ben Hecht, as he retraces his life as *A Child of the Century*, recalls a frenzied phone call from Bernie Hyman, then head of production at M.G.M. The studio chief begged author Hecht to suggest a "gimmick" to keep his hero and heroine from having sex right away; Bernie Hyman was at a loss to see any reason that would "keep a healthy pair of lovers from hitting the hay in Reel Two." The patient, though incredulous Hecht suggested to the baffled producer that "frequently a girl has moral concepts that keep her virtuous until a trip to the altar" and opined that there are even men "who prefer to wait for coitus until after they have married the girl they adore." Bernie Hyman was elated and hung up the phone saying, "Wonderful! We'll try it." Today's films about Catholic lovers assume that Bernie Hyman was right all along: healthy lovers hit the hay in Reel One. The miracle is if they reach the altar.

postscript

As this text goes to press, another spate of Catholic films is being readied for release. The trade papers are full of announcements for projects like *Agnes of God* and *Catholic Boys*. The advertisements for the latter, a Home Box Office co-production with Silver Screen Films, starring Donald Sutherland and John Heard, describe "an immaculate comedy about the conception of growing up" and picture uniformed choir boys sneaking puffs on cigarettes, pawing *Playboy* magazine, blowing elaborate bubbles from gum, picking their noses, and sporting glorious black eyes. Meanwhile, their demented looking choirmaster, an obviously ineffectual monk, stares heavenward in despair.

It's clear that the old stereotypes endure: insanity and pregnancy in the convent, inanity and impotency in the rectory, and mayhem and mischief in the pews. Roman Catholicism in American film still inhabits that mysterious domain Michael Wood so accurately describes in his *America in the Movies*, the special world of *the movies*, "an independent universe, self-created, self-perpetuated, a licensed zone of unreality, affectionately patronized by us all." In that Saturday afternoon world, little of Sunday's sermon lingers.

/elected /ource/

Adler, Renata. *A Year in the Dark.* New York: Berkley Medallion Books, 1971.

Agee, James. *Agee on Film.* Boston: Beacon Press, 1966.

Alfoldi, Andrew. *The Conversion of Constantine and Pagan Rome.* Trans. Harold Mattingly. London: Oxford University Clarendon Press, 1948.

Amberg, George, ed. *The New York Times Film Reviews, A One Volume Selection 1913-1970.* New York: Arno Press, 1971.

Anger, Kenneth. *Hollywood Babylon.* New York: Simon and Schuster, 1975.

Anson, Jay. *The Amityville Horror:* A True Story. New York: Bantam Books, 1977.

Asbury, Herbert. *The Great Illusion: An Informal History of Prohibition.* Garden City, N.Y.: Doubleday and Company, 1950.

Averson, Richard and David Manning White. *The Celluloid Weapon: Social Comment in the American Film.* Boston: Beacon Press, 1972.

Baldwin, James. *The Devil Finds Work.* New York: The Dial Press, 1976.

Balio, Tino, ed. *The American Film Industry.* Madison: The University of Wisconsin Press, 1976.

Baritz, Loren. *The Culture of the Twenties.* Indianapolis, Indiana: Bobbs-Merrill Educational Publishing, 1970.

Barry, Iris. *D. W. Griffith: American Film Master.* New York: The Museum of Modern Art, 1940.

Baxter, John. *Hollywood in the Thirties.* New York: A. S. Barnes, 1968.

_____. *Hollywood in the Sixties.* New York: A. S. Barnes, 1972.

Behlmer, Rudy. *America's Favorite Movies: Behind the Scenes.* New York: Frederick Ungar, 1982.

Bergman, Andrew. *We're in the Money: Depression America and Its Films.* New York: Harper and Row, 1971.

Bernstein, Marcelle. *The Nuns*. Philadelphia: J. B. Lippincott Company, 1976.

Bessie, Alvah. *Inquisition in Eden*. Berlin: Seven Seas Books, 1967.

Bird, Michael, and John R. May, eds. *Religion in Film*. Knoxville: The University of Tennessee Press, 1982.

Biró, Yvette, Trans. Imre Goldstein. *Profane Mythology: The Savage Mind of the Cinema*. Bloomington: Indiana University Press, 1982.

Biskind, Peter. *Seeing Is Believing: How Hollywood Taught Us to Stop Worrying and Love the Fifties*. New York: Pantheon, 1983.

Bitzer, G. W. *Billy Bitzer: His Story*. New York: Farrar, Straus, and Giroux, 1973.

Blatty, William Peter. *The Exorcist*. New York: Harper and Row, 1971.

——. *I'll Tell Them I Remember You*. New York: Signet Books, 1973.

——. *Legion*. New York: Simon and Schuster, 1983.

——. "There is Goodness in *The Exorcist*." *America*, 130 (1974), 131-32.

——. *William Peter Blatty on The Exorcist: From Novel to Film*. New York: Bantam Books, 1974.

Bluestone, George. *Novels into Film*. Berkeley: University of California Press, 1957.

Bogdanovich, Peter. *Fritz Lang in America*. New York: Praeger Books, 1967.

Bohn, Thomas W., and Richard L. Stromgren. *Light and Shadows: A History of Motion Pictures*. New York: Alfred Publishing, 1975.

Bowles, Stephen E. "Damnation and Purgation: *The Exorcist* and *Jaws*." *Literature/Film Quarterly*, 4 (Summer 1976), 196-215.

Bowser, Eileen, ed. *Film Notes*. New York: The Museum of Modern Art, 1969.

Brosnan, John. *The Horror People*. New York: Signet, 1976.

Brown, Karl. *Adventures with D. W. Griffith*. New York: Farrar, Straus, and Giroux, 1973.

Browne, Henry J. "A History of the Catholic Church in the United States." In Louis J. Putz, *The Catholic Church, U.S.A.* Chicago: Fides Publishers Association, 1956.

Brownlow, Kevin. *The Parade's Gone By*. New York: Ballantine Books, 1968.

Butler, Ivan, *Religion in the Cinema*. New York: A. S. Barnes, 1969.

Cagney, James. *Cagney by Cagney*. Garden City, N.Y.: Doubleday and Company, 1976.

Callahan, Daniel. *The New Church: Essays in Catholic Reform.* New York: Charles Scribner's Sons, 1966.

Callahan, Daniel, ed. *The Secular City Debate.* New York: MacMillan Company, 1966.

Campbell, Richard H., and Michael R. Pitts. *The Bible on Film: A Checklist 1897-1980.* Metuchen, New Jersey: The Scarecrow Press, 1981.

Campbell-Jones, Suzanne. *In Habit: A Study of Working Nuns.* New York: Pantheon Books, 1978.

Carey, Gary. *All the Stars in Heaven.* New York: E. P. Dutton, 1981.

Carroll David. *The Matinee Idols.* New York: Arbor House, 1972.

Cascone, Gina. *Pagan Babies and Other Catholic Memories.* New York: St. Martin's Press, 1982.

Cavell, Stanley. *The World Viewed: Reflections on the Ontology of Film.* New York: The Viking Press, 1971.

Ceplair, Larry, and Steven Englund. *The Inquisition in Hollywood: Politics in the Film Community 1930-1960.* Berkeley: University of California Press, 1979.

Chabrol, Claude, and Eric Rohmer. *Hitchcock: The First Forty-four Films.* Trans. Stanley Hochman. New York: Frederick Ungar Publishing Co., 1979.

Champlin, Charles. "What Will H. Hayes Begot." *American Film,* October 1980.

Clarens, Carlos. *Crime Movies.* New York: W. W. Norton, 1979.

Coffey, Thomas M. *The Long Thirst: Prohibition in America 1920-1933.* New York: W. W. Norton, 1975.

Cogley, John. *Catholic America.* New York: Doubleday and Company, 1973.

Cohen, Henry. *The Public Enemy.* Madison: University of Wisconsin Press, 1981.

Cooke, David A. *A History of Narrative Film.* New York: W. W. Norton, 1981.

Cooper, John C. and Carl Skrade. *Celluloid and Symbols.* Philadelphia: Fortress Press, 1970.

Corliss, Richard. *The Hollywood Screenwriters.* New York: Avon Books, 1970.

_____. *Talking Pictures.* New York: Penguin Books, 1975.

Coughlin, Robert. "Konklave in Kokomo." In Isabel Leighton, ed. *The Aspirin Age 1919-1941.* New York: Simon and Schuster, 1965.

Cox, Harvey. *The Secular City.* New York: The MacMillan Company, 1965.

Cripps, Thomas. "The Movie Jew as Image of Assimiliation." *Journal of Popular Film*, 4 (Fall 1975), 197.

Crowther, Bosley. *Vintage Films*. New York: G. P. Putnam, 1977.

De Grazia, Edward and Roger K. Newman. *Banned Films: Movies, Censors, and the First Amendment*. New York: R. R. Bowker, 1982.

DeMille, Cecil B. *The Autobiography*, Donald Hayne, ed. Englewood Cliffs, N.J.: Prentice-Hall, 1959.

De Wohl, Louis. *Founded on a Rock: A History of the Catholic Church*. Philadelphia: J. B. Lippincott, 1961.

Dickinson, Thorald. *A Discovery of Cinema*. London: Oxford University Press, 1971.

Dooley, Roger. *From Scarface to Scarlett: American Films in the 1930s*. New York: Harcourt, Brace, Jovanovich, 1979.

Douglas, Lloyd C. *The Robe*. Boston: Houghton Mifflin, 1942.

Dowdy, Andrew. *The Films of the Fifties: The American State of Mind*. New York: William Morrow, 1973.

Durgnat, Raymond. *Films and Feelings*. Cambridge, Mass.: Massachusetts Institute of Technology Press, 1971.

Ebon, Martin. *Exorcism: Fact Not Fiction*. New York: Signet Books, 1974.

Eisenstein, Sergei. *Film Form*. Trans. Jay Leyda. New York: Harcourt, Brace, and World, Inc., 1949.

Ellis, John Tracy. *American Catholicism*. Chicago: The University of Chicago Press, 1956.

Essoe, Gabe, and Raymond Lee. *DeMille: The Man and His Pictures*. New York: Castle Books, 1970.

Evans, Walter. "Monster Movies: A Sexual Theory." *Journal of Popular Film*, 2 (Fall 1973), 353-66.

Everson, William K. *American Silent Film*. New York: Oxford University Press, 1978.

_____. *Love in the Film*. Secaucus, N.J.: Citadel Press, 1979.

Farber, Manny. *Negative Space*. New York: Praeger Publishers, 1971.

Farber, Stephen. *The Movie Rating Game*. Washington, D.C.: Public Affairs Press, 1972.

Figenshu, Tom. "Screams of a Summer Night." *Film Comment*, 15 (Sept.-Oct. 1979), 49-54.

Flaherty, Joe. "Rocky's Road." *Film Comment*, 18 (July-Aug. 1982), 58-64.

Fosburgh, Lacey. *Closing Time: The True Story of the 'Goodbar' Murder*. New York: Dell Publishing Co., 1975.

Franklin, Joe. *Classics of the Silent Screen*. New York: Cadillac Publishing, 1959.

French, Philip. *The Movie Moguls: An Informal History of the Hollywood Tycoons*. Chicago: Henry Regnery Company, 1969.

Friedman, Lester D. *Hollywood's Image of the Jew*. New York: Frederick Ungar, 1982.

Froug, William, ed. *The Screenwriter Looks at the Screenwriter*. New York: Dell Publishing Co., 1972.

Fuchs, Lawrence H. *John F. Kennedy and American Catholicism*. New York: Meredith Press, 1967.

Furhammar, Leif, and Saksson Folke. *Politics and Film*. New York: Praeger Books, 1971.

Geduld, Harry M. ed. *Authors on Film*. Bloomington: Indiana University Press, 1972.

Gelmis, Joseph. *The Film Director as Superstar*. Garden City, N.Y.: Doubleday and Company, 1970.

Gessner, Robert. *The Moving Image: A Guide to Cinematic Literacy*. New York: E. P. Dutton, 1970.

Gish, Lillian. *Dorothy and Lillian Gish*. New York: Charles Scribner's Sons, 1973.

_____. *The Movies, Mr. Griffith, and Me*. Englewood Cliffs, N.Y.: Prentice Hall, Inc., 1969.

Glazer, Nathan, and Daniel Moynihan. *Beyond the Melting Pot*. Cambridge, Mass.: The Massachusetts Institute of Technology Press, 1963.

Goethals, Gregor T. *The TV Ritual: Worship at the Video Altar*. Boston: Beacon Press, 1981.

Gow, Gordon. *Hollywood in the Fifties*. New York: A. S. Barnes, 1971.

Graham, Frank. *Al Smith, American: An Informal Biography*. New York: G. P. Putnam's Son, 1945.

Granfield, Patrick. *Ecclesial Cybernetics: A Study of Democracy in the Church*. New York: The MacMillan Company, 1973.

Grant, Barry K., ed. *Film Genre: Theory and Criticism*. Metuchen, N.J.: The Scarecrow Press, 1977.

Greeley, Andrew M. *The American Catholic: A Social Portrait*. New York: Basic Books, 1977.

_____. *The Catholic Experience: An Interpretation of the History of American Catholicism*. New York: Doubleday and Company, 1967.

_____. *Come Blow Your Mind With Me: Provocative Reflections on the*

American Religious Scene. New York: Doubleday and Company, 1971

———. *The Jesus Myth.* New York: Doubleday and Company, 1971.

———. *That Most Distressful Nation: The Taming of the American Irish.* Chicago: Quadrangle Books, 1972.

Greenberg, Joel and Charles Higham. *Hollywood in the Forties.* New York: A. S. Barnes, 1968.

Greenburg, Harvey R. *The Movies on Your Mind.* New York: E. P. Dutton, 1975.

Greene, Graham. *Graham Greene on Film.* Ed. John Russell Taylor. New York: Simon and Schuster, 1972.

Guild, Leo. *Zanuck: Hollywood's Last Tycoon.* Los Angeles: Holloway House Publishing, 1970.

Guiles, Fred Lawrence. *Hanging on in Paradise.* New York: McGraw-Hill, 1975.

Hall, Stephen S. "Italian-Americans: Coming into their Own." *New York Times Magazine,* 15 May 1983, pp. 28-50.

Halliwell, Leslie. *Film Guide.* London: Granada Publishing, 1977.

Hecht, Ben. *A Child of the Century.* New York: Simon and Schuster, 1954.

Henderson, Robert M. *D. W. Griffith: His Life and Work.* New York: Oxford University Press, 1972.

Hennesey, James. *American Catholics: A History of the Roman Catholic Community in the United States.* New York: Oxford University Press, 1981.

Higham, Charles. *The Art of the American Film.* Garden City, N.Y.: Anchor Press, 1974.

———. *Cecil B. DeMille.* New York: Charles Scribner's Sons, 1973.

———. *Hollywood Cameramen: Sources of Light.* Bloomington: Indiana University Press, 1970.

Higham, Charles and Joel Greenberg, eds. *The Celluloid Muse: Hollywood Directors Speak.* New York: New American Library, 1972.

Hitchcock, James. *The Decline and Fall of Radical Catholicism.* New York: Herder and Herder, 1973.

Hochman, Stanley, ed. *American Film Directors: A Library of Film Criticism.* New York: Frederick Ungar, 1974.

Hoffer, Eric. *The True Believer.* New York: Harper and Row, 1951.

Holzer, Hans. *Murder in Amityville.* New York: A Belmont Tower Book, 1979.

Howard, Joseph. *Damien: Omen II.* From the screenplay by Stanley Mann and Michael Hodges. New York: New American Library, 1978.

Huff, Theodore. *Intolerance, the Film by David Wark Griffith: Shot-by-Shot Analysis.* New York: The Museum of Modern Art, 1966.

Hulme, Kathryn. *The Nun's Story.* Boston: Little, Brown, and Company, 1956.

Hurley, Neil. "Cinematic Transfiguration of Jesus." In Bird, Michael and John R. May, *Religion in Film,* Knoxville: The University of Tennessee Press, 1982, pp. 64-66.

_____. *Theology Through Film.* Re-titled *Toward a Film Humanism.* New York: Delta Books, 1970.

Huss, Roy, and T. J. Ross. *Focus on the Horror Film.* Englewood Cliffs, N.J.: Prentice Hall, 1972.

Hutchinson, Ray. *The Gospel According to Madison Avenue.* New York: The Bruce Publishing Company, 1969.

Jacobs, Lewis. *The Emergence of Film Art.* Second Edition. New York: W. W. Norton, 1979.

_____. *The Rise of the American Film.* New York: Teachers College Press, 1969.

Jewell, Richard B. and Vernon Harbin. *The RKO Story.* New York: New York: Arlington House, 1982.

Johnson, Glen M. "Sharper Than an Irish Serpent's Tooth: Leo McCarey's *My Son John.*" *The Journal of Popular Film and Television,* 8 (Spring 1980), 44-50.

Jordan, Rene. *Clark Gable.* New York: Galahad Books, 1973.

_____. *Marlon Brando.* New York: Galahad Books, 1973.

Jowett, Garth. "Bullets, Beers, and the Hays Office." In John E. O'Connor and Martin A. Jackson, eds. *American History/American Film: Interpreting the Hollywood Image.* New York: Frederick Ungar, 1979, pp. 57-77.

Jung, Carl Gustav. *Psychology and Religon.* New Haven: Yale University Press, 1938.

Kael, Pauline. *Reeling.* Boston: Little, Brown, and Company, 1976.

Kaminsky, Stuart M. *American Film Genres: Approaches to a Critical Theory of Popular Film.* New York: Dell, 1977.

Kanfer, Stefan. *A Journal of the Plague Years.* New York: Atheneum, 1973.

Kaplan, E. Ann. *Women and Film: Both Sides of the Camera.* London: Methuen, 1983.

Kauffman, Stanley. *American Film Criticism*. New York: Liveright, 1972.

Kavanaugh, James. *The Birth of God*. New York: The Trident Press, 1969.

——. *A Modern Priest Looks at His Outdated Church*. New York: Trident Press, 1967.

Keeler, Greg. "Saturday Night Fever: Crossing the Verrazano Bridge." *Journal of Popular Film and Television*, 6 (1979), 158-68.

Kellogg, Gene. *The Vital Tradition*. Chicago: Loyola University Press, 1970.

Kelly, Mary Pat. *Martin Scorsese, The First Decade*. Pleasantville, N.Y.: Redgrave Publishing Company, 1980.

Kobler, John. *Ardent Spirits: The Rise and Fall of Prohibition*. New York: G. P. Putnam's Sons, 1973.

Kolbenschlag, Madonna C. "The Female Grotesque: Gargoyles in the Cathedrals of Cinema." *Journal of Popular Film*, 6 (1978), 328-42.

Kosnick, Anthony. *Human Sexuality: New Directions in American Catholic Thought*. New York: Paulist Press, 1977.

Koszarski, Richard, ed. *Hollywood Directors 1941-1976*. New York: Oxford University Press, 1977.

Kotre, John N. *The Best of Times, The Worst of Times: Andrew Greeley and American Catholicism 1950-1975*. Chicago: Nelson-Hall Company, 1978.

Krafsur, Richard P., ed. *The American Film Institute Catalog of Motion Pictures: Feature Films 1961-1970*. New York: R. R. Bowker and Company, 1976.

Laistner, M. L. W. *Christianity and Pagan Culture in the Later Roman Empire*. Ithaca, N.Y.: Cornell University Press, 1951.

Lawson, John Howard. *Film: The Creative Process*. Second Edition. New York: Hill and Wang, 1967.

Leab, Daniel. "The Blue Collar Ethnic in Bicentennial America: Rocky." In O'Connor and Jackson, eds. *American History; American Film*, Ungar Film Library, 1979, pp. 257-73.

Leach, Michael. *I Know It When I See It: Pornography, Violence, and Public Sensitivity*. Philadelphia: The Westminster Press, 1975.

Leighton, Isabel, ed. *The Aspirin Age 1919-1941*. New York: Simon and Schuster, 1965.

LeRoy, Mervyn. *Take One*. New York: Hawthorn Books, Inc., 1974.

Levin, Ira. *Rosemary's Baby*. New York: Dell Books, 1967.

Lindsay, Vachel. *The Art of the Moving Picture*. New York: Liveright, 1970.

Liu, William T., and Nathaniel J. Pallone. *Catholics/U.S.A.: Perspectives on Social Change*. New York: John Wiley and Sons, 1970.

LoBello, Nino. *Vatican, U.S.A.* New York: Trident Press, 1972.

Loos, Anita. *Kiss Hollywood Goodbye*. New York: The Viking Press, 1974.

McArthur, Colin. *Underworld U.S.A.* New York: The Viking Press, 1972.

McAvoy, Thomas T. *A History of the Catholic Church in the United States*. Notre Dame, Indiana: The University of Notre Dame Press, 1969.

McCarthy, Todd. "The Exorcism of *The Heretic:* Why They Had to Destroy This Film in Order to Save It." *Film Comment*, 13 (Sept.-Oct. 1977), 47-55.

McConnell, Frank. *Storytelling and Mythmaking*. New York: Oxford University Press, 1979.

MacGowan, Kenneth. *Behind the Screen: The History and Technique of the Motion Picture*. New York: Delta Books, 1965.

McLoughlin, Emmett. *Crime and Immorality in the Catholic Church*. New York: Lyle Stuart, 1962.

Manvell, Roger. *Films and the Second World War*. New York: Dell Publishing, 1974.

Marcus, Sheldon. *Father Coughlin: The Tumultuous Life of the Priest of the Little Flower*. Boston: Little, Brown, and Company, 1973.

Martin, Malachi. *The Decline and Fall of the Roman Church*. New York: Bantam Books, 1983.

_____. *Hostage to the Devil*. New York: Thomas Y. Crowell, 1976.

Martin, Thomas M. *Image and the Imageless: A Study in Religious Consciousness and Film*. Lewisburg: Bucknell University Press, 1981.

Mast, Gerald. *Film/Cinema/Movie: A Theory of Experience*. New York: Harper and Row, 1977.

_____, ed. *The Movies in Our Midst: Documents in the Cultural History of Film in America*. Chicago: The University of Chicago Press, 1982.

Mate, Ken, and Pat McGilligan. "W. R. Burnett." *Film Comment*, 19 (Jan.-Feb. 1983).

Mayersburg, Paul. *Hollywood and the Haunted House*. New York: Ballantine Books, 1967.

Miller, Gabriel. *Screening the Novel: Rediscovering American Fiction in Film*. New York: Frederick Ungar, 1980.

Miller, Randall M., ed. *The Kaleidoscopic Lens: How Hollywood Views Ethnic Groups*. New York: Jerome S. Oyer, 1980.

Morella, Joe, Edward Z. Epstein, and John Griggs. *The Films of World War II*. Introd. Judith Crist. Secaucus, N.J.: The Citadel Press, 1980.

Morris, George. "McCarey and McCarthy: *My Son John.*" *Film Comment*, 12 (Jan.-Feb. 1976), 16-21.

Munden, Kenneth W., ed. *The American Film Institute Catalog of Motion Pictures Produced in the United States Feature Films 1921-1930.* New York: R. R. Bowker, 1971.

Munn, Mike. *Great Film Epics.* London: Illustrated Publications Company Limited, 1982.

Myers, Eric. "Stroheim and *Queen Kelly.*" *Cinema Journal*, 15 (Spring 1976), 73-79.

Navasky, Victor S. *Naming Names.* New York: The Viking Press, 1980.

New York Times Film Reviews 1913-1968. Six volumes. New York: New York Times and Arno Press, 1970.

Nichols, Peter. *The Pope's Divisions.* New York: Penguin Books, 1981.

Niver, Kemp. *The First Twenty Years: A Segment of Film History.* Los Angeles: Artisan Books, 1968.

——. *Klaw and Erlanger Present Famous Plays in Pictures.* Los Angeles: Locare Research Group, 1976.

North, Sterling, and C. B. Boutell. *Speak of the Devil.* Garden City, N.Y.: Doubleday, Doran and Company, Inc., 1945

O'Brien, David J. *The Renewal of American Catholicism.* New York: Oxford University Press, 1972.

O'Connor, John E., and Martin A. Jackson. *American History/American Film: Interpreting the Hollywood Image.* New York: Frederick Ungar, 1979.

O'Dell, Paul. *Griffith and the Rise of Hollywood.* New York: Castle Books, 1970.

Otto, Rudolf. *The Idea of the Holy: An Inquiry into the Non-rational Factor in the Idea of the Divine and its Relation to the Rational.* New York: Oxford University Press, 1923.

Oursler, Fulton, and Will Oursler. *Father Flanagan of Boys Town.* Garden City, N.Y.: Doubleday and Company, Inc., 1949.

Peary, Gerald, and Roger Shatzkin. *The Classic American Novel and the Movies.* New York: Frederick Ungar, 1977.

Peary, Gerald, ed. *Little Caesar.* Madison: University of Wisconsin Press, 1981.

Pells, Richard. *Radical Visions and American Dreams: Culture and Social Thought in the Depression Years.* New York: Harper and Row, 1973.

Perlmutter, Ruth. "For God, Country, and Whoopee: DeMille and the Floss." *Film Comment*, 12 (Jan.-Feb. 1976), 24-28.

Phelan, John B. *Disenchantment: Meaning and Morality in the Media.* New York: Hasting House, 1980.

Phillips, Gene D. *Graham Greene: The Films of His Fiction.* New York: Teachers College Press, 1974.

_____. *Hemingway and Film.* New York: Frederick Ungar, 1980.

Pirie, David, ed. *Anatomy of the Movies.* New York: MacMillan, 1981.

Powdermaker, Hortense. *Hollywood: The Dream Factory. An Anthropologist Looks at the Movie-Makers.* New York: Little, Brown, and Company, 1950.

Powers. J. F. *Morte d'Urban.* Garden City, N.Y.: Doubleday, 1956.

Pratley, Gerald. *The Cinema of Otto Preminger.* New York: Castle Books, 1971.

Preminger, Otto. *Preminger: An Autobiography.* Garden City, N.Y.: Doubleday, 1977.

Putz, Louis J. *The Catholic Church, U.S.A.* Chicago: Fides Publishers Association, 1956.

Puzo, Mario. *The Godfather.* Greenwich, Conn.: Fawcett Crest Books, 1969.

_____. *The Godfather Papers and Other Confessions.* Greenwich, Conn.: Fawcett Publications, 1972.

Ramsaye, Terry. *A Million and One Nights: A History of the Motion Picture through 1925.* New York: Simon and Schuster, 1926.

Rapping, Elayne. "The View from Hollywood: The American Family and the American Dream." *Socialist Review,* 13 (Jan.-Feb. 1983), 71-92.

Rhode, Eric. *The History of the Cinema from Its Origins to 1970.* New York: Hill and Wang, 1976.

Ringgold, Gene, and DeWitt Bodeen. *The Films of Cecil B. DeMille.* New York: Cadillac Publishing Co., 1969.

Robinson, David. *Hollywood in the Twenties.* New York: A. S. Barnes, 1968.

Rosenbaum, Jonathan. *Moving Places, A Life at the Movies.* New York: Harper and Row, 1980.

Rossner, Judith. *Looking for Mr. Goodbar.* New York: Pocket Books, 1975.

Rosten, Leo, ed. *Religions of America: Ferment and Faith in an Age of Crisis.* New York: Simon and Schuster, 1975.

Rotha, Paul. *The Film Till Now: A Survey of World Cinema.* London: Spring Books, 1967.

Russo, Vito. *The Celluloid Closet: Homosexuality in the Movies.* New York: Harper and Row, 1981.

Sabrames, Demostenes. *The Satanizing of Woman: Religion Versus Sexuality.* Trans. Martin Ebon. Garden City, N.Y.: Doubleday, 1974.

Schulberg, Budd. *On the Waterfront.* Carbondale: Southern Illinois University Press, 1980.

Schumach, Murray. *The Face on the Cutting Room Floor.* New York: William Morrow and Company, 1964.

Schwartz, Tony. *Media: the Second God.* New York: Random House, 1981.

Seldes, Gilbert. *The Movies Come From America.* New York: Charles Scribner's Sons, 1937.

Seltzer, David. *The Omen.* New York: New American Library, 1976.

Selznick, David O. *Memo from: David O. Selznick.* Ed. Rudy Behlmer. New York: Avon Books, 1972.

Sennett, Ted. *Warner Brothers Presents.* New York: Castle Books, 1971.

Shadoian, Jack. *Dreams and Dead Ends: The American Gangster/Crime Film.* Cambridge, Mass.: Massachusetts Institute of Technology Press, 1979.

Silva, Fred, ed. *Focus on The Birth of a Nation.* Englewood Cliffs, N.J.: Prentice Hall, 1971.

Silver, Alain, and Elizabeth Ward, eds. *Film Noir: An Encyclopedic Reference to the American Style.* Woodstock, N.Y.: The Overlook Press, 1979.

Sklar, Robert. *Movie-Made America: A Cultural History of American Movies.* New York: Vintage Books, 1976.

Slide, Anthony. *Early American Cinema.* New York: A. S. Barnes, 1970.

Smith, Julian. *Looking Away: Hollywood and Vietnam.* New York: Charles Scribner's Sons, 1975.

Sobchack, Thomas. "Genre Film: A Classical Experience." In Grant, ed., *Film Genre.* New York: Scarecrow, 1977.

Solomon, Stanley J. *Beyond Formula: American Film Genres.* New York: Harcourt, Brace, Jovanovich, Inc., 1976.

Spears, Jack. *Hollywood: The Golden Era.* New York: A. S. Barnes, 1971.

Spoto, Donald. *Camerado: Hollywood and the American Man.* New York: New American Library, 1978.

Stanley, Robert H. *The Celluloid Empire.* New York: Hasting House, 1978.

Steen, Mike. *Hollywood Speaks!* An Oral History. New York: G. P. Putnam's Sons, 1974.

Talbot, Daniel, ed. *Film: An Anthology.* Berkeley: University of California Press, 1966.

Taylor, John Russell, ed. *Graham Greene on Film: Collected Film Criticism 1935-1940.* New York: Simon and Schuster, 1972.

Thomas, John L. "Nationalities and American Catholicism." In Putz, Louis, *The Catholic Church, U.S.A.* Chicago: Fides Publishers Association, 1956.

Thompson, Charles. *Bing: The Authorized Biography.* New York: David McKay, 1975.

Thomson, David. *Overexposures: The Crisis in American Filmmaking.* New York: William Morrow and Company, Inc., 1981.

Thorp, Margaret Farrand. *America at the Movies.* New Haven: Yale University Press, 1939.

Tozzi, Romana. *Spencer Tracy.* New York: Galahad Books, 1973.

Travers, Peter, and Stephanie Reiff. *The Story Behind The Exorcist.* New York: Crown Publishers, 1974.

Truffaut, Francois. *Hitchcock.* New York: Simon and Schuster, 1967.

Tyler, Parker. *The Hollywood Hallucination.* New York: Simon and Schuster, 1944.

_____. *Screening the Sexes.* New York: Doubleday, 1972.

_____. *The Shadow of an Airplane Climbs the Empire State Building: A World Theory of Film.* New York: Doubleday, 1973.

Unger, Merrill Frederick. *Biblical Demonology.* Wheaton, Ill.: Van Kampen Press, Inc., 1952.

Valentini, Norberto, and Clara di Meglio. *Sex and the Confesional.* New York: Stein and Day, 1974.

Vance, Malcolm. *The Movie Ad Book.* Minneapolis: Control Data Publishing, 1981.

Vermilye, Jerry. *The Films of the Thirties.* Secaucus, N.J.: The Citadel Press, Inc., 1982.

Vizzard, Jack. *See No Evil.* New York: Simon and Schuster, 1970.

Vogel, Amos. *Film as a Subversive Art.* New York: Random House, 1974.

Walker, Alexander. *Sex in the Movies: The Celluloid Sacrifice.* Baltimore: Penguin Books, 1966.

_____. *The Shattered Silents.* New York: William Morrow and Company, Inc., 1979.

Wall, James M. *Church and Cinema: A Way of Viewing Film.* Grand Rapids, Mich.: William B. Eerdmans Publishing Company, 1971.

Walsh, William Thomas. *Our Lady of Fatima.* New York: Image Books, 1947.

Warshow, Robert. *The Immediate Experience.* New York: Atheneum, 1970.

Wenden, D. J. *The Birth of the Movies.* New York: E. P. Dutton, 1974.

Wills, Garry. *Bare Ruined Choirs: Doubt, Prophecy, and Radical Religion.* New York: Doubleday, 1971.

Wilson, Robert, ed. *The Film Criticism of Otis Ferguson.* Philadelphia: Temple University Press, 1971.

Wood, Michael. *America in the Movies.* New York: Delta Books, 1975.

Wood, Robin. "Democracy and *Shpontanuity:* McCarey and the Hollywood Tradition." *Film Comment,* 12 (Jan.-Feb. 1976), 6-16.

———. "Gods and Monsters: The Private Films of Larry Cohen." *Film Comment,* 14 (Sept.-Oct. 1978), 19-27.

———. *Hitchcock's Films.* New York: Castle Books, 1969.

———. *Howard Hawks.* Garden City, N.Y.: Doubleday, 1968.

———. "Return of the Repressed." *Film Comment,* 14 (July-Aug. 1978), 24-33.

Workman, Herbert B. *Persecution in the Early Church,* 1906. Rpt. New York: Oxford University Press, 1980.

Zukor, Adolph. "Origin and Growth of the Industry." In Joseph P. Kennedy, ed., *The Story of the Films.* New York: A. W. Shaw Company, 1927.

index